Samuel Johnson, Thomas Davies

Miscellaneous and Fugitive Pieces

Vol. 2, Second Edition

Samuel Johnson, Thomas Davies

Miscellaneous and Fugitive Pieces
Vol. 2, Second Edition

ISBN/EAN: 9783337217525

Printed in Europe, USA, Canada, Australia, Japan

Cover: Foto ©Thomas Meinert / pixelio.de

More available books at **www.hansebooks.com**

MISCELLANEOUS

AND

FUGITIVE PIECES.

VOLUME the SECOND.

THE SECOND EDITION, CORRECTED.

LONDON,

Printed for T. Davies, in Ruffel-Street, Covent-Garden, Bookseller to the Royal Academy.
MDCCLXXIV.

CONTENTS

OF THE

SECOND VOLUME.

Prologue

CONTENTS.

A THIRD VOLUME OF

MISCELLANEOUS

AND

FUGITIVE PIECES

IS IN THE PRESS,

AND

WILL BE PUBLISHED VERY SPEEDILY.

A N

E S S A Y

ON THE

ORIGIN and IMPORTANCE

O F

SMALL TRACTS and FUGITIVE PIECES.

Written for the INTRODUCTION to the

HARLEIAN MISCELLANY.

THOUGH the Scheme of the following *Miscellany* is so obvious, that the Title alone is sufficient to explain it; and though several Collections have been formerly attempted upon Plans, as to the Method, very little, but, as to the Capacity and Execution, very different from ours; we, being possessed of the greatest Variety for such a Work, hope for a more general Reception than those confined Schemes had the Fortune to meet with; and, therefore, think it not wholly unnecessary to explain our Intentions, to display the Treasure of Materials out of which this *Miscellany* is to be compiled, and to exhibit a general Idea of the Pieces which we intend to insert in it.

There is, perhaps, no Nation in which it is so necessary, as in our own, to assemble, from time to time, the small Tracts and fugitive Pieces, which are occasionally published: For, besides the general Subjects of Enquiry, which are cultivated by us, in common with every other learned Nation, our Constitution in Church and State naturally gives Birth to a Multitude of Performances, which would either not have been written, or could not have been made publick in any other Place.

The Form of our Government, which gives every Man, that has Leisure, or Curiosity, or Vanity, the Right of enquiring into the Propriety of publick Measures, and, by Consequence, obliges those who are intrusted with the Administration of national Affairs, to give an Account of their Conduct to almost every Man who demands it, may be reasonably imagined to have occasioned innumerable Pamphlets, which would never have appeared under arbitrary Governments, where every Man lulls himself in Indolence under Calamities, of which he cannot promote the Redress, or thinks it prudent to conceal the Uneasiness, of which he cannot complain without Danger.

The Multiplicity of religious Sects tolerated among us, of which every one has found Opponents and Vindicators, is another Source of unexhaustible Publication, almost peculiar to ourselves ; for Controversies cannot be long continued, nor frequently revived, where an Inquisitor has a Right to shut up the Disputants in Dungeons; or where Silence can be imposed on either Party, by the Refusal of a Licence.

Not that it should be inferred from hence, that political or religious Controversies are the only Products of the Liberty of the British Press; the Mind once let loose to Enquiry, and suffered to operate without Restraint, necessarily deviates into peculiar Opinions, and wanders in new Tracks, where she is indeed sometimes lost in a Labyrinth; from which though

though she cannot return, and scarce knows how to proceed; yet, sometimes, makes useful Discoveries, or finds out nearer Paths to Knowledge.

The boundless Liberty with which every Man may write his own Thoughts, and the Opportunity of conveying new Sentiments to the Publick, without Danger of suffering either Ridicule or Censure, which every Man may enjoy, whose Vanity does not incite him too hastily to own his Performances, naturally invites those who employ themselves in Speculation, to try how their Notions will be received by a Nation, which exempts Caution from Fear, and Modesty from Shame; and it is no Wonder, that where Reputation may be gained, but needs not be lost, Multitudes are willing to try their Fortune, and thrust their Opinions into the Light; sometimes with unsuccessful Haste, and sometimes with happy Temerity.

It is observed, that, among the Natives of England, is to be found a greater Variety of Humour, than in any other Country; and, doubtless, where every Man has a full Liberty to propagate his Conceptions, Variety of Humour must produce Variety of Writers; and, where the Number of Authors is so great, there cannot but be some worthy of Distinction.

All these, and many other Causes, too tedious to be enumerated, have contributed to make Pamphlets and small Tracts a very important Part of an *English* Library; nor are there any Pieces, upon which those, who aspire to the Reputation of judicious Collectors of Books, bestow more Attention, or greater Expence; because many Advantages may be expected from the Perusal of these small Productions, which are scarcely to be found in that of larger Works.

If we regard History, it is well known, that most political Treatises have for a long Time appeared in

this

this Form, and that the firſt Relations of Tranſactions, while they are yet the Subject of Conver-
ſation, divide the Opinions, and employ the Conjectures of Mankind, are delivered by theſe petty
Writers, who have Opportunities of collecting the
different Sentiments of Diſputants, of enquiring the
Truth from living Witneſſes, and of copying their
Repreſentations from the Life; and, therefore, they
preſerve a Multitude of particular Incidents, which
are forgotten in a ſhort Time, or omitted in formal
Relations, and which are yet to be conſidered as
Sparks of Truth, which, when united, may afford
Light in ſome of the darkeſt Scenes of State, as we
doubt not, will be ſufficiently proved in the Courſe
of this *Miſcellany*; and which it is, therefore, the
Intereſt of the Publick to preſerve unextinguiſhed.

The ſame Obſervation may be extended to Subjects of yet more Importance. In Controverſies that
relate to the Truths of Religion, the firſt Eſſays of
Reformation are generally timorous; and thoſe, who
have Opinions to offer, which they expect to be
oppoſed, produce their Sentiments, by Degrees;
and, for the moſt Part, in ſmall Tracts: By Degrees, that they may not ſhock their Readers with
too many Novelties at once; and in ſmall Tracts,
that they may be eaſily diſperſed, or privately printed: Almoſt every Controverſy, therefore, has been,
for a Time carried on in Pamphlets, nor has ſwelled
into larger Volumes, till the firſt Ardor of the Diſputants has ſubſided, and they have recollected their
Notions with Coolneſs enough to digeſt them into
Order, conſolidate them into Syſtems, and fortify
them with Authorities.

From Pamphlets, conſequently, are to be learned
the Progreſs of every Debate; the various State to
which the Queſtions have been changed; the Artifices and Fallacies which have been uſed, and the
Subterfuges, by which Reaſon has been eluded: In
ſuch

fuch Writings may be feen how the Mind has been opened by Degrees, how one Truth has led to another, how Error has been difentangled, and Hints improved to Demonftration, which Pleafure, and many others, are loft by him that only reads the larger Writers, by whom thefe fcattered Sentiments are collected, who will fee none of the Changes of Fortune which every Opinion has paffed through, will have no Opportunity of remarking the tranfient Advantages which Error may fometimes obtain, by the Artifices of its Patron, or the fuccefsful Rallies, by which Truth regains the Day, after a Repulfe; but will be to him, who traces the Difpute through into particular Gradations, as he that hears of a Victory, to him that fees the Battle.

Since the Advantages of preferving thefe fmall Tracts are fo numerous, our Attempt to unite them in Volumes cannot be thought either ufelefs or unfeafonable; for there is no other Method of fecuring them from Accidents; and they have already been fo long neglected, that this Defign cannot be delayed, without hazarding the Lofs of many Pieces, which deferve to be tranfmitted to another Age.

The Practice of publifhing Pamphlets on the moft important Subjects, has now prevailed more than two Centuries among us; and therefore it cannot be doubted, but that, as no large Collections have been yet made, many curious Tracts muft have perifhed; but it is too late to lament that Lofs; nor ought we to reflect upon it, with any other View, than that of quickening our Endeavours, for the Prefervation of thofe that yet remain; of which we have now a greater Number, than was, perhaps, ever amaffed by any one Perfon.

The firft Appearance of Pamphlets among us, is generally thought to be at the new Oppofition raifed againft the Errors and Corruptions of the Church of *Rome*. Thofe who were firft convinced of the

Reafon-

Reasonablenefs of the new Learning, as it was then called, propagated their Opinions in fmall Pieces, which were cheaply printed; and, what was then of great Importance, eafily concealed. Thefe Treatifes were generally printed in foreign Countries, and are not, therefore, always very correct. There was not then that Opportunity of printing in private; for, the Number of Printers were fmall, and the Preffes were eafily overlooked by the Clergy, who fpared no Labour or Vigilance for the Suppreffion of Herefy. There is, however, Reafon to fufpect, that fome Attempts were made to carry on the Propagation of Truth by a fecret Prefs; for one of the firft Treatifes in Favour of the Reformation, is faid, at the End, to be printed at *Greenwich, by the Permiffion of the Lord of Hofts.*

In the Time of King *Edward the Sixth* the Preffes were employed in Favour of the Reformed Religion, and fmall Tracts were difperfed over the Nation, to reconcile them to the new Forms of Worfhip. In this Reign, likewife, Political Pamphlets may be faid to have been begun, by the Addrefs of the Rebels of *Devonfhire*; all which Means of propagating the Sentiments of the People fo difturbed the Court, that no fooner was Queen *Mary* refolved to reduce her Subjects to the *Romifh* Superftition, but fhe artfully, by a Charter * granted to certain Freemen of *London*, in whofe Fidelity, no doubt, fhe confided, intirely prohibited *all* Preffes, but what fhould be licenfed by them; which Charter is that by which the Corporation of *Stationers*, in *London*, is at this Time incorporated.

Under the Reign of Queen *Elizabeth*, when Liberty again began to flourifh, the Practice of writ-

---

* Which begins thus, *Know ye, that We, confidering, and manifeftly perceiving, that feveral feditious and heretical Books or Tracts — againft the Faith and found Catholic Doctrine of holy Mother, the Church, &c.*

ing

ing Pamphlets became more general; Preſſes were multiplied, and Books were diſperſed; and, I believe, it may properly be ſaid, that the Trade of Writing began at that Time, and that it has ever ſince gradually increaſed in the Number, though, perhaps, not in the Style of thoſe that followed it.

In this Reign was erected the firſt *ſecret* Preſs againſt the Church as now eſtabliſhed, of which I have found any certain Account. It was employed by the *Puritans*, and conveyed from one Part of the Nation to another, by them, as they found themſelves in Danger of Diſcovery. From this Preſs iſſued moſt of the Pamphlets againſt *Whitgift* and his Aſſociates, in the Eccleſiaſtical Government; and, when it was at laſt ſeized at *Mancheſter*, it was employed upon a Pamphlet called *More Work for a Cooper*.

In the peaceable Reign of King *James*, thoſe Minds which might, perhaps, with leſs Diſturbance of the World, have been engroſſed by War, were employed in Controverſy; and Writings of all Kinds were multiplied among us. The Preſs, however, was not wholly engaged in Polemical Performances, for more innocent Subjects were ſometimes treated; and it deſerves to be remarked, becauſe it is not generally known, that the Treatiſes of *Huſbandry* and *Agriculture*, which were publiſhed about that Time, are ſo numerous, that it can ſcarcely be imagined by whom they were written, or to whom they were ſold.

The next Reign is too well known to have been a Time of Confuſion, and Diſturbance, and Diſputes of every Kind; and the Writings, which were produced, bear a natural Proportion to the Number of Queſtions that were diſcuſſed at that Time; each Party had its Authors and its Preſſes, and no Endeavours were omitted to gain Proſelytes to every Opinion. I know not whether this may not properly be

B 4   called,

called, *The Age of Pamphlets*; for, though they, perhaps, may not arise to such Multitudes as Mr. *Rawlinson* imagined, they were, undoubtedly, more numerous than can be conceived by any who have not had an Opportunity of examining them.

After the Restoration, the same Differences, in Religious Opinions, are well known to have subsisted, and the same Political Struggles to have been frequently renewed; and, therefore, a great Number of Pens were employed, on different Occasions, till, at length, all other Disputes were absorbed in the Popish Controversy.

From the Pamphlets which these different Periods of Time produced, it is proposed, that this *Miscellany* shall be compiled; for which it cannot be supposed that Materials will be wanting; and, therefore, the only Difficulty will be in what Manner to dispose them.

Those who have gone before us, in Undertakings of this Kind, have ranged the Pamphlets, which Chance threw into their Hands, without any Regard either to the Subject on which they treated, or the Time in which they were written; a Practice in no wise to be imitated by us, who want for no Materials; of which we shall choose those we think best for the particular Circumstances of Times and Things, and most instructing and entertaining to the Reader.

Of the different Methods which present themselves, upon the first View of the great Heaps of Pamphlets which the *Harleian* Library exhibits, the two which merit most Attention are, to distribute the Treatises according to their Subjects, or their Dates; but neither of these Ways can be conveniently followed. By ranging our Collection in Order of Time, we must necessarily publish those Pieces first, which least engage the Curiosity of the Bulk of Mankind; and our Design must fall to the Ground, for Want of Encouragement,

ragement, before it can be so far advanced as to obtain general Regard: By confining ourselves for any long Time to any single Subject, we shall reduce our Readers to one Class; and, as we shall lose all the Grace of Variety, shall disgust all those who read chiefly to be diverted. There is likewise one Objection of equal Force, against both these Methods, that we shall preclude ourselves from the Advantage of any future Discoveries; and we cannot hope to assemble at once all the Pamphlets which have been written in any Age, or on any Subject.

It may be added, in Vindication of our intended Practice, that it is the same with that of *Photius*, whose Collections are no less Miscellaneous than ours; and who declares, that he leaves it to his Reader, to reduce his Extracts under their proper Heads.

Most of the Pieces, which shall be offered in this Collection to the Public, will be introduced by short Prefaces, in which will be given some Account of the Reasons for which they are inserted; Notes will be sometimes adjoined, for the Explanation of obscure Passages, or obsolete Expressions; and Care will be taken to mingle Use and Pleasure through the whole Collection. Notwithstanding every Subject may not be relished by every Reader; yet the Buyer may be assured that each Number will repay his generous Subscription.

An ACCOUNT of the

HARLEIAN LIBRARY.

TO folicit a Subfcription for a Catalogue of
Books expofed to Sale, is an Attempt for
which fome Apology cannot but be neceffary; for
few would willingly contribute to the Expence of
Volumes, by which neither Inftruction nor Entertainment could be afforded, from which only the
Bookfeller could expect Advantage, and of which
the only Ufe muft ceafe, at the Difperfion of the
Library.

Nor could the Reafonablenefs of an univerfal Re-
jection of our Propofal be denied, if this Catalogue
were to be compiled with no other View, than that
of promoting the Sale of the Books which it enume-
rates, and drewn up with that Innacuracy and Confufion which may be found in thofe that are daily
publifhed.

But our Defign, like our Propofal, is uncommon;
and to be profecuted at a very uncommon Expence;
it being intended, that the Books fhall be diftributed
into their diftinct Claffes, and every Clafs ranged
with fome Regard to the Age of the Writers; that
every Book fhall be accurately defcribed; that the
Peculiarities of Editions fhall be remarked, and Obfervations from the Authors of Literary Hiftory oc-
cafionally interfperfed; that, by this Catalogue, we
may inform Pofterity of the Excellence and Value of
this great Collection, and promote the Knowledge
of fcarce Books, and elegant Editions. For this
Purpofe Men of Letters are engaged, who cannot
even

even be fupplied with Amanuenfes, but at an Expence above that of a common Catalogue.

To fhew that this Collection deferves a particular Degree of Regard from the Learned and the Studious, that it excels any Library that was ever yet offered to public Sale in the Value as well as Number of the Volumes which it contains ; and that therefore this Catalogue will not be of lefs Ufe to Men of Letters, than thofe of the *Thuanian*, *Heinfian*, or *Barberinian* Libraries, it may not be improper to exhibit a general Account of the different Claffes, as they are naturally divided by the feveral Sciences.

By this Method we can indeed exhibit only a general Idea, at once magnificent and confufed ; an Idea of the Writings of many Nations, collected from diftant Parts of the World, difcovered fometimes by Chance, and fometimes by Curiofity, amidft the Rubbifh of forfaken Monafteries, and the Repofitories of ancient Families, and brought hither from every Part, as to the univerfal Receptacle of Learning.

It will be no unpleafing Effect of this Account, if thofe, that fhall happen to perufe it, fhould be inclined by it to reflect on the Character of the late Proprietors, and to pay fome Tribute of Veneration to their Ardor for Literature, to that generous and exalted Curiofity which they gratified with inceffant Searches and immenfe Expence, and to which they dedicated that Time, and that Superfluity of Fortune, which many others of their Rank employ in the Purfuit of contemptible Amufements, or the Gratification of guilty Paffions. And, furely, every Man, who confiders Learning as ornamental and advantageous to the Community, muft allow them the Honour of public Benefactors, who have introduced amongft us Authors not bitherto well known, and added to the Literary Treafures of their native Country.

. That

That our Catalogue will excite any other Man to emulate the Collectors of this Library, to prefer Books and Manuscripts to Equipage and Luxury, and to forsake Noise and Diversion for the Conversation of the Learned, and the Satisfaction of extensive Knowledge, we are very far from presuming to hope; but shall make no Scruple to assert, that, if any Man should happen to be seized with such laudable Ambition, he may find in this Catalogue Hints and Informations which are not easily to be met with; he will discover, that the boasted *Bodleian* Library is very far from a perfect Model, and that even the learned *Fabricius* cannot completely instruct him in the early Editions of the Classic Writers.

But the Collectors of Libraries cannot be numerous; and, therefore, Catalogues cannot very properly be recommended to the Public, if they had not a more general and frequent Use, an Use which every Student has experienced, or neglected to his Loss. By the Means of Catalogues only can it be known, what has been written on every Part of Learning, and the Hazard avoided of encountering Difficulties which have already been cleared, discussing Questions which have already been decided, and digging in Mines of Literature which former Ages have exhausted.

How often this has been the Fate of Students, every Man of Letters can declare; and, perhaps, there are very few who have not sometimes valued as new Discoveries, made by themselves, those Observations, which have long since been published, and of which the World therefore will refuse them the Praise; nor can the Refusal be censured as any enormous Violation of Justice; for, why should they not forfeit by their Ignorance, what they might claim by their Sagacity.

To illustrate this Remark, by the Mention of obscure Names, would not much confirm it; and to vilify for this Purpose the Memory of Men truly
great,

great, would be to deny them the Reverence which they may juftly claim from thofe whom their Writings have inftructed. May the Shade at leaft, of one great *Englifh* Critic reft without Difturbance; and may no Man prefume to infult his Memory, who wants his Learning, his Reafon, or his Wit.

From the vexatious Difappointment of meeting Reproach, where Praife is expected, every Man will certainly defire to be fecured; and therefore that Book will have fome Claim to his Regard, from which he may receive Informations of the Labours of his Predeceffors, fuch as a Catalogue of the *Harleian* Library will copioufly afford him.

Nor is the Ufe of Catalogues of lefs Importance to thofe whom Curiofity has engaged in the Study of Literary Hiftory, and who think the intellectual Revolutions of the World more worthy of their Attention, than the Ravages of Tyrants, the Defolation of Kingdoms, the Rout of Armies, and the Fall of Empires. Thofe who are pleafed with obferving the firft Birth of new Opinions, their Struggles againft Oppofition, their filent Progrefs under Perfecution, their general Reception, and their gradual Decline, or fudden Extinction; thofe that amufe themfelves with remarking the different Periods of human Knowledge, and obferve how Darknefs and Light fucceed each other; by what Accident the moft gloomy Nights of Ignorance have given Way in the Dawn of Science, and how Learning has languifhed and decayed, for Want of Patronage and Regard, or been overborne by the Prevalence of fafhionable Ignorance, or loft amidft the Tumults of Invafion, and the Storms of Violence. All thofe who defire any Knowledge of the literary Tranfactions of paft Ages, may find in Catalogues, like this at leaft, fuch an Account as is given by Annalifts, and Chronologers of Civil Hiftory.

How

How the Knowledge of the Sacred Writings has been diffused, will be obferved from the Catalogue of the various Editions of the Bible, from the firft Impreffion by *Fuft*, in 1462, to the prefent Time; in which will be contained the Polyglot Editions of *Spain*, *France*, and *England*, thofe of the original *Hebrew*, the *Greek Septuagint*, and the *Latin Vulgate*; with the Verfions which are now ufed in the remoteft Parts of *Europe*, in the Country of the *Grifons*, in *Lithuania*, *Bohemia*, *Finland*, and *Iceland*.

With regard to the Attempts of the fame Kind made in our own Country, there are few whofe Expectations will not be exceeded by the Number of *Englifh* Bibles, of which not one is forgotten, whether valuable for the Pomp and Beauty of the Impreffion, or for the Notes with which the Text is accompanied, or for any Controverfy or Perfecution that it produced, or for the Peculiarity of any fingle Paffage. With the fame Care have the various Editions of the Book of Common-Prayer been felected, from which all the Alterations which have been made in it may be eafily remarked.

Amongft a great Number of *Roman* Miffals and Breviaries, remarkable for the Beauty of their Cuts and Illuminations, will be found the *Mofarabic* Miffal and Breviary, that raifed fuch Commotions in the Kingdom of *Spain*.

The Controverfial Treatifes written in *England*, about the Time of the Reformation, have been diligently collected, with a Multitude of remarkable Tracts, fingle Sermons, and fmall Treatifes; which, however worthy to be preferved, are, perhaps, to be found in no other Place.

The Regard which was always paid, by the Collectors of this Liberary, to that remarkable Period of Time, in which the Art of Printing was invented, determined them to accumulate the ancient Impreffions of the Fathers of the Church; to which the later

Additions

Additions are added, left Antiquity should have seemed more worthy of Esteem than Accuracy.

History has been considered with the Regard due
to that Study by which the Manners are most easily
formed, and from which the most efficacious In-
struction is received ; nor will the most extensive Curiosity fail of Gratification in this Library ; from
which no Writers have been excluded, that relate
either to the religious or civil Affairs of any Nation.

Not only those Authors of Ecclesiastical History
have been procured, that treat of the State of Religion in general, or deliver Accounts of Sects or Nations, but those likewise who have confined themselves to particular Orders of Men in every Church ;
who have related the Original, and the Rules of
every Society, or recounted the Lives of its Founder
and its Members ; those who have deduced in every
Country the Succession of Bishops, and those who
have employed their Abilities in celebrating the Piety
of particular Saints, or Martyrs, or Monks, or Nuns.

The Civil History of all Nations has been amassed
together ; nor is it easy to determine which has been
thought most worthy of Curiosity.

Of *France*, not only the general Histories and ancient Chronicles, the Accounts of celebrated Reigns,
and Narratives of remarkable Events, but even the
Memorials of single Families, the Lives of private
Men, the Antiquities of particular Cities, Churches,
and Monasteries, the Topography of Provinces, and
the Accounts of Laws, Customs, and Prescriptions,
are here to be found.

The several States of *Italy* have, in this Treasury,
their particular Historians, whose Accouns are, perhaps, generally more exact, by being less extensive ;
and more interesting, by being more particular.

Nor has less Regard been paid to the different Nations of the *Germanic* Empire, of which neither the
Bohemians, nor *Hungarians,* nor *Austrians,* nor *Ba-*
varians,

varians, have been neglected; nor have their Antiquities, however generally difregarded, been lefs ftudioufly fearched, than their prefent State.

The Northern Nations have fupplied this Collection, not only with Hiftory, but Poetry, with *Gothic*
Antiquities, and *Runic* Infcriptions ; which at leaft
have this Claim to Veneration, above the Remains
of the *Roman* Magnificence, that they are the Works
of thofe Heroes, by whom the *Roman* Empire was
deftroyed ; and which may plead, at leaft in this
Nation, that they ought not to be neglected by thofe
that owe to the Men whofe Memories they preferve,
their Conftitution, their Properties, and their Liberties.

The Curiofity of thefe Collectors extend equally
to all Parts of the World; nor did they forget to add
to the Northern the Southern Writers, or to adorn
their Collection with Chronicles of *Spain*, and the
Conqueft of *Mexico*.

Even of thofe Nations with which we have lefs Intercourfe, whofe Cuftoms are lefs accurately known,
and whofe Hiftory is lefs diftinctly recounted, there
are in this Library repofited fuch Accounts as the
Europeans have been hitherto able to obtain ; nor are
the *Mogul*, the *Tartar*, the *Turk*, and the *Saracen*,
without their Hiftorians.

That Perfons fo inquifitive, with Regard to the
Tranfactions of other Nations, fhould enquire yet
more ardently after the Hiftory of their own, may be
naturally expected ; and, indeed, this Part of the
Library is no common Inftance of Diligence and
Accuracy. Here are to be found, with the ancient
Chronicles, and larger Hiftories of *Britain*, the
Narratives of fingle Reigns, and the Accounts of
remarkable Revolutions, the topographical Hiftories
of Counties, the Pedigrees of Families, the Anti-
quities of Churches and Cities, the Proceedings of
Parliaments, the Records of Monafteries, and the

Lives

Lives of particular Men, whether eminent in the Church or the State, or remarkable in private Life; whether exemplary for their Virtues, or deteſtable for their Crimes; whether perſecuted for Religion, or executed for Rebellion.

That memorable Period of the *Engliſh* Hiſtory, which begins with the Reign of King *Charles* the Firſt, and ends with the Reſtoration, will almoſt furniſh a Library alone, ſuch is the Number of Volumes, Pamphlets, and Papers, which were publiſhed by either Party; and ſuch is the Care with which they have been preſerved.

Nor is Hiſtory without the neceſſary Preparatives and Attendants, Geography and Chronology: Of Geography, the beſt Writers and Delineators have been procured, and Pomp and Accuracy have both been regarded: The Student of Chronology may here find likewiſe thoſe Authors who ſearched the Records of Time, and fixed the Periods of Hiſtory.

With the Hiſtorians and Geographers may be ranked the Writers of Voyages and Travels, which may be read here in the *Latin, Engliſh, Dutch, German, French, Italian,* and *Spaniſh* Languages.

The Laws of different Countries, as they are in themſelves equally worthy of Curioſity with their Hiſtory, have, in this Collection, been juſtly regarded; and the Rules by which the various Communities of the World are governed, may be here examined and compared. Here are the ancient Editions of the Papal Decretals, and the Commentators on the Civil Law, the Edicts of *Spain,* and the Statutes of *Venice.*

But with particular Induſtry have the various Writers on the Laws of our own Country been collected, from the moſt ancient to the preſent Time, from the Bodies of the Statutes to the minuteſt Treatiſe; not only the Reports, Precedents, and Readings of our own Courts, but even the Laws of our

West-Indian Colonies, will be exhibited in our Catalogue.

But neither History nor Law have been so far able to engross this Library, as to exclude Physic, Philosophy, or Criticism. Those have been thought, with Justice, worthy of a Place, who have examined the different Species of Animals, delineated their Forms, or described their Properties and Instincts, or who have penetrated the Bowels of the Earth, treated on its different Strata, and analysed its Metals; or who have amused themselves with less laborious Speculations, and planted Trees, or cultivated Flowers.

Those that have exalted their Thoughts above the minuter Parts of the Creation, who have observed the Motions of the heavenly Bodies, and attempted Systems of the Universe, have not been denied the Honour which they deserved by so great an Attempt, whatever has been their Success. Nor have those Mathematicians been rejected, who have applied their Science to the common Purposes of Life; or those that have deviated into the kindred Arts, of Tactics, Architecture, and Fortification.

Even Arts of far less Importance have found their Authors, nor have these Authors been despised by the boundless Curiosity of the Proprietors of the *Harleian* Library. The Writers on Horsemanship and Fencing are more numerous, and more bulky, than could be expected by those who reflect how seldom those excel in either, whom their Education has qualified to compose Books.

The Admirer of *Greek* and *Roman* Literature will meet, in this Collection, with Editions little known to the most inquisitive Critics, and which have escaped the Observation of those whose great Employment has been the Collation of Copies; not will he find only the most ancient Editions of *Faustus, Jenson, Spira, Sweynheim,* and *Pannartz,* but the

the moſt accurate likewiſe and beautiful of *Colinæus*,
the *Juntæ*, *Plantin*, *Aldus*, the *Stephens*, and *El-
ſevir*, with the Commentaries and Obſervations of
the moſt learned Editors.

Nor are they accompanied only with the Illuſtra-
tions of thoſe who have confined their Attempts to
particular Writers, but of thoſe likewiſe who have
treated on any Part of the *Greek*, or *Roman* Antiquities, their Laws, their Cuſtoms, their Dreſs, their
Buildings, their Wars, their Revenues, or the
Rites and Ceremonies of their Worſhip, and thoſe
that have endeavoured to explain any of their Authors from their Statues or their Coins.

Next to the Ancients, thoſe Writers deſerve to be
mentioned, who, at the Reſtoration of Literature,
imitated their Language and their Stile with ſo great
Succeſs, or who laboured with ſo much Induſtry to
make them underſtood : Such were *Philelphus* and
Politian, *Scaliger* and *Buchanan*, and the Poets of the
Age of *Leo* the Tenth ; theſe are likewiſe to be
found in this Library, together with the *Deliciæ*, or
Collections of all Nations.

Painting is ſo nearly allied to Poetry, that it cannot
be wondered that thoſe who have ſo much eſteemed
the one, have paid an equal Regard to the other ;
and therefore it may be eaſily imagined, that the Collection of Prints is numerous in an uncommon Degree ; but ſurely, the Expectation of every Man will
be exceeded, when he his informed that there are
more than forty thouſand engraven from *Raphael*, *Ti-
tian*, *Guido*, the *Carraches*, and a thouſand others by
Nauteuil, *Hollar*, *Callet*, *Edelinck*, and *Dorigny*, and
other Engravers of equal Reputation.

There is alſo a great Collection of original Draw-
ings, of which three ſeem to deſerve a particular
Mention ; the firſt exhibits a Repreſentation of the
Inſide of St. *Peter*'s Church at *Rome* ; the ſecond, of
that of St. *John Lateran* ; and the third, of the high

Altar

Altar of St. *Ignatius*; all painted with the utmost. Accuracy, in their proper Colours.

As the Value of this great Collection may be conceived from this Account, however imperfect, as the Variety of Subjects muſt engage the Curioſity of Men of different Studies, Inclinations, and Employments, it may be thought of very little Uſe to mention any ſlighter Advantages, or to dwell on the Decorations and Embelliſhments which the Generoſity of the Proprietors has beſtowed upon it ; yet, ſince the Compiler of the *Thuanian* Catalogue thought not even that Species of Elegance below his Obſervation, it may not be improper to obſerve, that the *Harleian* Library, perhaps, excels all others, not more in the Number and Excellence, than in the Splendor of its Volumes.

We may now ſurely be allowed to hope, that our Catalogue will not be thought unworthy of the public Curioſity ; that it will be purchaſed as a Record of this great Collection, and preſerved as one of the Memorials of Learning.

The Patrons of Literature will forgive the Purchaſer of this Library, if he preſumes to aſſert ſome Claim to their Protection and Encouragement, as he may have been inſtrumental in continuing to this Nation the Advantage of it. The Sale of *Voſſius's* Collection into a foreign Country, is, to this Day, regretted by Men of Letters ; and if this Effort for the Prevention of another Loſs of the ſame Kind ſhould be diſadvantageous to him, no Man will hereafter willingly riſque his Fortune in the Cauſe of Learning.

A DIS-

A DISSERTATION on AUTHORS.

Scire velim qùare toties mihi, Nævole, triſtis
Occuris fronte obductâ, ceu Marſya victus. Juv.

THERE is no Gift of Nature, or Effect of
Art, however beneficial to Mankind, which,
either by caſual Deviations, or fooliſh Perverſions,
is not ſometimes miſchievous. Whatever may be
the Cauſe of Happineſs, may be made likewiſe the
Cauſe of Miſery. The Medicine, which rightly applied, has Power to cure, has, when Raſhneſs or
Ignorance preſcribes it, the ſame Power to deſtroy.

I have computed, at ſome Hours of Leiſure, the
Loſs and Gain of Literature, and ſet the Pain which
it produces againſt the Pleaſure. Such Calculations
are indeed at a great Diſtance from mathematical
Exactneſs, as they ariſe from the Induction of a few
Particulars, and from Obſervations made rather according to the Temper of the Computiſt, than the
Nature of Things. But ſuch a narrow Survey as
can be taken, will eaſily ſhew that Letters cauſe many
Bleſſings, and inflict many Calamities ; that there is
ſcarcely an Individual who may not conſider them as
immediately or mediately influencing his Life, as
they are chief Inſtruments of conveying Knowledge,
and tranſmitting Sentiments ; and almoſt every Man
learns, by their Means, all that is right or wrong
in his Sentiments and Conduct.

If Letters were conſidered only as Means of Pleaſure, it might well be doubted in what Degree of
Eſtimation they ſhould be held ; but when they are
referred to Neceſſity, the Controverſy is at an End :
It ſoon appears, that though they may ſometimes in-

commode

commode us; yet human Life would fcarcely rife, without them, above the common Exiftence of animal Nature: We might indeed breathe and eat in univerfal Ignorance; but muft want all that gives Pleafure or Security, all the Embellifhments and Delights, and moft of the Conveniencies and Comforts of our prefent Condition.

Literature is a Kind of intellectual Light, which, like the Light of the Sun, may fometimes enable us to fee what we do not like; but who would wifh to efcape unpleafing Objects, by condemning himfelf to perpetual Darknefs?

Since, therefore, Letters are thus indifpenfably neceffary, fince we cannot perfuade ourfelves to lofe their Benefits for the Sake of efcaping their Mifchiefs, it is worth our ferious Enquiry, how their Benefits may be increafed, and their Mifchiefs leffened; by what Means the Harveft of our Studies may afford us more Corn, and lefs Chaff; and how the Rofes of the Gardens of Science may gratify us more with their Fragrance, and prick us lefs with their Thorns.

I fhall not, at prefent, mention the more formidable Evils which the Mifapplication of Literature produces; nor fpeak of Churches infected with Herefy, States inflamed with Sedition, or Schools infatuated with hypothetical Fictions. Thefe are Evils which Mankind have always lamented; and which, till Mankind grow wife and modeft, they muft, I am afraid, continue to lament, without Hope of Remedy. I fhall now touch only on fome lighter and lefs extenfive Evils, yet fuch as are fufficiently heavy to thofe that feel them; and are of late fo widely diffufed, as to deferve, though perhaps not the Notice of the Legiflature, yet the Confideration of thofe whofe Benevolence inclines them to a voluntary Care of public Happinefs.

It was long ago obferved by *Virgil*, and I fuppofe by many before him, that *Bees do not make Honey for*
their

their own Use: The Sweets which they collect in their laborious Excursions, and store up in their Hives with so much Skill, are seized by those who have contributed neither Toil nor Art to the Collection; and the poor Animals are either destroyed by the Invader, or left to shift without a Supply. The Condition is nearly the same of the Gatherer of Honey and the Gatherer of Knowledge The *Bee* and the *Author* work alike for others, and often lose the Profit of their Labour. The Case, therefore, of Authors, however hitherto neglected, may claim Regard. Every Body of Men is important according to the joint Proportion of their Usefulness and their Number. Individuals, however they may excel, cannot hope to be considered singly as of great Weight in the political Balance; and Multitudes, though they may, merely by their Bulk, demand some Notice, are yet not of much Value, unless they contribute to ease the Burthen of Society, by co-operating to its Prosperity.

Of the Men, whose Condition we are now examining, the Usefulness never was disputed: They are known to be the great Disseminators of Knowledge, and Guardians of the Commonwealth; and of late their Numbers have been so much increased, that they are become a very conspicuous Part of the Nation. It is not now, as in former Times, when Men studied long, and passed through the Severities of Discipline, and the Probation of public Trials, before they presumed to think themselves qualified for Instructors of their Countrymen: There is found a nearer Way to Fame and Erudition, and the Inclosures of Literature are thrown open to every Man whom Idleness disposes to loiter, or whom Pride inclines to set himself to View. The Sailor publishes his Journal; the Farmer writes the Process of his annual Labour: He that succeeds in his Trade thinks his Wealth a Proof of his Understanding, and

boldly

boldly tutors the Public: He that fails, confiders his Mifcarriage as the Confequence of a Capacity too great for the Bufinefs of a Shop, and amufes himfelf in the Fleet with Writing or Tranflating. The laft Century imagined, that a Man compofing in his Chariot was a new Object of Curiofity; but how much would the Wonder have been increafed, by a Footman ftudying behind it? There is now no Clafs of Men without its Authors, from the Peer to the Threfher; nor can the Sons of Literature be confined any longer to *Grubftreet* or *Moorfields*; they are fpread over all the Town and all the Country, and fill every Stage of Habitation from the Cellar to the Garret.

It is well known, that the Price of Commodities muft always fall as the Quantity is increafed, and that no Trade can allow its Profeffors to be multiplied beyond a certain Number. The great Mifery of Writers proceeds from their Multitude. We eafily perceive that in a Nation of Clothiers no Man could have any Cloth to make but for his own Back; that in a Community of Bakers every Man muft ufe his own Bread; and what can be the Cafe of a Nation of Authors, but that every Man muft be content to read his Book to himfelf? For furely it is in vain to hope, that of Men labouring at the fame Occupation, any will prefer the Work of his Neighbour to his own; yet this Expectation, wild as it is, feems to be indulged by many of the Writing Race; and therefore it can be no Wonder that, like all other Men who fuffer their Minds to form inconfiderate Hopes, they are harraffed and dejected with frequent Difappointments.

If I were to form an Adage of Mifery, or fix the loweft Point to which Humanity could fall, I fhould be tempted to name the Life of an Author. Many univerfal Comparifons there are by which Mifery is expreffed. We talked of a Man teazed like a Bear at the

the Stake, tormented like a Toad under a Harrow, or hunted like a Dog with a Stick at his Tail : All thefe are indeed States of Uneafinefs; but what are they to the Life of an Author! of an Author worried by Critics, tormented by his Bookfeller, and hunted by his Creditors. Yet fuch muft be the Cafe of many among the Retailers of Knowledge, while they continue thus to fwarm over the Land; and whether it be by Propagation or Contagion, produce new Writers to heighten the general Diftrefs, to increafe Confufion, and haften Famine.

Having long ftudied the Varieties of Life, I can guefs by every Man's Walk, or Air, to what State of the Community he belongs. Every Man has noted the Legs of a Taylor, and the Gait of a Seaman; and a little Extenfion of his phyfiognomical Acquifitions will teach him to diftinguifh the Countenance of an Author. It is my Practice, when I am in Want of Amufement, to place myfelf for an Hour at *Temple-Bar*, or any other narrow Pafs much frequented, and examine one by one the Looks of the Paffengers; and I have commonly found, that, between the Hours of Eleven and Four, every Sixth Man is an Author. They are feldom to be feen very early in the Morning, or late in the Evening; but about Dinner-time they are all in Motion, and have one uniform Eagernefs in their Faces, which gives little Opportunity of difcerning their Hopes or Fears, their Pleafures or their Pains.

But, in the Afternoon, when they have all dined, or compofed themfelves to pafs the Day without a Dinner, their Paffions have full Play, and I can perceive one Man wondering at the Stupidity of the Public, by which his new Book has been totally neglected; another curfing the *French*, who fright away literary Curiofity by their Threats of an Invafion; another fwearing at his Bookfeller, who will advance no Money without Copy; another perufing,

6

ing, as he walks, his Publisher's Bill ; another murmuring at an unanswerable Criticism; another determining to write no more to a Generation of Barbarians; and another resolving to try once again, whether he cannot awake the drowsy World to a Sense of his Merit.

It sometimes happens, that there may be remarked among them a Smile of Complacence, or a Strut of Elevation : But if these Favourites of Fortune are carefully watched for a few Days, they seldom fail to shew the Transitoriness of human Felicity ; the Crest falls, the Gaiety is ended, and there appear evident Tokens of a successful Rival, or a fickle Patron.

But of all Authors, those are the most wretched, who exhibit their Productions on the Theatre, and who are to propitiate first the Manager, and then the Public. Many an humble Visitant have I followed to the Doors of these Lords of the Drama, seen him touch the Knocker with a shaking Hand ; and, after long Deliberation, adventure to solicit Entrance by a single Knock : But I never staid to see them come out from their Audience ; because my Heart is tender, and being subject to Frights in Bed, I would not willingly dream of an Author.

That the Number of Authors is disproportionate to the Maintenance which the Public seems willing to assign them ; that there is neither Praise nor Meat for all who write, is apparent from this ; that, like Wolves in long Winters, they are forced to prey one on another. The *Reviewers* and *Critical Reviewers*, the *Remarkers* and *Examiners*, can satisfy their Hunger only by devouring their Brethren. I am far from imagining that they are naturally more ravenous or blood-thirsty than those on whom they fall with so much Violence and Fury; but they are hungry, and Hunger must be satisfied ; and these Savages, when
their

their Bellies are full, will fawn on thofe whom they now bite.

The Refult of all thefe Confiderations amounts only to this ; that the Number of Writers muft at laft be leffened ; but by what Method this great Defign can be accomplifhed, is not eafily difcovered. It was lately propofed that every Man who kept a Dog fhould pay a certain Tax, which, as the Contriver of Ways and Means very judicioufly obferved, would either deftroy the Dogs, or bring in Money. Perhaps it might be proper to lay fome fuch Tax upon Authors; only the Payment muft be leffened in Proportion as the Animal, upon which it is raifed, is lefs neceffary ; for many a Man that would pay for his Dog, will difmifs his Dedicator. Perhaps if every one, who employed or harboured an Author, was affeffed a Groat a Year, it would fufficiently leffen the Nuifance without deftroying the Species.

But no great Alteration is to be attempted rafhly. We muft confider how the Authors, which this Tax fhall exclude from their Trade, are to be employed. The Nets ufed in the Herring Fifhery can furnifh Work but for few, and not many can be employed as Labourers at the Foundation of the new Bridge. There muft, therefore, be fome other Scheme formed for their Accommodation, which the prefent State of Affairs may eafily fupply. It is well known, that great Efforts have been lately made to man the Fleet, and augment the Army, and loud Complaints are made of ufeful Hands forced away from their Families into the Service of the Crown. This offenfive Exertion of Power may be eafily avoided, by opening a few Houfes for the Entertainment of difcarded Authors, who would enter into the Service with great Alacrity, as moft of them are zealous Friends of every prefent Government ; many of them are Men of able Bodies, and ftrong Limbs, qua'ified at leaft as well for the Mufket as the Pen; They are, perhaps,

haps, at prefent a little emaciated and enfeebled; but would foon recover their Strength and Flefh with good Quarters and prefent Pay.

There are fome Reafons for which they may feem particularly qualified for a military Life. They are ufed to fuffer Want of every Kind; they are accuftomed to obey the Word of Command from their Patrons and their Bookfellers; they have always paffed a Life of Hazard and Adventure, uncertain what may be their State on the next Day; and, what is of yet more Importance, they have long made their Minds familiar to Danger, by Defcriptions of bloody Battles, daring Undertakings, and wonderful Efcapes. They have their Memories ftored with all the Stratagems of War, and have, over and over, practifed in their Clofets the Expedients of Diftrefs, the Exultation of Triumph, and the Refignation of Heroes fentenced to Deftruction.

Some indeed there are, who, by often changing Sides in Controverfy, may give juft Sufpicion of their Fidelity, and whom I fhould think likely to defert for the Pleafure of Defertion, or for a Farthing a Month advanced in their Pay. Of thefe Men I know not what Ufe can be made; for they can never be trufted but with Shackles on their Legs. There are others whom long Depreffion, under fupercilious Patrons, has fo humbled and crufhed, that they will never have Steadinefs to keep their Ranks. But for thefe Men there may be found Fifes and Drums, and they will be well enough pleafed to inflame others to Battle, if they are not obliged to fight themfelves.

It is more difficult to know what can be done with the Ladies of the Pen, of whom this Age has produced greater Numbers than any former Time. It is indeed common for Women to follow the Camp; but no prudent General will allow them in fuch Numbers as the Breed of Authoreffes would furnifh. Authoreffes are feldom famous for clean Linen; there-

fore

fore they cannot make Laundreffes: They are rarely
fkilful at their Needle, and cannot make a Soldier's
Shirt: They will make bad Suttlers, being not
much accuftomed to eat. I muft therefore propofe,
that they fhall form a Regiment of themfelves, and
garrifon the Town which is fuppofed to be in moft
Danger of a *French* Invafion. They will probably
have no Enemies to encounter; but, if they are once
fhut up together, they will foon difincumber the
Public, by tearing out the Eyes of one another.

The great Art of Life is to play for much, and to
ftake little; which Rule I have kept in View through
this whole Project: For, if our Authors, and Authoreffes defeat our Enemies, we fhall obtain all the
ufual Advantages of Victory; and if they fhould be
deftroyed in War, we fhall lofe only thofe who had
wearied the Public, and whom, whatever be their
Fate, nobody will mifs.

The PLAN of a

DICTIONARY

OF THE

ENGLISH LANGUAGE.

To the Right Honourable *Philip Dormer*, Earl of *Chesterfield*, one of His Majesty's Principal Secretaries of State.

My LORD,

WHEN first I undertook to write an *English* Dictionary, I had no Expectation of any higher Patronage than that of the Proprietors of the Copy, nor Prospect of any other Advantage than the Price of my Labour. I knew that the Work in which I engaged is generally considered as Drudgery for the Blind, as the proper Toil of artless Industry; a Task that requires neither the Light of Learning, nor the Activity of Genius, but may be successfully performed without any higher Quality than that of bearing Burthens with dull Patience, and beating the Track of the Alphabet with sluggish Resolution.

Whether this Opinion, so long transmitted, and so widely propagated, had its Beginning from Truth and Nature, or from Accident and Prejudice; whether it be decreed by the Authority of Reason, or the Tyranny of Ignorance, that of all the Candidates for literary Praise, the unhappy Lexicographer holds the lowest Place, neither Vanity nor Interest incited me to enquire. It appeared that the Province allotted me was, of all the Regions of Learning,

ing,

ing, generally confessed to be the least delightful, that it was believed to produce neither Fruits nor Flowers; and that, after a long and laborious Cultivation, not even the barren Laurel had been found upon it.

Yet on this Province, my Lord, I entered, with the pleasing Hope, that, as it was low, it likewise would be safe. I was drawn forward with the Prospect of Employment, which, though not splendid, would be useful; and which, though it could not make my Life envied, would keep it innocent; which would awaken no Passion, engage me in no Contention, nor throw in my Way any Temptation to disturb the Quiet of others by Censure, or my own by Flattery.

I had read indeed of Times, in which Princes and Statesmen thought it Part of their Honour to promote the Improvement of their native Tongues; and in which Dictionaries were written under the Protection of Greatness. To the Patrons of such Undertakings I willingly paid the Homage of believing that they, who were thus solicitous for the Perpetuity of their Language, had Reason to expect that their Actions would be celebrated by Posterity, and that the Eloquence which they promoted would be employed in their Praise. But I consider such Acts of Beneficence as Prodigies, recorded rather to raise Wonder than Expectation; and content with the Terms that I had stipulated, had not suffered my Imagination to flatter me with any other Encouragement, when I found that my Design had been thought by your Lordship of Importance sufficient to attract your Favour.

How far this unexpected Distinction can be rated among the happy Incidents of Life, I am not yet able to determine. Its first Effect has been to make me anxious, lest it should fix the Attention of the Public too much upon me, and, as it once happened

to

to an Epic Poet of *France*, by raifing the Reputation of the Attempt, obftruct the Reception of the
Work. I imagine what the World will expect from
a Scheme, profecuted under your Lordfhip's Influence; and I know that Expectation, when her
Wings are once expanded, eafily reaches Heights
which Performance never will attain; and when fhe
has mounted the Summit of Perfection, derides her
Follower, who dies in the Purfuit.

Not therefore to raife Expectation, but to reprefs
it, I here lay before your Lordfhip the Plan of my
Undertaking, that more may not be demanded than
I intend; and that, before it is too far advanced to
be thrown into a new Method, I may be advertifed
of its Defects or Superfluities. Such Informations I
may juftly hope, from the Emulation with which
thofe, who defire the Praife of Elegance or Difcernment, muft contend in the Promotion of a Defign
that you, my Lord, have not thought unworthy to
fhare your Attention with Treaties and with Wars.

In the firft Attempt to methodife my Ideas I found
a Difficulty, which extended itfelf to the whole
Work. It was not eafy to determine by what Rule of
Diftinction the Words of this Dictionary were to be
chofen. The chief Intent of it is to preferve the Purity,
and afcertain the Meaning of our *Englifh* Idiom; and
this feems to require nothing more than that our Language be confidered, fo far as it is our own; that the
Words and Phrafes ufed in the general Intercourfe
of Life, or found in the Works of thofe whom we
commonly ftile polite Writers, be felected, without
including the Terms of particular Profeffions; fince,
with the Arts to which they relate, they are generally derived from other Nations, and are very often
the fame in all the Languages of this Part of the
World. This is, perhaps, the exact and pure Idea
of a grammatical Dictionary; but in Lexicography,
as in other Arts, naked Science is too delicate for
the

the Purpofes of Life. The Value of a Work muft be eftimated by its Ufe : It is not enough that a Dictionary delights the Critic, unlefs, at the fame Time, it inftructs the Learner ; as it is to little Purpofe that an Engine amufes the Philofopher by the Subtilty of its Mechanifm, if it requires fo much Knowledge in its Application, as to be of no Advantage to the common Workman.

The Title which I prefix to my Work has long conveyed a very mifcellaneous Idea, and they that take a Dictionary into their Hands, have been accuftomed to expect from it a Solution of almoft every Difficulty. If foreign Words therefore were rejected, it could be little regarded, excepted by Critics, or thofe who afpire to Criticifm ; and however it might enlighten thofe that write, would be all Darknefs to them that only read. The Unlearned much oftner confult their Dictionaries for the Meaning of Words, than for their Structures or Formations ; and the Words that moft want Explanation are generally Terms of Art ; which, therefore, Experince has taught my Predeceffors to fpread with a Kind of pompous Luxuriance over their Productions.

The Academicians of *Franse*, indeed, rejected Terms of Science in their firft Effay, but found afterwards a Neceffity of relaxing the Rigour of their Determination ; and, though they would not naturalize them at once by a fingle Act, permitted them by Degrees to fettle themfelves among the Natives, with little Oppofition ; and it would furely be no Proof of Judgment to imitate them in an Error which they have now retracted, and deprive the Book of its chief Ufe, by fcrupulous Diftinctions.

On fuch Words, however, all are not equally to be confidered as Parts of our Language ; for fome of them are naturalized and incoporated, but others ftill continue Aliens, and are rather Auxiliaries then

Subjects. This Naturalization is produced either by an Admiſſion into common Speech, in ſome metaphorical Signification, which is the Acquiſition of a Kind of Property among us; as we ſay, the Zenith of Advancement, the Meridian of Life, the * Cynoſure of neighbouring Eyes; or it is the Conſequence of long Intermixture and frequent Uſe, by which the Ear is accuſtomed to the Sound of Words, till their Original is forgotten, as in Equator, Satellites; or of the Change of a foreign into an *Engliſh* Termination, and a Conformity to the Laws of the Speech into which they are adopted; as in Category, Chachexy, Peripneumony.

Of thoſe which ſtill continue in the State of Aliens, and have made no Approaches towards Aſſimilation, ſome ſeem neceſſary to be retained; becauſe the Purchaſers of the Dictionary will expect to find them. Such are many Words in the Common Law, as *Capias, Habeas Corpus, Prædmunire, Niſi Prius:* Such are ſome Terms of Controverſial Divinity, as Hypoſtaſis; and of Phyſick, as the Names of Diſeaſes; and in general, all Terms which can be found in Books not written profeſſedly upon particular Arts, or can be ſuppoſed neceſſary to thoſe who do not regularly ſtudy them. Thus, when a Reader not ſkilled in Phyſick happens in *Milton* upon this Line,

———————————————— pining Atrophy,
Maraſmus, and wide-waſting Peſtilence,

he will, with equal Expectation, look into his Dictionary for the Word Maraſmus, as for Atrophy, or Peſtilence; and will have Reaſon to complain if he does not find it.

It ſeems neceſſary to the Completion of a Dictionary deſigned not merely for Critics, but for popular Uſe, that it ſhould compriſe, in ſome Degree,

* *Milton.*

the

the peculiar Words of every Profeffion ; that the Terms of War and Navigation fhould be inferted, fo far as they can be required by Readers of Travels, and of Hiftory ; and thofe of Law, Merchandife, and mechanical Trades, fo far as they can be fuppofed ufeful in the Occurrences of common Life.

But there ought, however, to be fome Diftinction made between the different Claffes of Words ; and therefore it will be proper to print thofe which are incorporated into the Language in the ufual Character, and thofe which are ftill to be confidered as foreign, in the *Italick* Letter.

Another Queftion may arife with regard to Appellatives, or the Names of Species. It feems of no great Ufe to fet down the Words Horfe, Dog, Cat, Willow, Alder, Dafy, Rofe, and a thoufand others, of which it will be hard to give an Explanation, not more obfcure than the Word itfelf. Yet it is to be confidered, that, if the Names of Animals be inferted, we muft admit thofe which are more known, as well as thofe with which we are, by Accident, lefs acquainted ; and if they are all rejected, how will the Reader be relieved from Difficulties produced by Allufions to the Crocodile, the Camæleon, the Ichneumon, and the Hyæna ? If no Plants are to be mentioned, the moft pleafing Part of Nature will be excluded, and many beautiful Epithets be unexplained. If only thofe which are lefs known are to be mentioned, who fhall fix the limits of the Reader's Learning ? The Importance of fuch Explications appears from the Miftakes which the Want of them has occafioned. Had *Shakefpeare* had a Dictionary of this Kind, he had not made the Woodbine entwine the Honeyfuckle ; nor would *Milton*, with fuch Affiftance, have difpofed fo improperly of his Ellops and his Scorpion.

Befides, as fuch Words, like others, require that their Accents fhould be fettled, their Sounds afcer-

tained,

tained, and their Etymologies deduced, they cannot be properly omitted in the Dictionary. And though the Explanations of some may be censured as trivial because they are almost universally understood, and those of others as unnecessary, because they will seldom occur, yet it seems not proper to omit them, since it is rather to be wished that many Readers should find more than they expect, than that one should miss what he might hope to find.

When all the Words are selected and arranged, the first Part of the Work to be considered is the Orthography, which was long vague and uncertain; which at last, when its Fluctuation ceased, was in many Cases settled but by Accident; and in which according to your Lordship's Observation, there is still great Uncertainty among the best Critics: Nor is it easy to state a Rule by which we may decide between Custom and Reason, or between the equiponderant Authorities of Writers alike eminent for Judgment and Accuracy.

The great orthographical Contest has long subsisted between Etymology and Pronunciation. It has been demanded, on one Hand, that Men should write as they speak; but, as it has been shewn that this Conformity never was attained in any Language, and that it is not more easy to persuade Men to agree exactly in speaking than in writing, it may be asked with equal Propriety, why Men do not rather speak as they write. In *France*, where this Controversy was at its greatest Height, neither Party, however ardent, durst adhere steadily to their own Rule; the Etymologist was often forced to spell with the People; and the Advocate for the Authority of Pronunciation found it sometimes deviating so capriciously from the received Use of Writing, that he was constrained to comply with the Rule of his Adversaries, lest he should lose the End by the Means, and be left alone by following the Crowd.

When

When a Queſtion of Orthography is dubious, that Practice has, in my Opinion, a Claim to Preference which preſerves the greateſt Number of radical Letters, or ſeems moſt to comply with the general Cuſtom of our Language. But the chief Rule which I propoſe to follow is, to make no Innovation, without a Reaſon ſufficient to balance the Inconvenience of Change; and ſuch Reaſons I do not expect often to find. All Change is of itſelf an Evil, which ought not be hazarded but for evident Advantage; and as Inconſtancy is in every Caſe a Mark of Weakneſs, it will add nothing to the Reputation of our Tongue. There are, indeed, ſome who deſpiſe the Inconveniences of Confuſion, who ſeem to take Pleaſure in departing from Cuſtom, and to think Alteration deſirable for its own Sake, and the Reformation of our Orthography, which theſe Writers have attempted, ſhould not paſs without its due Honours, but that I ſuppoſe they hold a Singularity its own Reward, or may dread the Faſcination of laviſh Praiſe.

The preſent Uſage of Spelling, where the preſent Uſage can be diſtinguiſhed, will therefore, in this Work, be generally followed; yet there will be often Occaſion to obſerve, that it is in itſelf inaccurate, and tolerated rather than choſen; particularly when, by a Change of one Letter, or more, the Meaning of a Word is obſcured; as in *Farrier*, or *Ferrier*, as it was formerly written, from *Ferrum*, or *Fer*; in *Gibberiſh*, for *Gebriſh*, the Jargon of *Geber*, and his chymical Followers, underſtood by none but their own Tribe. It will be likewiſe ſometimes proper to trace back the Orthography of different Ages, and ſhew by what Gradations the Word departed from its Original.

Cloſely connected with Orthography is Pronunciation, the Stability of which is of great Importance to the Duration of a Language, becauſe the firſt Change will naturally begin by Corruptions in

the

the living Speech. The Want of certain Rules for the Pronunciation of former Ages, has made us wholly ignorant of the metrical Art of our ancient Poets; and since those who study their Sentiments regret the Loss of their Numbers, it is surely Time to provide that the Harmony of the Moderns may be more permanent.

A new Pronunciation will make almost a new Speech; and therefore, since one great End of this Undertaking is to fix the *English* Language, Care will be taken to determine the Accentuation of all Polysyllables by proper Authorities, as it is one of those capricious Phænomena which cannot be easily reduced to Rules. Thus there is no antecedent Reason for Difference of Accent in the Words *dolorous* and *sonorous*; yet of the one *Milton* gives the Sound in this Line:

He pass'd o'er many a Region *dolorous*,

and that of the other in this,

Sonorous Metal blowing martial Sounds.

It may likewise be proper to remark metrical Licenses, such as Contractions, *generous*, *gen'rous*; *reverend*, *rev'rend*; and Coalitions, as *Region*, *Question*.

But it is still more necessary to fix the Pronunciation of Monosyllables, by placing with them Words of correspondent Sound, that one may guard the other against the Danger of that Variation, which, to some of the most common, has already happened; so that the Words *Wound* and *Wind*, as they are now frequently pronounced, will not rhyme to *Sound* and *Mind*. It is to be remarked, that many Words written alike are differently pronounced, as *Flow*, and *Brow*; which may be thus registered, *Flow*, *Woe*, *Brow*, *now*; or of which the Exemplification may be generally given by a Distich: Thus the Words

tear,

tear, or lacerate, and *Tear*, the Water of the Eye, have the fame Letters, but may be diftinguifhed thus, *tear, dare* ; *Tear, Peer*.

. Some Words have two Sounds, which may be equally admitted, as being equally defenfible by Authority. Thus *great* is differently ufed.

For *Swift* and him defpis'd the Farce of State, The fober Follies of the Wife and *Great*. POPE.

As if Misfortune made the Throne her Seat, And none could be unhappy but the *Great*. ROWE.

The Care of fuch minute Particulars may be cenfured as trifling ; but thefe Particulars have not been thought unworthy of Attention in more polifhed Languages.

The Accuracy of the *French*, in ftating the Sounds of their Letters, is well known ; and, among the *Italians, Crefcembeni* has not thought it unneceffary to inform his Countrymen of the Words which, in Compliance with different Rhymes, are allowed to be differently fpelt, and of which the Number is now fo fixed, that no modern Poet is fuffered to encreafe it.

When the Orthography and Pronunciation are adjufted, the Etymology or Derivation is next to be confidered, and the Words are to be diftinguifhed according to their different Claffes, whether fimple, as *Day, Light*, or compound, as *Day-light* ; whether primitive, as, to *act*, or derivative, as *Action, actionable, active, Activity*. This will much facilitate the Attainment of our Language, which now ftands in our Dictionaries a confufed Heap of Words without Dependence, and without Relation.

When this Part of the Work is performed, it will be neceffary to enquire how our Primitives are to be deduced from foreign Languages, which may be often very fuccefsfully performed by the Affiftance of our own Etymologifts. This Search will give Oc-
D 4 cafion

cafion to many curious Difquifitions, and fometimes
perhaps to Conjectures, which to Readers unacquainted with this Kind of Study, cannot but appear improbable and capricious.   But it may be reafonably imagined, that what is fo much in the Power
of Men as Language, will very often be capricioufly
conducted.   Nor are thefe Difquifitions and Conjectures to be confidered altogether as wanton Sports
of Wit, or vain Shews of Learning; our Language
is well known not to be primitive or felf-originated,
but to have adopted Words of every Generation,
and, either for the Supply of its Neceffities, or the
Encreafe of its Copioufnefs, to have received Additions from very diftant Regions; fo that in Search
of the Progenitors of our Speech, we may wander
from the Tropic to the Frozen Zone, and find fome
in the Valleys of *Paleftine*, and fome upon the Rocks
of *Norway*.

Befides the Derivation of particular Words, there
is likewife an Etymology of Phrafes.   Expreffions
are often taken from other Languages; fome apparently, as to *run a Rifque, courier un Rifque*; and
fome even when we do not feem to borrow their
Words; thus, to *bring about* or accomplifh, appears
an *Englifh* Phrafe, but in Reality our native Word
about has no fuch Import, and is only a *French* Expreffion, of which we have an Example in the common Phrafes *venir à bout d'une affaire*.

In exhibiting the Defcent of our Language, our
Etymologifts feem to have been too lavifh of their
Learning, having traverfed almoft every Word
through various Tongues, only to fhew what was
fhewn fufficiently by the firft Derivation.   This
Practice is of great Ufe in fynoptical Lexicons, where
mutilated and doubtful Languages are explained by
their Affinity to others more certain and extenfive,
but is generally fuperfluous in *Englifh* Etymologies.
When the Word is eafily deduced from a *Saxon*
Original,

Original, I shall not often enquire further, since we know not the Parent of the *Saxon* Dialect ; but when it is borrowed from the *French*, I shall shew whence the *French* is apparently derived. Where a *Saxon* Root cannot be found, the Defect may be supplied from kindred Languages, which will be generally furnished with much Liberality by the Writers of our Glossaries ; Writers who deserve often the highest Praise, both of Judgment and Industry, and may expect at least to be mentioned with Honour by me, whom they have freed from the greatest Part of a very laborious Work, and on whom they have imposed, at worst, only the easy Task of rejecting Superfluities.

By tracing in this Manner every Word to its Original, and not admitting, but with great Caution, any of which no Original can be found, we shall secure our Language from being over-run with Cant, from being crouded with low Terms, the Spawn of Folly or Affectation, which arise from no just Principles of Speech, and of which therefore no legitimate Derivation can be shewn.

When the Etymology is thus adjusted, the Analogy of our Language is next to be considered ; when we have discovered whence our Words are derived, we are to examine by what Rules they are governed, and how they are inflected through their various Terminations. The Terminations of the *English* are few, but those few have hitherto remained unregarded by the Writers of our Dictionaries. Our Substantives are declined only by the plural Termination, our Adjectives admit no Variation but in the Degrees of Comparison, and our Verbs are conjugated by auxiliary Words, and are only changed in the Preter Tense.

To our Language may be with great Justness applied the Observation of *Quintilian*, that Speech was not formed by an Analogy sent from heaven. It did

not

not defcend to us in a State of Uniformity and Perfection, but was produced by Neceſſity, and enlarged by Accident ; and is therefore compoſed of
diffimilar Parts ; thrown together by Negligence, by
Affectation, by Learning, or by Ignorance.

Our Inflections therefore are by no Means conftant, but admit of numberlefs Irregularities, which
in this Dictionary will be diligently noted.   Thus
Fox makes in the Plural *Foxes*, but *Ox* makes *Oxen.*
Sheep is the fame in both Numbers.   Adjectives are
fometimes compared by changing the laft Syllable,
as *proud, prouder, proudeſt* ; and fometimes by Particles prefixed, as *ambitious, more* ambitious, *moſt*
ambitious.   The Forms of our Verbs are fubject to
great Variety ; fome end their Preter Tenfe in *ed*, as
I *love*, I *lov'd*, I have *loved* ; which may be called
the regular Form, and is followed by moft of our
Verbs of fouthern Original.   But many depart from
this Rule, without agreeing in any other ; as I
ſhake, I *ſhook*, I have *ſhaken*, or *ſhook*, as it is fometimes written in Poetry ;   I *make*, I *made*, I have
made ; I *bring*, I *brought*, I *wring*, I *wrung*, and
many others, which, as they cannot be reduced to
Rules, muft be learned from the Dictionary rather
than the Grammar.

The Verbs are likewife to be diftinguifhed according to their Qualities, as Actives from Neuters ; the
Neglect of which has already introduced fome Bar-
barities in our Converfation, which if not obviated
by juft Animadverfions, may in Time creep into our
Writings.

Thus, my Lord, will our Language be laid
down, diftinct in its minuteft Subdivifions, and refolved into its elemental Principles.   And who upon
this Survey can forbear to wifh, that thefe fundamen-
tal Atoms of our Speech might obtain the Firmnefs
and Immutability of the primogenial and conftituent
Particles of Matter, that they might retain their Subftance

ftance while they alter their Appearance, and be varied and compounded, yet not deftroyed.

But this is a Privilege which Words are fcarcely to expect: for, like their Author, when they are not gaining Strength, they are generally lofing it. Tho' Art may fometimes prolong their Duration, it will rarely give them Perpetuity; and their Changes will be almoft always informing us, that Language is the Work of Man, of a Being from whom Permanence and Stability cannot be derived.

Words having been hitherto confidered as feparate and unconnected, are now to be likewife examined as they are ranged in their various Relations to others by the Rules of Syntax or Conftruction, to which I do not know that any Regard has been yet fhewn in *Englifh* Dictionaries, and in which the Grammarians can give little Affiftance. The Syntax of this Language is too inconftant to be reduced to Rules, and can be only learned by the diftinct Confideration of particular Words as they are ufed by the beft Authors. Thus, we fay, according to the prefent Modes of Speech, The Soldier died *of* his Wounds, and the Sailor perifhed *with* Hunger: and every Man acquainted with our Language would be offended by a Change of thefe Particles, which yet feem originally affigned by Chance, there being no Reafon to be drawn from Grammar why a Man may not, with equal Propriety, be faid to die *with* a Wound, or perifh *of* Hunger.

Our Syntax therefore is not to be taught by general Rules, but by fpecial Precedents; and in examining whether *Addifon* has been with Juftice accufed of a Solecifm in this Paffage,

The poor Inhabitant ———
Starves in the midft of Nature's Bounty curft,
And in the loaden Vineyard *dies for Thirft,*

it

it is not in our Power to have recourse to any eſtabliſhed Laws of Speech; but we muſt remark how the Writers of former Ages have uſed the ſame Word, and conſider whether he can be acquitted of Impropriety, upon the Teſtimony of *Davies*, given in his Favour by a ſimilar Paſſage.

She loaths the wat'ry Glaſs wherein ſhe gaz'd,
And ſhuns it ſtill, although *for Thirſt ſhe dye.*

When the Conſtruction of a Word is explained, it is neceſſary to purſue it through its Train of Phraſeology, through thoſe Forms where it is uſed in a Manner peculiar to our Language, or in Senſes not to be compriſed in the general Explanations; as from the Verb *make* ariſe theſe Phraſes, to *make Love*, to *make an End*, to *make Way*; as, He *made Way* for his Followers, The Ship *made Way* before the Wind; to *make a Bed*, to *make merry*, to *make a Mock*, to *make Preſents*, to *make a Doubt*, to *make out an Aſſertion*, to *make good* a Breach, to *make good* a Cauſe, to *make nothing* of an Attempt, to *make Lamentation*, to *make a Merit*, and many others which will occur in reading with that View, and which only their Frequency hinders from being generally remarked.

The great Labour is yet to come, the Labour of interpreting theſe Words and Phraſes with Brevity, Fullneſs, and Perſpicuity; a Taſk of which the Extent and Intricacy is ſufficiently ſhewn by the Miſcarriage of thoſe who have generally attempted it. This Difficulty is increaſed by the Neceſſity of explaining the Words in the ſame Language; for there is often only one Word for one Idea; and though it be eaſy to tranſlate the Words *bright, ſweet, ſalt, bitter*, into another Language, it is not eaſy to explain them.

With regard to the Interpretation, many other Queſtions have required Conſideration. It was

ſome

some Time doubted whether it be necessary to explain the Things implied by particular Words; as under the Term *Baronet*, whether, instead of this Explanation, *a Title of Honour next in Degree to that of Baron*, it would be better to mention more particularly the Creation, Privileges, and Rank of Baronets; and whether, under the Word *Barometer*, instead of being satisfied with observing that it is *an Instrument to discover the Weight of the Air*, it would be fit to spend a few Lines upon its Invention, Construction, and Principles. It is not to be expected, that with the Explanation of the one the Herald should be satisfied, or the Philosopher with that of the other; but since it will be required by common Readers, that the Explications should be sufficient for common Use; and since, without some Attention to such Demands, the Dictionary cannot become generally valuable, I have determined to consult the best Writers, for Explanations real, as well as verbal; and perhaps I may at last have Reason to say, after one of the Augmenters of *Furetier*, that my Book is more learned than its Author.

In explaining the general and popular Language, it seems necessary to sort the several Senses of each Word, and to exhibit first its natural and primitive Signification; as,

'To *arrive*, to reach the Shore in a Voyage: He *arrived* at a safe Harbour.

Then to give its consequential Meaning, *to arrive*, to reach any Place, whether by Land or Sea; as, He *arrived* at his Country-Seat.

Then its metaphorical Sense, to obtain any Thing desired; as, He *arrived* at a Peerage.

Then to mention any Observation that arises from the Comparison of one Meaning with another; as, it may be remarked of the Word *arrive*, that, in consequence of its original and etymological Sense, it cannot be properly applied but to Words signifying fomething defirable: Thus we fay a Man *arrived* at Happinefs; but cannot fay, without a Mixture of Irony, he *arrived* at Mifery.

Ground, the Earth, generally as oppofed to the Air or Water. He fwam till he reached *Ground*. The Bird fell to the *Ground*.

Then follows the accidental or confequential Signification, in which *Ground* implies any Thing that lies under another; as he laid Colours upon a rough *Ground*. This Silk had blue Flowers on a red *Ground*.

Then the remoter, or metaphorical Signification; as, the *Ground* of his Opinion was a falfe Computation. The *Ground* of his Work was his Father's Manufcript.

After having gone through the natural and figurative Senfes, it will be proper to fubjoin the poetical Senfe of each Word, where it differs from that which is in common Ufe; as, *wanton*, applied to any Thing of which the Motion is irregular without Terror; as,

In *wanton* Ringlets curl'd her Hair.

To the poetical Senfe may fucceed the familiar; as of *Toaft*, ufed to imply the Perfon whofe Health is drank; as,

The wife Man's Paffion, and the vain Man's *Toaft*.
POPE.

The familiar may be followed by the burlefque; as of *mellow*, applied to good Fellowfhip.

In all thy Humours, whether grave or *mellow*.
ADDISON.

Or of *Bite*, ufed for *Cheat*.

——More a Dupe than Wit,
Sappho can tell you how this Man was *bit*. POPE.

And,

And, laſtly, may be produced the peculiar Senſe, in which a Word is found in any great Author : As Faculties, in Shakeſpeare, ſignifies the Powers of Authority.

——This Duncan
Has born his Faculties ſo meek, has been
So clear in his great Office, that, &c.

The Signification of Adjectives may be often aſcertained by uniting them to Subſtantives ; as, ſimple Swain, ſimple Sheep. Sometimes the Senſe of a Subſtantive may be elucidated by the Epithets annexed to it in good Authours ; as, the boundleſs Ocean, the open Lawns : And where ſuch Advantage can be gained by a ſhort Quotation, it is not to be omitted.
The Difference of Signification in Words generally accounted ſynonimous, ought to be carefully obſerved ; as in Pride, Haughtineſs, Arrogance ; and the ſtrict and critical Meaning ought to be diſtinguiſhed from that which is looſe and popular ; as in the Word Perfection, which, though, in its philoſophical and exact Senſe, it can be of little Uſe among human Beings, is often ſo much degraded from its original Signification, that the Academicians have inſerted in their Work, the Perfection of a Language, and, with a little more Licentiouſneſs, might have prevailed on themſelves to have added the Perfection of a Dictionary.
There are many other Characters of Words which it will be of uſe to mention. Some have both an active and paſſive Signification ; as fearful, that which gives or feels Terror ; a fearful Prodigy, a fearful Hare. Some have a perſonal, ſome a real Meaning ; as in Oppoſition to old, we uſe the Adjective young, of animated Beings, and new of other Things. Some are reſtrained to the Senſe of Praiſe, and others to that of Diſapprobation ; ſo commonly, though not always, we exhort to good Actions, we
instigate

inftigate to ill ; we *animate, incite,* and *encourage* indifferently to good or bad. So we ufually *afcribe* Good, but *impute* Evil ; yet neither the Ufe of thefe Words, nor, perhaps, of any other in our licentious Language, is fo eftablifhed as not to be often reverfed by the correcteft Writers. I fhall therefore, fince the Rules of Stile, like thofe of Law, arife from Precedents often repeated, collect the Teftimonies on both Sides, and endeavour to difcover and promulgate the Decrees of Cuftom, who has fo long poffefied, whether by Right or by Ufurpation, the Sovereignty of Words.

It is neceffary likewife to explain many Words by their Oppofition to others ; for Contraries are beft feen when they ftand together. Thus the Verb *ftand* has one Senfe, as oppofed to *fall,* and another as oppofed to *fly* ; for want of attending to which Diftinction, obvious as it is, the learned Dr. *Bentley* has fquandered his Criticifm to no Purpofe, on thefe Lines of *Paradife Loft :*

——— In Heaps
Chariot and Charioteer lay overturn'd,
And fiery foaming Steeds. *What flood, recoil'd,*
O'erwearied, through the faint, Satanic Hoft,
Defenfive fcarce, or with pale Fear furpris'd,
Fled ignominious———

' Here,' fays the Critic, ' as the Sentence is now ' read, we find that what *ftood, fled :*' And therefore he propofes an Alteration, which he might have fpared if he had confulted a Dictionary, and found that nothing more was affirmed than that thofe *fled* who did *not fall.*

In explaining fuch Meanings as feem accidental and adventitious, I fhall endeavour to give an Account of the Means by which they were introduced. Thus, to *eke out* any Thing, fignifies to lengthen it beyond its juft Dimenfions, by fome low Artifice ;

becaufe

becaufe the Word *eke* was the ufual Refuge of our old Writers, when they wanted a Syllable. And *buxom*, which means only *obedient*, is now made, in familiar Phrafes, to ftand for *wanton*; becaufe in an ancient Form of Marriage, before the Reformation, the Bride promifed Complaifance and Obedience, in thefe Terms : ' I will be bonair and *buxom*, in bed ' and at board.'

I know well, my Lord, how trifling many of thefe Remarks will appear, feparately confidered, and how eafily they may give Occafion to the contemptuous Merriment of fportive Idlenefs, and the gloomy Cenfures of arrogant Stupidity ; but Dulnefs it is eafy to defpife, and Laughter it is eafy to repay. I fhall not be follicitous what is thought of my Work by fuch as know not the Difficulty or Importance of philological Studies ; nor fhall think thofe that have done nothing, qualified to condemn me for doing little. It may not, however, be improper to remind them, that no terreftrial Greatnefs is more than an Aggregate of little Things ; and to inculcate, after the *Arabian* Proverb, that Drops, added to Drops, conftitute the Ocean.

There remains yet to be confidered the Diftribution of Words into their proper Claffes, or that Part of Lexicography which is ftrictly critical.

The popular Part of the Language, which includes all Words not appropriated to particular Sciences, admits of many Diftinctions and Subdivifions ; as, into Words of general Ufe, Words employed chiefly in Poetry, Words obfolete, Words which are admitted only by particular Writers, yet not in themfelves improper ; Words ufed only in burlefque Writing, and Words impure and barbarous.

Words of general Ufe will be known by having no Sign of Particularity, and their various fenfes will be fupported by Authorities of all Ages.

The Words appropriated to Poetry will be diſtinguiſhed by ſome Mark prefixed, or will be known by having no Authorities but thoſe of Poets.

Of antiquated, or obſolete Words, none will be inſerted but ſuch as are to be found in Authors who wrote ſince the Acceſſion of *Elizabeth,* from which we date the golden Age of our Language; and of theſe many might be omitted, but that the Reader may require, with an Appearance of Reaſon, that no Difficulty ſhould be left unreſolved in Books which he finds himſelf invited to read, as confeſſed and eſtabliſhed Models of Stile. Theſe will be likewiſe pointed out by ſome Note of Excluſion, but not of Diſgrace.

The Words which are found only in particular Books, will be known by the ſingle Name of him that has uſed them; but ſuch will be omitted, unleſs either their Propriety, Elegance, or Force, or the Reputation of their Authours affords ſome extraordinary Reaſon for their Reception.

Words uſed in burleſque and familiar Compoſitions, will be likewiſe mentioned with their proper Authorities; ſuch as *dudgeon,* from *Butler,* and *leaſing,* from *Prior*; and will be diligently characteriſed by Marks of Diſtinction.

Barbarous, or impure Words and Expreſſions, may be branded with ſome Note of Infamy, as they are carefully to be eradicated wherever they are found; and they occur too frequently even in the beſt Writers: As in *Pope*:

———in endleſs Error hurl'd,
'Tis *theſe* that early taint the female Soul.

In *Addiſon*:
Attend to what a *leſſer* Muſe indites.

And

And in *Dryden* .

> A dreadful Quiet felt, and *worfer* far
> Than Arms——

If this Part of the Work can be well performed it will be equivalent to the Propofal made by *Boileau* to the Academicians, that they fhould review all their polite Writers, and correct fuch Impurities as might be found in them, that their Authority might not contribute, at any diftant Time, to the Depravation of the Language.

With Regard to Queftions of Purity, or Propriety, I was once in doubt whether I fhould not attribute too much to myfelf, in attempting to decide them, and whether my Province was to extend beyond the Propofition of the Queftion, and the Difplay of the Suffrages on each Side ; but I have been fince determined, by your Lordfhip's Opinion, to interpofe my own Judgment, and fhall therefore endeavour to fupport what appears to me moft confonant to Grammar and Reafon. *Aufonius* thought that Modefty forbad him to plead Inability for a Tafk to which *Cæfar* had judged him equal.

> *Cur me poffe negem poffe quod ille putat ?*

And I may hope, my Lord, that fince you, whofe Authority in our Language is fo generally acknowledged, have commiffioned me to declare my own Opinion, I fhall be confidered as exercifing a Kind of vicarious Jurifdiction, and that the Power which might have been denied to my own Claim, will be readily allowed me as the Delegate of your Lordfhip.

In citing Authorities, on which the Credit of every Part of this Work muft depend, it will be proper to obferve fome obvious Rules ; fuch as of preferring Writers of the firft Reputation to thofe of an inferior Rank ; of noting the Quotations with Accu-

racy ;

racy; and of felecting, when it can be conveniently
done, fuch Sentences, as, befides their immediate
Ufe, may give Pleafure or Inftruction, by conveying
fome Elegance of Language, or fome Precept of
Prudence, or Piety.

It has been afked, on fome Occafions, who fhall
judge the Judges? And fince, with regard to this
Defign, a Queftion may arife by what Authority the
Authorities are felected, it is neceffary to obviate it,
by declaring that many of the Writers whofe Teftimonies will be alledged, were felected by Mr. *Pope*;
of whom, I may be juftified in affirming, that were
he ftill alive, follicitous as he was for the Succefs of
this Work, he would not be difpleafed that I have
undertaken it.

It will be proper that the Quotations be ranged according to the Ages of their Authours; and it will
afford an agreeable Amufement, if, to the Words
and Phrafes which are not of our own Growth, the
Name of the Writer who firft introduced them can
be affixed; and if, to Words which are now antiquated, the Authority be fubjoined of him who laft
admitted them. Thus, for *fcathe* and *buxom*, now
obfolete, *Milton* may be cited.

> ――――Thee Mountain Oak
> Stands *fcath'd* to Heaven――――
> ――――He with broad Sails
> Winnow'd the *buxom* Air――――

By this Method every Word will have its Hiftory,
and the Reader will be informed of the gradual
Changes of the Language, and have before his Eyes
the Rife of fome Words, and the Fall of others.
But Obfervations fo minute and accurate are to be
defired rather than expected: And if Ufe be carefully fupplied, Curiofity muft fometimes bear its
Difappointments.

8   This,

This, my Lord, is my Idea of an *English* Dictionary; a Dictionary by which the Pronunciation of our Language may be fixed, and its Attainment facilitated; by which its Purity may be preferved, its Ufe afcertained, and its Duration lengthened. And though, perhaps, to correct the Language of Nations by Books of Grammar, and amend their Manners by Difcourfes of Morality, may be Tafks equally difficult; yet, as it is unavoidable to wifh, it is natural likewife to hope, that your Lordfhip's Patronage may not be wholly loft; that it may contribute to the Prefervation of ancient, and the Improvement of modern Writers; that it may promote the Reformation of thofe Tranflators, who, for Want of underftanding the characteriftical Difference of Tongues, have formed a chaotic Dialect of heterogeneous Phrafes; and awaken to the Care of purer Diction fome Men of Genius, whofe Attention to Argument makes them negligent of Stile, or whofe rapid Imagination, like the *Peruvian* Torrents, when it brings down Gold, mingles it with Sand.

When I furvey the Plan which I have laid before you, I cannot, my Lord, but confefs, that I am frighted at its Extent, and, like the Soldiers of *Cæfar*, look on *Britain* as a new World, which it is almoft Madnefs to invade. But I hope, that though I fhould not complete the Conqueft, I fhall at leaft difcover the Coaft, civilize Part of the Inhabitants, and make it eafy for fome other Adventurer to proceed farther, to reduce them wholly to Subjection, and fettle them under Laws.

We are taught by the great *Roman* orator, that every Man fhould propofe to himfelf the higheft Degree of Excellence, but that he may ftop with Honour at the Second or the Third: Though therefore my Performance fhould fall below the Excellence of other Dictionaries, I may obtain, at leaft, the Praife of having endeavoured well; nor fhall I think it any

Reproach

Reproach to my Diligence, that I have retired without a Triumph, from a Contest with united Academies, and long Successions of learned Compilers. I cannot hope, in the warmest Moments, to preserve so much Caution through so long a Work, as not often to sink into Negligence, or to obtain so much Knowledge of all its Parts, as not frequently to fail by Ignorance. I expect that sometimes the Desire of Accuracy will urge me to Superfluities, and sometimes the Fear of Prolixity betray me to Omissions; that in the Extent of such Variety, I shall be often bewildered; and in the Mazes of such Intricacy, be frequently entangled; that in one Part Refinement will be subtilised beyond Exactness, and Evidence dilated in another beyond Perspicuity. Yet I do not despair of Approbation from those who, knowing the Uncertainty of Conjecture, the Scantiness of Knowledge, the Fallibility of Memory, and the Unsteadiness of Attention, can compare the Causes of Error with the Means of avoiding it, and the Extent of Art with the Capacity of Man; and whatever be the Event of my Endeavours, I shall not easily regret an Attempt which has procured me the Honour of appearing thus publickly,

My Lord,

Your Lordship's most obedient,

And most humble Servant,

SAM. JOHNSON.

'PREFACE

TO

The FOLIO EDITION of

Dr. JOHNSON's DICTIONARY.

IT is the Fate of thofe who toil at the lower Employments of Life, to be rather driven by the Fear of Evil, than attracted by the Profpect of Good; to be expofed to Cenfure, without Hope or Praife; to be difgraced by Mifcarriage, or punifhed for Neglect, where Succefs would have been without Applaufe, and Diligence without Reward.

Among thefe unhappy Mortals is the Writer of Dictionaries; whom Mankind have confidered, not as the Pupil, but the Slave of Science, the Pioneer of Literature, doomed only to remove Rubbifh and clear Obftructions from the Paths of Learning and Genius, who prefs forward to Conqueft and Glory, without beftowing a Smile on the humble Drudge who facilitates their Progrefs. Every other Author may afpire to Praife; the Lexicographer can only hope to efcape Reproach, and even this negative Recompence has been yet granted to very few.

I have, notwithftanding this Difcouragement, attempted a Dictionary of the *Englifh* Language, which, while it was employed in the Cultivation of every Species of Literature, has itfelf been hitherto neglected, fuffered to fpread, under the Direction of Chance, into wild Exuberance, refigned to the Tyranny of Time and Fafhion, and expofed to the Corruptions of Ignorance, and Caprices of Innovation.

When

When I took the first Survey of my Undertaking, I found our Speech copious without Order, and energetic without Rules : wherever I turned my View, there was Perplexity to be disentangled, and Confusion to be regulated ; Choice was to be made out of boundless Variety, without any established Principle of Selection ; Adulterations were to be detected, without a settled Test of Purity ; and Modes of Expression to be rejected or received, without the Suffrages of any Writers of classical Reputation or acknowledged Authority.

Having therefore no Assistance but from general Grammar, I applied myself to the Perusal of our Writers ; and noting whatever might be of Use to ascertain or illustrate any Word or Phrase, accumulated in Time the Materials of a Dictionary, which, by Degrees, I reduced to Method, establishing to myself, in the Progress of the Work, such Rules as Experience and Analogy suggested to me ; Experience, which Practice and Observation were continually increasing ; and Analogy, which, though in some Words obscure, was evident in others.

In adjusting the Orthography, which has been to this Time unsettled and fortuitous, I found it necessary to distinguish those Irregularities that are inherent in our Tongue, and perhaps coeval with it, from others which the Ignorance or Negligence of later Writers has produced. Every Language has its Anomalies, which, though inconvenient, and in themselves once unnecessary, must be tolerated among the Imperfections of human Things, and which require only to be registered, that they may not be increased ; and ascertained, that they may not be confounded : But every Language has likewise its Improprieties and Absurdities, which it is the Duty of the Lexicographer to correct or proscribe.

As Language was at its Beginning merely oral, all Words of necessary or common Use were spoken before

fore they were written ; and while they were unfixed by any visible Signs, must have been spoken with great Diversity, as we now observe those who cannot read to catch Sounds imperfectly, and utter them negligently.   When this wild and barbarous Jargon was first reduced to an Alphabet, every Penman endeavoured to express, as he could, the Sounds which he was accustomed to pronounce or to receive, and vitiated in Writing such Words as were already vitiated in Speech.   The Powers of the Letters, when they were applied to a new Language, must have been vague and unsettled ; and therefore different Hands would exhibit the same Sound by different Combinations.

From this uncertain Pronunciation arise, in a great Part, the various Dialects of the same Country, which will always be observed to grow fewer, and less different, as Books are multiplied ; and from this arbitrary Representation of Sounds by Letters, proceeds that Diversity of Spelling observable in the *Saxon* Remains, and I suppose in the first Books of every Nation, which perplexes or destroys Analogy, and produces anomalous Formations ; which, being once incorporated, can never be afterwards dismissed or reformed.

Of this Kind are the Derivatives *Length* from *long*, *Strength* from *strong*, *Darling* from *dear*, *Breadth* from *broad* ; from *dry*, *Drought*, and from *high*, *Height* ; which *Milton*, in Zeal for Analogy, writes *Highth* : *Quid te exempta juvat spinis de pluribus una* ; to change all would be too much, and to change one is nothing.

This Uncertainty is most frequent in the Vowels, which are so capriciously pronounced, and so differently modified, by Accident or Affectation, not only in every Province, but in every Mouth, that to them, as is well known to Etymologists, little Regard is to
be

be shewn in the Deduction of one Language from another.

Such Defects are not Errours in Orthography, but Spots of Barbarity impressed so deep in the *English* Language, that Criticism can never wash them away; these, therefore, must be permitted to remain untouched: but many Words have likewise been altered by Accident, or depraved by Ignorance, as the Pronunciation of the Vulgar has been weakly followed : and some still continue to be variously written, as Authours differ in their Care or Skill : Of these it was proper to enquire the true Orthography, which I have always considered as depending on their Derivation, and have therefore referred them to their original Languages : Thus I write *enchant*, *Enchantment*, *Enchanter*, after the *French*, and *Incantation* after the *Latin*; thus *entire* is chosen rather than *intire*, because it passed to us not from the *Latin integer*, but from the *French entier*.

Of many Words it is difficult to say whether they were immediately received from the *Latin* or the *French*; since at the Time when we had Dominions in *France*, we had *Latin* Service in our Churches. It is, however, my Opinion, that the *French* generally supplied us : for we have few *Latin* Words, among the Terms of domestick Use, which are not *French*; but many *French*, which are very remote from *Latin*.

Even in Words of which the Derivation is apparent, I have been often obliged to sacrifice Uniformity to Custom : Thus I write, in Compliance with a numberless Majority, *convey* and *inveigh*, *Deceit* and *Receipt*, *Fancy* and *Phantom*; sometimes the Derivative varies from the Primitive, as *explain* and *Explanation*, *repeat* and *Repetition*.

Some Combinations of Letters having the same Power, are used indifferently without any discoverable Reason of Choice ; as in *choak*, *choke*; *Soap*, *Sope*;

Fewel,

Fewel, Fuel; and many others ; which I have some-times inserted twice, that those who search for them under either Form, may not search in vain.

In examining the Orthography of any doubtful Word, the Mode of Spelling by which it is inserted in the Series of the Dictionary, is to be considered as that to which I give, perhaps not often rashly, the Preference. I have left, in the Examples, to every Authour his own Practice unmolested, that the Reader may balance Suffrages, and judge between us : But this Question is not always to be deter-mined by reputed or by real Learning ; some Men, intent upon greater Things, have thought little on Sounds and Derivations ; some, knowing in the an-cient Tongues, have neglected those in which our Words are commonly to be sought. Thus *Hammond* writes *Feciblenefs* for *Feafiblenefs*, because I suppose he imagined it derived immediately from the *Latin*; and some Words, such as *dependant, dependent* ; *Depend-ance, Dependence*, vary their final Syllable, as one or other Language is present to the Writer.

In this Part of the Work, where Caprice has long wantoned without Controul, and Vanity sought Praise by petty Reformation, I have endeavoured to proceed with a Scholar's Reverence for Antiquity, and a Grammarian's Regard to the Genius of our Tongue. I have attempted few Alterations, and among those few, perhaps the greater Part is from the modern to the ancient Practice ; and I hope I may be allow-ed to recommend to those, whose Thoughts have been, perhaps, employed too anxiously on verbal Singularities, not to disturb, upon narrow Views, or for minute Propriety, the Orthography of their Fathers. It has been asserted, that for the Law to be *known*, is of more Importance than to be *right*. ' Change,' says *Hooker*, ' is not made without In-' convenience, even from worse to better.' There is in Constancy and Stability a general and lasting Advantage,

vantage, which will always overbalance the flow Improvements of gradual Correction. Much lefs ought our written Language to comply with the Corruptions of oral Utterance, or copy that which every Variation of Time or Place makes different from itfelf, and imitate thofe Changes, which will again be changed, while Imitation is employed in obferving them.

This Recommendation of Steadinefs and Uniformity does not proceed from an Opinion, that particular Combinations of Letters have much Influence on human Happinefs; or that Truth may not be fuccefsfully taught by Modes of Spelling fanciful and erroneous: I am not yet fo loft in Lexicography, as to forget that *Words are the Daughters of Earth, and that Things are the Sons of Heaven.* Language is only the Inftrument of Science, and Words are but the Signs of Ideas: I wifh, however, that the Inftrument might be lefs apt to decay, and that the Signs might be permanent, like the Things which they denote.

In fettling the Orthography, I have not wholly neglected the Pronunciation, which I have directed, by putting an Accent upon the acute or elevated Syllable. It will fometimes be found, that the Accent is placed by the Authour quoted, on a different Syllable from that marked in the alphabetical Series; it is then to be underftood that Cuftom has varied, or that the Authour has, in my Opinion, pronounced wrong: Short Directions are fometimes given where the Sound of Letters is irregular; and if they are fometimes omitted, Defect in fuch minute Obfervations will be more eafily excufed than Superfluity.

In the Inveftigation both of the Orthography and Signification of Words, their Etymology was necefsarily to be confidered, and they were therefore to be divided into Primitives and Derivatives. A primitive Word is that which can be traced no further to any *Englifh* Root; thus *circumfpect, circumvent, Circumftance,*

cumſtance, *delude,* *concave,* and *complicate,* though
Compounds in the *Latin,* are to us Primitives. De-
rivatives are all thoſe that can be referred to any
Word in *Engliſh* of greater Simplicity.

The Derivatives I have referred to their Primitives, with an Accuracy ſometimes needleſs ; for who
does not ſee that *Remoteneſs* comes from *remote, love-*
ly from *Love, Concavity* from *concave,* and *demonſtra-*
tive from *demonſtrate ?* but this grammatical Exuberance the Scheme of my Work did not allow me to
repreſs. It is of great Importance in examining the
general Fabrick of a Language, to trace one Word
from another, by noting the uſual Modes of Derivation and Inflection ; and Uniformity muſt be
preſerved in ſyſtematical Works, though ſometimes at the Expence of particular Propriety.

Among other Derivatives I have been careful to
inſert and elucidate the anomalous Plurals of Nouns
and Preterites of Verbs, which in the *Teutonick* Dialects are very frequent ; and though familiar to thoſe
who have always uſed them, interrupt and embarraſs
the Learners of our Language.

The two Languages from which our Primitives
have been derived, are the *Roman* and *Teutonick :*
Under the *Roman* I comprehend the *French* and Pro-
vincial Tongues ; and under the *Teutonick* range the
Saxon, German, and all their kindred Dialects.
Moſt of our Polyſyllables are *Roman,* and our Words
of one Syllable are very often *Teutonick.*

In aſſigning the *Roman* Original, it has perhaps
ſometimes happened that I have mentioned only the
Latin, when the Word was borrowed from the *French;*
and conſidering myſelf as employed only in the Illuſtration of my own Language, I have not been very
careful to obſerve whether the *Latin* Word be pure
or barbarous, or the *French* elegant or obſolete.

For the *Teutonick* Etymologies I am commonly indebted to *Junius* and *Skinner,* the only Names which
I have

I have forborne to quote when J copied their Books;
not that I might appropriate their Labours to ufurp
their Honours, but that I might fpare a perpetual
Repetition by one general Acknowledgment. Of
thefe, whom I ought not to mention but with the
Reverence due to Inftructors and Benefactors, *Junius*
appears to have excelled in Extent of Learning, and
Skinner in Rectitude of Underftanding. *Junius* was
accurately fkilled in all the northern Languages.
Skinner probably examined the ancient and remoter
Dialects only by occafional Infpection into Dictionaries; but the Learning of *Junius* is often of no other
Ufe than to fhew him a Track by which he may deviate from his Purpofe, to which *Skinner* always
preffes forward by the fhorteft Way. *Skinner* is often
ignorant, but never ridiculous: *Junius* is always
full of Knowledge; but his Variety diftracts his
Judgment, and his Learning is very frequently difgraced by his Abfurdities.

The Votaries of the northern Mufes will not perhaps eafily reftrain their Indignation, when they find
the Name of *Junius* thus degraded by a difadvan-
tageous Comparifon; but whatever Reverence is due
to his Diligence, or his Attainments, it can be no
criminal Degree of Cenforioufnefs to charge that
Etymologift with Want of Judgment, who can ferioufly derive *Dream* from *Drama*, becaufe *Life is a
Drama, and a Drama is a Dream*; and who declares
with a Tone of Defiance, that no Man can fail to
derive *Moan* from μὸνⓈ, *monos*, who confiders that
Grief naturally loves to be *alone* *.

* That I may not appear to have fpoken too irreverently of *Junius*,
I have here fubjoined a few Specimens of his etymological Extravagance.

Banish, *religare, ex banno vel territorio exigere,* in *exilium agere.*
G. *bannir.* It. *bandire, bandeggiare.* H. *bandir.* B. *bannen.* Ævi
medii fcriptores *bannire* dicebant. V. Spelm. in Bannum & in Ban-
lenga. Quoniam verò regionum urbiumq; limites arduis plerumq;
montibus, aliis fluminibus, longis deniq; flexuofifq; anguftiffima-
rum viarum amfractibus includebantur, fieri poteft id genus limites
ban

Our Knowledge of the Northern Literature is fo fcanty, that of Words undoubtedly *Teutonick*, the Original is not always to be found in any ancient Language; and I have therefore inferted *Dutch* or *German* Subftitutes, which I confider not as radical, but parallel; not as the Parents, but Sifters of the *Englifh*.

The Words which are reprefented as thus related by Defcent or Cognation, do not always agree in Senfe; for it is incident to Words, as to their Authours, to degenerate from their Anceftors, and to change their Manners when they change their Country. It is fufficient, in etymological Enquiries, if the Senfes of kindred Words be found, fuch as may eafily pafs into each other, or fuch as may both be referred to one general Idea.

The Etymology, fo far as it is yet known, was eafily found in the Volumes where it is particularly and profeffedly delivered; and, by proper Attention to the Rules of Derivation, the Orthography was

ban dici ab eo quod Βανιᾶται & Βάνατροι Tarentinis olim, ficuti tradit Hefychius, vocabantur αἱ λεξὶι ἡ μὴ ἰθυτετεῖς ὁδοι, "obliquæ ac "minimè in rectum tendentes viæ." Ac fortaffe quoque huc facit quod Βανὸς, eodem Hefychio tefte, dicebant ὅρη ϛραγγύλη montes arduos.

EMPTY, emtie, *vacuus, incnis.* A. S. Æmtig. Nefcio an fint ab ἐμέω vel ἐμετάω. Vomo, evomo, vomitu evacuo. Videtur interim etymologiam hanc non obfcurè firmare codex Rufh. Mat. xii. 22. ubi antiquè fcriptum invenimus ʒemoeteð hiʒ emeʒiʒ. "Invenit am "vacantem."

HILL, *mons, collis.* A. S. hyll. Quod videri poteft abfciffum ex κολώνη vel κολωνὸς. Collis, tumulus, locus in plano editior. Hom. Il. b. v. 811, ἔϛι δὲ τις προπάροιθε πόλεϟ- αἰπεῖα, κολώνη. Ubi authori brevium fcholiorum κολώνη exp. τόπϟ- εἰς ὕψϟ- ἀνήκων, γεώλοϟϟ- ἐξοχή.

NAP, *to take a Nap. Dormire, condormifcere.* Cym. heppian. A. S. hnæppan. Quod poftremum videri poteft defumptum ex κνέφας, obfcuritas, tenebræ: nihil enim æque folet conciliare fomnum, quàm caliginofa profundæ notis obfcuritas.

STAMMERER, Balbus, blæfus Goth. STAMMS. A. S. ϛamen. ϛamun. D. ftam. B. ftameler. Su. ftamma. Ifl. ftamr. Sunt a ϛομμιλεῖν vel ϛωμύλλειν, nimiâ loquacitate alios offendere; quod impedirè loquentes libentiffimè garrire foleant; vel quòd aliis nimii femper videantur, etiam parciffimè loquentes.

foon

foon adjufted. But to collect the Words of our Language was a Tafk of greater Difficulty: The Deficiency of Dictionaries was immediately apparent ; and when they were exhaufted, what was yet wanting muft be fought by fortuitous and unguided Excurfions into Book, and gleaned as Induftry fhould find, or Chance fhould offer it, in the boundlefs Chaos of a living Speech. My Search, however, has been either fkilful or lucky ; for I have much augmented the Vocabulary.

As my Defign was a Dictionary, common or appellative, I have omitted all Words which have Relation to proper Names; fuch as *Arian, Socinian, Calvinift, Benedictine, Mahometan* : but have retained thofe of a more general Nature ; as *Heathen, Pagan.*

Of the Terms of Art, I have received fuch as could be found either in Books of Science, or technical Dictionaries ; and have often inferted, from philofophical Writers, Words which are fupported perhaps only by a fingle Authority ; and which being not admitted into general Ufe, ftand yet as Candidates or Probationers, and muft depend for their Adoption on the Suffrage of Futurity.

The Words which our Authours have introduced by their Knowledge of foreign Languages, or Ignorance of their own, by Vanity or Wantonnefs, by Compliance with Fafhion, or Luft of Innovation, I have regiftered as they occurred, though commonly only to cenfure them, and warn others againft the Folly of naturalizing ufelefs Foreigners, to the Injury of the Natives.

I have not rejected any by Defign, merely becaufe they were unneceffary or exuberant ; but have received thofe which by different Writers have been differently formed ; as *vifcid*, and *Vifcidity* ; *vifcous*, and *Vifcofity.*

Compounded or double Words I have feldom noted, except when they obtain a Signification different

ferent

ferent from that which the Components have in their simple State. Thus *Highwayman, Woodman,* and *Horsecourser* require an Explication ; but of *Thieflike* or *Coachdriver* no Notice was needed, becauſe the Primitives contain the Meaning of the Compounds.

Words arbitrarily formed by a conſtant and ſettled Analogy, like diminutive Adjectives in *iſh,* as *greeniſh, blueſh,* Adverbs in *ly,* as *dully, openly* ; Subſtantives in *neſs* ; as *Vileneſs, Faultineſs,* were leſs diligently ſought ; and many ſometimes have been omitted, when I had no Authority that invited me to inſert them ; not that they are not genuine and regular Offsprings of *Engliſh* Roots, but becauſe their Relation to the Primitive being always the ſame, their Signification cannot be miſtaken.

The verbal Nouns in *ing,* ſuch as the *Keeping* of the *Caſtle,* the *Leading* of the *Army,* are always neglected, or placed only to illuſtrate the Senſe of the Verb, except when they ſignify Things as well as Actions, and have therefore a plural Number, as *Dwelling, Living* ; or have an abſolute and abſtract Signification, as *Colouring, Painting, Learning.*

The Participles are likewiſe omitted, unleſs, by ſignifying rather Qualities than Action, they take the Nature of Adjectives ; as, a *thinking* Man, a Man of Prudence ; a *pacing* Horſe, a Horſe that can pace : Theſe I have ventured to call *participial Adjectives.* But neither are theſe always inſerted, becauſe they are commonly to be underſtood, without any Danger of Miſtake, by conſulting the Verb.

Obſolete Words are admitted, or when they have found in Authours not obſolete, or when they have any Force or Beauty that may deſerve Revival.

As Compoſition is one of the chief Characteriſticks of a Language, I have endeavoured to make ſome Reparation for the univerſal Negligence of my Predeceſſors, by inſerting great Numbers of com-

pounded

pounded Words, as may be found under *after*, *fore*,·
new, *night*, *fair*, and many more. Thefe, numerous as they are, might be multiplied, but that Ufe
and Curiofity are here fatisfied, and the Frame of our
Language, and Modes of our Combination, amply
difcovered.

Of fome Forms of Compofition, fuch as that by
which *re* is prefixed to note *Repetition*, and *un* to fig-
nify *Contrariety* or *Privation*, all the Examples cannot be accumulated, becaufe the Ufe of thefe Particles, if not wholly arbitrary, is fo little limited, that
they are hourly affixed to new Words as Occafion
requires, or is imagined to require them.

There is another Kind of Compofition more frequent in our Language than perhaps in any other,
from which arifes to Foreigners the greateft Difficulty. We modify the Signification of many Verbs
by a Particle fubjoined ; as, to *come off*, to efcape by
a Fetch ; to *fall on*, to attack ; to *fall off*, to apo-
ftatize ; to *break off*, to ftop abruptly ; to *bear out*,
to juftify ; to *fall in*, to comply ; to *give over*, to
ceafe ; to *fet off*, to embellifh ; to *fet in*, to begin
a continual Tenour ; to *fet out*, to begin a Courfe or
Journey ; to *take off*, to copy ; with innumerable Expreffions of the fame Kind ; of which fome appear
wildly irregular, being fo far diftant from the Senfe
of the fimple Words, that no Sagacity will be able
to trace the Steps by which they arrived at the prefent Ufe. Thefe I have noted with great Care ; and
though I cannot flatter myfelf that the Collection is
complete, I believe I have fo far affifted the Students
of our Language, that this Kind of Phrafeology will
be no longer infuperable ; and the Combinations of
Verbs and Particles, by Chance omitted, will be
eafily explained by Comparifon with thofe that may
be found.

Many Words yet ftand fupported only by the
Name of *Bailey*, *Ainfworth*, *Philips*, or the contracted
Dict.

Dict. for *Dictionaries*, subjoined : Of these I am not always certain that they are read in any Book but the Works of Lexicographers. Of such I have omitted many, because I had never read them ; and many I have inserted, because they may perhaps exist, though they have escape my Notice : They are however, to be yet considered as resting only upon the Credit of former Dictionaries. Others, which I considered as useful, or know to be proper, though I could not at present suppport them by Authorities I have suffered to stand upon my own Attestation, claiming the same Privilege with my Predecessors, of being sometimes credited without Proof.

The Words, thus selected and disposed, are grammatically considered : They are referred to the different Parts of Speech ; traced when they are irregularly inflected, through their various Terminations ; and illustrated by Observations, not indeed of great or striking Importance, separately considered, but necessary to the Elucidation of our Language, and hitherto neglected or forgotten by *English* Grammarians.

That Part of my Work on which I expect Malignity most frequently to fasten, is the *Explanation* ; in which I cannot hope to satisfy those, who are, perhaps, not inclined to be pleased, since I have not always been able to satisfy myself. To interpret a Language by itself is very difficult ; many Words cannot be explained by Synonymes, because the Idea signified by them has not more than one Appellation ; nor by Paraphrase, because simple Ideas cannot be described. When the Nature of Things is unknown, or the Notion unsettled and indefinite, and various in various Minds, the Words by which such Notions are conveyed, or such Things denoted, will be ambiguous and perplexed. And such is the Fate of hapless Lexicography, that not only Darkness, but Light, impedes and distresses it ; Things may

be

be not only too little, but too much known, to be happily illuftrated.   To explain, requires the Ufe of Terms lefs abftrufe than that which is to be explained ;   and fuch Terms cannot always be found :   For as nothing can be proved but by fuppofing fomething intuitively known and evident without Proof, fo nothing can be defined but by the Ufe of Words too plain to admit a Definition.

Other Words there are, of which the Senfe is too fubtle and evanefcent to be fixed in a Paraphrafe ;   fuch are all thofe which are by the Grammarians termed *Expletives*, and, in dead Languages, are fuffered to pafs for empty Sounds, of no other Ufe than to fill a Verfe, or to modulate a Period, but which are eafily perceived in living Tongues to have Power, and Emphafis, though it be fometimes fuch as no other Form of Expreffion can convey.

My Labour has likewife been much increafed by a Clafs of Verbs too frequent in the *Englifh* Language of which the Signification is fo loofe and general, the Ufe fo vague and indeterminate, and the Senfes detorted fo widely from the firft Idea, that it is hard to trace them through the Maze of Variation, to catch them on a Brink of utter Inanity, to circumfcribe them by any Limitations, or interpret them by any Words of diftinct and fettled Meaning :   Such are *bear*, *break*, *come*, *caft*, *fall*, *get*, *give*, *do*, *put*, *fet*, *go*, *run*, *make*, *take*, *turn*, *throw*.   If of thefe the whole Power is not accurately delivered, it muft be remembered, that while our Language is yet living, and variable by the Caprice of every one thar fpeaks it, thefe Words are hourly fhifting their Relations, and can no more be afcertained in a Dictionary, than a Grove, in the Agitation of a Storm, can be accurately delineated from its Picture in the Water.

The Particles are, among all Nations, applied with fo great Lattitude, that they are not eafily reducible

ducible under any regular Scheme of Explication: This Difficulty is not lefs, nor perhaps greater, in *Englifh*, than in other Languages. I have laboured them with Diligence, I hope with Succefs; fuch at leaft as can be expected in a Tafk, which no Man, however learned or fagacious, has yet been able to perform.

Some Words there are which I cannot explain, becaufe I do not underftand them; thefe might have been omitted very often with little Inconvenience; but I would not fo far indulge my Vanity as to decline this Confeffion: For when *Tully* owns himfelf ignorant whether *leffus*, in the Twelve Tables, means a *funeral Song*, or *mourning Garment*; and *Ariftotle* doubts whether οὖρευς, in the *Iliad*, fignifies a *Mule*, or *Muleteer*, I may freely, without Shame, leave fome Obfcurities to happier Induftry, or future Information.

The Rigour of interpretative Lexicography requires that the *Explanation, and the Word explained, fhould be always reciprocal*; this I have always endeavoured, but could not always attain. Words are feldom exactly fynonymous; a new Term was not introduced, but becaufe the former was thought inadequate: Names, therefore, have often many Ideas, but few Ideas have many Names. It was then neceffary to ufe the proximate Word, for the Deficiency of fingle Terms can very feldom be fupplied by Circumlocution; nor is the Inconvenience great of fuch mutilated Interpretations, becaufe the Senfe may eafily be collected entire from the Examples.

In every Word of extenfive Ufe it was requifite to make the Progrefs of its Meaning, and fhow by what Gradations of intermediate Senfe it has paffed from its primitive, to its remote and accidental Signification; fo that every foregoing Explanation fhould tend to that which follows, and the Series be regularly concatenated from the firft Notion to the laft.

F 3 This

This is specious, but not always practicable; kindred Senses may be so interwoven, that the Perplexity cannot be disentangled, nor any Reason be assigned why one should be ranged before the other. When the radical Idea branches out into parallel Ramifications, how can a consecutive Series be formed of Senses in their Nature collateral? The Shades of Meaning sometimes pass imperceptibly into each other; so that though on one Side they apparently differ, yet it is impossible to mark the Point of Contact. Ideas of the same Race, though not exactly alike, are sometimes so little different, that no Words can express the Dissimilitude, though the Mind easily perceives it, when they are exhibited together; and sometimes there is such a Confusion of Acceptations, that Discernment is wearied, and Distinction puzzled, and Perseverance herself hurries to a End, by crouding together what she cannot separate.

These Complaints of Difficulty will, by those that have never considered Words beyond their popular Use, be thought only the Jargon of a Man willing to magnify his Labours, and procure Veneration to his Studies by Involution and Obscurity. But every Art is obscure to those that have not learned it: This Uncertainty of Terms, and Commixture of Ideas, is well known to those who have joined Philosophy with Grammar; and if I have not expressed them very clearly, it must be remembered that I am speaking of that which Words are insufficient to explain.

The original Sense of Words is often driven out of Use by their metaphorical Acceptations, yet must be inserted for the Sake of a regular Origination. Thus I know not whether *Ardour* is used for *material Heat*, or whether *flagrant*, in *English*, ever signifies the same with *burning*; yet such are the primitive Ideas of these Words, which are therefore set first, though without Examples, that the figurative Senses may be commodiously deduced.

Such

Such is the Exuberance of Signification which many Words have obtained, that it was scarcely possible to collect all their Senses; sometimes the Meaning of Derivatives must be sought in the Mother Term, and sometimes deficient Explanations of the Primitive may be supplied in the Train of Derivation. In any Case of Doubt or Difficulty, it will be always proper to examine all the Words of the same Race; for some Words are slightly passed over to avoid Repetition, some admitted easier and clearer Explanation than others, and all will be better understood, as they are considered in greater Variety of Structures and Relations.

All the Interpretations of Words are not written with the same Skill, or the same Happiness: Things equally easy in themselves, are not all equally easy to any single Mind. Every Writer of a long Work commits Errours, where there appears neither Ambiguity to mislead, nor Obscurity to confound him; and in a Search like this, many Felicities of Expression will be casually overlooked, many convenient Parallels will be forgotten, and many Particulars will admit Improvement from a Mind utterly unequal to the whole Performance.

But many seeming Faults are to be imputed rather to the Nature of the Undertaking, than the Negligence of the Performer. Thus some Explanations are unavoidably reciprocal or circular; as *Hind, the Female of the Stag*; *Stag, the Male of the Hind:* Sometimes easier Words are changed into harder; as *Burial* into *Sepulture* or *Interment*, *drier* into *desiccative*, *Dryness* into *Siccity* or *Aridity*, *Fit* into *Paroxysm*; for the easiest Word, whatever it be, cannot be translated into one more easy. But Easiness and Difficulty are merely relative; and if the present Prevalence of our Language should invite Foreigners to this Dictionary, many will be assisted by those Words which now seem only to encrease or procure Obscu-

rity,

rity. For this Reason I have endeavoured frequently to join a *Teutonick* and *Roman* Interpretation, as to CHEER, to *gladden*, or *exhilirate*, that every Learner of *English* may be assisted by his own Tongue.

The Solution of all Difficulties, and the Supply of all Defects, must be sought in the Examples, subjoined to the various Senses of each Word, and ranged according to the Time of their Authours.

When first I collected these Authorities, I was desirous that every Quotation should be useful to some other End than the Illustration of a Word; I therefore extracted from Philosophers Principles of Science; from Historians remarkable Facts; from Chymists complete Processes; from Divines striking Exhortations; and from Poets beautiful Descriptions. Such is Design, while it is yet at a Distance from Execution. When the Time called upon me to range this Accumulation of Elegance and Wisdom into an alphabetical Series, I soon discovered that the Bulk of my Volumes would fright away the Student, and was forced to depart from my Scheme of including all that was pleasing or useful in *English* Literature, and reduce my Transcripts very often to Clusters of Words, in which scarcely any Meaning is retained; thus to the Weariness of Copying, I was condemned to add the Vexation of Expunging. Some Passages I have yet spared, which may relieve the Labour of verbal Searches, and intersperse with Verdure and Flowers the dusty Desarts of barren Philology.

The Examples, thus mutilated, are no longer to be considered as conveying the Sentiments or Doctrine of their Authours; the Word for the Sake of which they are inserted, with all its appendant Clauses, has been carefully preserved; but it may sometimes happen, by hasty Detruncation, that the general Tendency of the Sentence may be changed: The Divine may desert his Tenets, or the Philosopher his System.

Some

Some of the Examples have been taken from Writers who were never mentioned as Mafters of Elegance or Models of Stile ; but Words muft be fought where they are ufed ; and in what Pages, eminent for Purity, can Terms of Manufacture or Agriculture be found ? Many Quotations ferve no other Purpofe, than that of proving the bare Exiftence of Words ; and are therefore felected with lefs Scrupuloufnefs than thofe which are to teach their Structures and Relations.

My Purpofe was to admit no Teftimony of living Authours, that I might not be mifled by Partiality, and that none of my Cotemporaries might have Reafon to complain ; nor have I departed from this Refolution, but when fome Performance of uncommon Excellence excited my Veneration, when my Memory fupplied me, from late Books, with an Example that was wanting, or when my Heart, in the Tendernefs of Friendfhip, folicited Amiffion for a favourite Name.

So far have I been from any Care to grace my Pages with modern Decorations, that I have ftudioufly endeavoured to collect Examples and Authorities from the Writers before the Reftoration, whofe Works I regard as *the Wells of Englifh undefiled*, as the pure Sources of genuine Diction. Our Language, for almoft a Century, has, by the Concurrence of many Caufes, been gradually departing from its original *Teutonick* Character, and deviating towards a *Gallick* Structure and Phrafeology, from which it ought to be our Endeavour to recal it, by making our ancient Volumes the Ground-work of Style, admitting among the Additions of later Times, only fuch as may fupply real Deficiencies, fuch as are readily adopted by the Genius of our Tongue, and incorporate eafily with our native Idioms.

But as every Language has a Time of Rudenefs antecedent to Perfection, as well as of falfe Refinement

ment and Declenfion, I have been cautious left my
Zeal for Antiquity might drive me into Times too
remote, and croud my Book with Words now no
longer underftood.   I have fixed *Sydney*'s Work for
the boundary, beyond which I make few Excurfions.   From the Authours which rofe in the Time
of *Elizabeth*, a Speech might be formed adequate to
all the Purpofes of Ufe and Elegance.   If the Language of Theology were extracted from *Hooker* and
the Tranflation of the Bible ; the Terms of Natural
Knowledge from *Bacon*; the Phrafes of Policy, War,
and Navigation, from *Raleigh*; the Dialect of Poetry and Fiction from *Spenfer* and *Sidney*; and the
Diction of common Life from *Shakefpeare* ; few Ideas
would be loft to Mankind, for want of *Englifh* Words,
in which they might be expreffed.

It is not fufficient that a Word is found, unlefs it
be fo combined as that its Meaning is apparently determined by the Tract and Tenour of the Sentence;
fuch Paffages I have therefore chofen ; and when it
happened that any Authour gave a Definition of a
Term, or fuch an Explanation as is equivalent to a
Definition, I have placed his Authority as a Sup-
plement to my own, without Regard to the chronological Order, that is otherwife obferved.

Some Words, indeed, ftand unfupported by any
Authority, but they are commonly derivative Nouns
or Adverbs, formed from their Primitives by regular
and conftant Analogy, or Names of Things feldom
occurring in Books, or Words of which I have Reafon to doubt the Exiftence.

There is more Danger of Cenfure from the Multiplicity than Pacuity of Examples ; Authorities will
fometimes feem to have been accumulated without
Neceffity or Ufe, and perhaps fome will be found,
which might, without Lofs, have been omitted.
But a Work of this Kind is not haftily to be charged
with Superfluities: Thofe Quotations which to care-

lefs

lefs or unfkilful Perufers appear only to repeat the
fame Senfe, will often exhibit, to a more accurate
Examiner, Diverfities of Signification, or, at leaft,
afford different Shades of the fame Meaning : One
will fhew the Word applied to Perfons, another to
Things ; one will exprefs an ill, another a good, and
a third a neutral Senfe; one will prove the Expreffion
genuine from an ancient Authour; another will fhew
it elegant from a modern : A doubtful Authority is
corroborated by another of more Credit; an ambiguous Sentence is afcertained by a Paffage clear and
determinate ; the Word, how often foever repeated,
appears with new Affociates and in different Combinations, and every Quotation contributes fomething
to the Stability or Enlargement of the Language.

When Words are ufed equivocally, I receive them
in either Senfe ; when they are metaphorical, I adopt them in their primitive Acceptation.

I have fometimes, though rarely, yielded to the
Temptation of exhibiting a Genealogy of Sentiments,
by fhewing how one Author copied the Thoughts
and Diction of another : Such Quotations are indeed
little more than Repetitions, which might juftly be
cenfured, did they not gratify the Mind, by affording
a Kind of intellectual Hiftory.

The various fyntactical Structures occurring in the
Examples have been carefully noted ; the Licence or
Negligence with which many Words have been hitherto ufed, has made our Style capricious and indeterminate ; when the different Combinations of the
fame Word are exhibited together, the Preference is
readily given to Propriety, and I have often endeavoured to direct the Choice.

Thus have I laboured to fettle the Orthography,
difplay the Analogy, regulate the Structures, and afcertain the Signification of *Englifh* Words, to perform all the Parts of a faithful Lexicographer : But
I have not always executed my own Scheme, or fatisfied

fied my own Expectations. The Work, whatever
Proofs of Diligence and Attention it may exhibit, is
yet capable of many Improvements : The Orthography which I recommend is still controvertible, the
Etymology which I adopt is uncertain, and perhaps
frequently erroneous; the Explanations are sometimes too much contracted, and sometimes too
much diffused; the Significations are distinguished rather with Subtility than Skill, and the Attention is
harrassed with unnecessary Minutenefs.

The Examples are too often injudiciously trun-
cated, and perhaps sometimes, I hope very rarely,
alledged in a mistaken Sense; for in making this Collection I trusted more to Memory, than, in a State
of Disquiet and Embarrassment, Memory can contain, and purposed to supply at the Review what was
left incomplete in the first Transcription.

Many Terms appropriated to particular Occupations, though neceffary and fignificant, are undoubtedly omitted; and of the Words most studioufly confidered and exemplified, many Senses have escaped
Obfervation.

Yet these Failures, however frequent, may admit
Extenuation and Apology. To have attempted much
is always laudable, even when the Enterprize is above
the Strength that undertakes it : To rest below his
own Aim is incident to every one whose Fancy is
active, and whose Views are comprehenfive ; nor is
any Man fatisfied with himself becaufe he has done
much, but becaufe he can conceive little. When
first I engaged in this Work, I resolved to leave neither Words nor Things unexamined, and pleased
myself with a Prospect of the Hours which I should
revel away in Feasts of Literature, the obscure Receffes of Northern Learning which I should enter and
ranfack, the Treafures with which I expected every
Search into those neglected Mines to reward my Labour, and the Triumph with which I should difplay
my Acquifitions to Mankind. When I had thus
enquired

enquired into the Original of Words, I refolved to
fhow likewife my Attention to Things ; to pierce
deep in every Science, to enquire the Nature of every
Subftance of which I inferted the Name, to limit
every Idea by a Definition ftrictly logical, and exhibit
every Production of Art or Nature in an accurate Defcription, that my Book might be in Place of all
other Dictionaries, whether appellative or technical.
But thefe were the Dreams of a Poet, doomed at
laft to wake a Lexicographer.   I foon found that it
is too late to look for Inftruments, when the Work
calls for Execution ; and that whatever Abilities I
had brought to my Tafk, with thofe I muft finally
perform it.   To deliberate whenever I doubted, to
enquire whenever I was ignorant, would have protracted the Undertaking without End, and, perhaps,
without much Improvement ; for I did not find by
my firft Experiments, that what I had not of my
own was eafily to be obtained : I faw that one Enquiry only gave Occafion to another, that Book referred to Book, that to fearch was not always to find,
and to find was not always to be informed ; and that
thus to purfue Perfection, was, like the firft Inhabitants of *Arcadia*, to chace the Sun, which, when
they had reached the Hill where he feemed to reft,
was ftill beheld at the fame Diftance from them.

I then contracted my Defign, determining to con-
fide in myfelf, and no longer to folicit Auxiliaries,
which produced more Incumbrance than Affiftance :
By this I obtained at leaft one Advantage, that I fet
Limits to my Work, which would in Time be finifhed, though not completed.

Defpondency has never fo far prevailed as to deprefs me to Negligence : Some Faults will at laft appear to be the Effects of anxious Diligence and per-
fevering Activity.   The nice and fubtle Ramifications of Meaning were not eafily avoided by a Mind
intent upon Accuracy, and convinced of the Neceffity

ceffity of difentangling Combinations, and feparat-
ing Similitudes. Many of the Diftinctions which to
common Readers appear ufelefs and idle, will be
found real and important by Men verfed in the School
Philofophy, without which no Dictionary ever fhall
be accurately compiled, or fkilfully examined.

Some Senfes however there are, which, though
not the fame, are yet fo nearly allied, that they are
often confounded. Moft Men think indiftinctly, and
therefore cannot fpeak with Exactnefs; and confequently fome Examples might be indifferently put to
either Signification: This Uncertainty is not to be
imputed to me, who do not form, but regifter the
Language; who do not teach Men how they fhould
think, but relate how they have hitherto expreffed
their Thoughts.

The imperfect Senfe of fome Examples I lamented, but could not remedy, and hope they will be
compenfated by innumerable Paffages felected with
Propriety, and preferved with Exactnefs; fome
fhining with Sparks of Imagination, and fome re-
plete with Treafures of Wifdom.

The Orthography and Etymology, though imperfect, are not imperfect for want of Care; but becaufe Care will not always be fuccefsful, and Recollection or Information come too late for Ufe.

That many Terms of Art and Manufacture are
omitted, muft be frankly acknowledged; but for
this Defect, I may boldly alledge that it was unavoidable; I could not vifit Caverns, to learn the
Miner's Language, nor take a Voyage, to perfect my
Skill in the Dialect of Navigation; nor vifit the
Warehoufes of Merchants, and Shops of Artificers,
to gain the Names of Wares, Tools, and Operations, of which no Mention is found in Books;
what favourable Accident, or eafy Enquiry, brought
within my Reach, has not been neglected; but it
had been a hopelefs Labour to glean up Words, by

courting

courting living Information, and contesting with the Sullenness of one, and the Roughness of another.

To furnish the Academicians *della Crusca* with Words of this Kind, a Series of Comedies, called *la Fiera*, or *the Fair*, was professedly written by *Buonaroti*; but I had no such Assistant, and therefore was content to want what they must have wanted likewise, had they not luckily been so supplied.

Nor are all Words which are not found in the Vocabulary, to be lamented as Omissions. Of the laborious and mercantile Part of the People, the Diction is in a great Measure casual and mutable; many of their Terms are formed for some temporary or local Convenience; and though current at certain Times and Places, are in others utterly unknown. This fugitive Cant, which is always in a State of Increase or Decay, cannot be regarded as any Part of the durable Materials of a Language, and therefore must be suffered to perish with other Things unworthy of Preservation.

Care will sometimes betray to the Appearance of Negligence. He that is catching Opportunities which seldom occur, will suffer those to pass by unregarded, which he expects hourly to return; he that is searching for rare and remote Things, will neglect those that are obvious and familiar: Thus many of the most common and cursory Words have been inserted with little Illustration, because in gathering the Authorities, I forbore to copy those which I thought likely to occur whenever they were wanted. It is remarkable that, in reviewing my Collection, I found the Word *Sea* unexemplified.

Thus it happens, that in Things difficult there is Danger from Ignorance, and in Things easy from Confidence; the Mind, afraid of Greatness, and disdainful of Littleness, hastily withdraws herself from painful Searches, and passes with scornful Rapidity

over

over Tasks not adequate to her Powers ; sometimes too secure for Caution, and again too anxious of vigorous Effort ; sometimes idle in a plain Path, and sometimes distracted in Labyrinths, and dissipated by different Intentions.

A large Work is difficult because it is large, even though all its Parts might singly be performed with Facility ; where there are many Things to be done, each must be allowed its Share of Time and Labour, in the Proportion only which it bears to the Whole ; nor can it be expected that the Stones which form the Dome of a Temple, should be squared and polished like the Diamond of a Ring.

Of the Event of this Work, for which, having laboured it with so much Application, I cannot but have some Degree of parental Fondness, it is natural to form Conjectures. Those who have been persuaded to think well of my Design, require that it should fix our Language, and put a Stop to those Alterations which Time and Chance have hitherto been suffered to make in it without Opposition. With this Consequence I will confess that I flattered myself for a while ; but now begin to fear that I have indulged Expectation, which neither Reason nor Experience can justify. When we see Men grow old and die, at a certain Time, one after another, from Century to Century, we laugh at the Elixir that promises to prolong Life to a thousand Years ; and with equal Justice may the Lexicographer be derided, who being able to produce no Example of a Nation that has preserved their Words and Phrases from Mutability, shall imagine that his Dictionary can embalm his Language, and secure it from Corruption and Decay ; that it is in his Power to change sublunary Nature, or clear the World at once from Folly, Vanity, and Affectation.

With this Hope, however, Academies have been instituted, to guard the Avenues of their Languages,

to

to retain Fugitives, and repulfe Intruders; but their Vigilance and Activity have hitherto been vain; Sounds are too volatile and fubtle for legal Reftraints; to enchain fyllables, and to lafh the Wind are equally the Undertakings of Pride, unwilling to meafure its Defires by its Strength. The *French* Language has vifibly changed under the Infpection of the Academy: the Stile of *Amelot's* Tranflation of Father *Paul* is obferved by *Le Courayer* to be *un peu pafsé*; and no *Italian* will maintain, that the Diction of any modern Writer is not perceptibly different from that of *Boccace*, *Machiavel*, or *Caro*.

Total and fudden Transformations of a Language feldom happen; Conquefts and Migrations are now very rare; but there are other Caufes of Change, which, though flow in their Operation, and invifible in their Progrefs, are perhaps as much fuperior to human Refiftance, as the Revolutions of the Sky, or Intumefcence of the Tide. Commerce, however neceffary, however lucrative, as it depraves the Manners, corrupts the Language; they that have frequent Intercourfe with Strangers, to whom they endeavour to accommodate themfelves, muft in Time learn a mingled Dialect, like the Jargon which ferves the Traffickers on the *Mediterranean* and *Indian* Coafts. This will not always be confined to the Exchange, the Warehoufe, or the Port, but will be communicated by Degrees to other Ranks of the People, and be at laft incorporated with the current Speech.

There are likewife internal Caufes equally forcible. The Language moft likely to continue long without Alteration, would be that of a Nation raifed a little, and but a little, above Barbarity, fecluded from Strangers, and totally employed in procuring the Conveniences of Life: either without Books, or, like fome of the *Mahometan* Countries, with very few: Men thus bufied and unlearned, having only

such Words as common Use requires, would perhaps long continue to express the same Notions by
the same Signs. But no such Constancy can be expected in a People polished by Arts, and classed by
Subordination, where one Part of the Community
is sustained and accommodated by the Labour of
the other. Those who have much Leisure to think,
will always be enlarging the stock of ideas, and every
Increase of Knowledge, whether real or fancied, will
produce new Words, or Combinations of Words.
When the Mind is unchained from Necessity, it
will range after Convenience ; when it is left at
large in the Fields of Speculation, it will shift Opinions ; as any Custom is disused, the Words that
expressed it must perish with it ; as any Opinion
grows popular, it will innovate Speech in the same
Proportion as it alters Practice.

As by the Cultivation of various Sciences a Language is amplified it will be more furnished with Words
deflected from their original Sense ; the Geometri-
cian will talk of a Courtier's Zenith, or the excen-
trick Virtue of a wild Hero ; and the Physician of
sanguine Expectations, and phlegmatick Delays.
Copiousness of Speech will give Opportunities to
capricious Choice, by which some Words will be
preferred, and others degraded ; Vicissitudes of Fashion will enforce the Use of new, or extend the
Signification of known Terms. The Tropes of
Poetry will make hourly Encroachments, and the
metaphorical will become the current Sense : Pronunciation will be varied by Levity or Ignorance,
and the Pen must at length comply with the Tongue ;
illiterate Writers will at one Time or other, by publick Infatuation, rise into Renown ; who, not knowing the original Import of Words, will use them
with colloquial Licentiousness, confound Distinction
and forget Propriety. As Politeness increases, some
Expressions will be considered as too gross and vul-

gar

gar for the Delicate, others as too formal and cere-
monious for the Gay and Airy; new Phrases are
therefore adopted, which must, for the same Reasons, be in Time dismissed. *Swift*, in his petty
Treatise on the *English* Language, allows that new
Words must sometimes be introduced, but proposes
that none should be suffered to become obsolete. But
what makes a Word obsolete, more than general
Agreement to forbear it? And how shall it be continued, when it conveys an offensive Idea, or recalled again into Mouths the Mankind, when it
has once by Disuse become unfamiliar, and by Un-
familiarity unpleasing.

There is another Cause of Alteration more prevalent than any other, which yet, in the present
State of the World, cannot be obviated. A Mixture of two Languages will produce a Third, distinct
from both, and they will always be mixed, where
the chief Part of Education, and the most conspicuous Accomplishment, is Skill in ancient or in
foreign Tongues. He that has long cultivated another Language, will find its Words and Combinations croud upon his Memory; and Haste and Negligence, Refinement and Affectation, will obtrude
borrowed Terms and exotick Expressions.

The great Pest of Speech is Frequency of Tranflation. No Book was ever turned from one Language into another, without imparting something of
its native Idiom; this is the most mischievous and
comprehensive Innovation; single Words may enter
by Thousands, and the Fabrick of the Tongue continue the same, but new Phraseology changes much
at once; it alters not the single Stones of the Building, but the Order of the Columns. If an Academy should be established for the Cultivation of our
Stile, which I, who can never wish to see Depend-
ance multiplied, hope the Spirit of *English* Liberty
will hinder or destroy, let them, instead of com-

piling

piling Grammars and Dictionaries, endeavour, with all their Influence, to stop the Licence of Translatours, whose Idleness and Ignorance, if it be suffered to proceed, will reduce us to babble a Dialect of *France*.

If the Changes that we fear be thus irresistible what remains but to acquiesce with Silence, as in the other insurmountable Distresses of Humanity ? It remains that we retard what we cannot repel, that we palliate what we cannot cure. Life may be lengthened by Care, though Death cannot be ultimately defeated: Tongues, like Governments, have a natural Tendency to Degeneration ; we have long preserved our Constitution, let us make some Struggles for our Language.

In Hope of giving Longevity to that which its own Nature forbids to be immortal, I have devoted this Book, the Labour of Years, to the Honour of my Country, that we may no longer yield the Palm of Philology to the Nations of the Continent. The chief Glory of every People arises from its Authours ! Whether I shall add any Thing by my own Writings to the Reputation of *English* Literature, must be left to Time : Much of my Life has been lost under the Pressures of Disease ; much has been trifled away ; and much has always been spent in Provision for the Day that was passing over me ; but I shall not think my Employment useless or ignoble, if by my Assistance foreign Nations, and distant Ages, gain Access to the Propagators of Knowledge, and understand the Teachers of Truth ; if my Labours afford Light to the Repositories of Science, and add Celebrity to *Bacon*, to *Hooker*, to *Milton* and to *Boyle*.

When I am animated by this Wish I look with Pleasure on my Book, however defective, and deliver it to the World with the Spirit of a Man that has endeavoured well. That it will immediately become

come popular, I have not promifed to myfelf: A few wild Blunders, and rifible Abfurdities, from which no Work of fuch Multiplicity was ever free, may for a Time furnifh Folly with Laughter, and harden Ignorance into Contempt; but ufeful Diligence will at laft prevail, and there never can be wanting fome who diftinguifh Defert; who will confider that no Dictionary of a living Tongue ever can be perfect, fince, while it is haftening to Publication, fome Words are budding, and fome falling away; that a whole Life cannot be fpent upon Syntax and Etymology; and that even a whole Life would not be fufficient; that he, whofe Defign includes whatever Language can exprefs, muft often fpeak of what he does not underftand; that a Writer will fometimes be hurried by Eagernefs to the End, and fometimes faint with Wearinefs under a Tafk, which *Scaliger* compares to the Labours of the Anvil and the Mine, that what is obvious is not always known, and what is known is not always prefent, that fudden Fits of Inadvertency will furprife Vigilance, flight Avocations will feduce Attention, and cafual Eclipfes of the Mind will darken Learning; and that the Writer fhall often in vain trace his Memory, at the Moment of Need, for that which Yefterday he knew with intuitive Readinefs, and which will come uncalled into his Thoughts To-morrow.

In this Work, when it fhall be found that much is omitted, let it not be forgotten that much likewife is performed; and though no Book was ever fpared out of Tendernefs to the Authour, and the World is little folicitous to know whence proceeded the Faults of that which it condemns; yet it may gratify Curiofity to inform it, that the *Englifh Dictionary* was written with little Affiftance of the Learned, and without any Patronage of the Great; not in the foft Obfcurities of Retirement, or under the Shelter of academick Bowers, but amidft Inconve-

nience

nience and Diſtraction, in Sickneſs and in Sorrow:
And it may repreſs the Triumph of malignant Criticiſm to obſerve, that if our Language is not here
fully diſplayed, I have only failed in an Attempt
which no human Powers have hitherto completed.
If the Lexicons of ancient Tongues, now immu-
tably fixed, and compriſed in a few Volumes, be
yet, after the Toil of ſucceſſive Ages, inadequate
and deluſive ; if the aggregated Knowledge, and co-
operating Diligence, of the *Italian* Academicians,
did not ſecure them from the Cenſure of *Beni* ; if
the embodied Criticks of *France*, when fifty Years
had been ſpent upon their Work, were obliged to
change its Œconomy, and give their ſecond Edition
another Form, I may ſurely be contented without
the Praiſe of Perfection, which, if I could obtain,
in this Gloom of Solitude, what would it avail me ?
I have protracted my Work till moſt of thoſe whom
I wiſhed to pleaſe have ſunk into the Grave, and
Succeſs and Miſcarriage are empty Sounds: I therefore diſmiſs it with frigid Tranquility, having little
to fear or hope from Cenſure or from Praiſe.

PROPOSALS

FOR PRINTING THE

DRAMATICK WORKS

OF

WILLIAM SHAKESPEARE.

Printed in the Year 1756.

WHEN the Works of *Shakefpeare* are, after fo many Editions, again offered to the Pub-lick, it will doubtlefs be enquired, why *Shakefpeare* ftands in more Need of critical Affiftance than any other of the *Englifh* Writers, and what are the Defi-ciencies of the late Attempts, which another Editor may hope to fupply.

The Bufinefs of him that republifhes an ancient Book is, to correct what is corrupt, and to explain what is obfcure. To have a Text corrupt in many Places, and in many doubtful, is, among the Au-thours that have written fince the Ufe of Types, al-moft peculiar to *Shakefpeare*. Moft Writers, by pub-lifhing their own Works, prevent all various Read-ings, and preclude all conjectural Criticifm. Books indeed are fometimes publifhed after the Death of him who produced them; but they are better fecured from Corruption than thefe unfortunate Compofi-tions. They fubfift in a fingle Copy, written or

G 4   revifed

revifed by the Authour; and the Faults of the printed Volume can be only Faults of one Defcent.

But of the Works of *Shakefpeare* the Condition has been far different: He fold them, not to be printed, but to be played. They were immediately copied for the Actors, and multiplied by Tranfcript after Tranfcript, vitiated by the Blunders of the Penman, or changed by the Affectation of the Player; perhaps enlarged to introduce a Jeft, or mutilated to fhorten the Reprefentation; and printed at laft without the Concurrence of the Authour, without the Confent of the Proprietor, from Compilations made by Chance or by Stealth out of the feparate Parts written for the Theatre: And thus thruft into the World furreptitioufly and haftily, they fuffered another Depravation from the Ignorance and Negligence of the Printers, as every Man who knows the State of the Prefs in that Age will readily conceive.

It is not eafy for Invention to bring together fo many Caufes concurring to vitiate the Text. No other Authour ever gave up his Works to Fortune and Time with fo little Care: No Books could be left in Hands fo likely to injure them, as Plays frequently acted, yet continued in Manufcript: No other Tranfcribers were likely to be fo little qualified for their Tafk as thofe who copied for the Stage, at a Time when the lower Ranks of the People were univerfally illiterate: No other Editions were made from Fragments fo minutely broken, and fo fortuitoufly reunited; and in no other Age was the Art of Printing in fuch unfkilful Hands.

With the Caufes of Corruption that make the Revifal of *Shakefpeare*'s Dramatick Pieces neceffary, may be enumerated the Caufes of Obfcurity, which may be partly imputed to his Age, and partly to himfelf.

When a Writer outlives his Contemporaries, and remains almoft the only unforgotten Name of a diftant Time, he is neceffarily obfcure. Every Age has

it

its Modes of Speech, and its Caſt of Thought ;
which, though eaſily explained when there are many
Books to be compared with each other, become ſometimes unintelligible, and always difficult, when there
are no parallel Paſſages that may conduce to their
Illuſtration. *Shakeſpeare* is the firſt conſiderable Authour of ſublime or familiar Dialogue in our Language. Of the Books which he read, and from
which he formed his Style, ſome perhaps have periſhed, and the reſt are neglected. His Imitations are
therefore unnoted, his Alluſions are undiſcovered,
and many Beauties, both of Pleaſantry and Greatneſs, are loſt with the Objects to which they were
united, as the Figures vaniſh when the Canvas has
decayed.

It is the great Excellence of *Shakeſpeare*, that he
drew his Scenes from Nature, and from Life. He
copied the Manners of the World then paſſing before
him, and has more Alluſions than other Poets to the
Traditions and Superſtition of the Vulgar; which
muſt therefore be traced before he can be underſtood.

He wrote at a Time when our poetical Language
was yet unformed, when the Meaning of our Phraſes
was yet in Fluctuation, when Words were adopted
at Pleaſure from the neighbouring Languages, and
while the *Saxon* was ſtill viſibly mingled in our Diction. The Reader is therefore embarraſſed at once
with dead and with foreign Languages, with Obſo-
leteneſs and Innovation. In that Age, as in all
others, Faſhion produced Phraſeology, which ſuc-
ceeding Faſhion ſwept away before its Meaning was
generally known, or ſufficiently authoriſed: And in
that Age, above all others, Experiments were made
upon our Language, which diſtorted its Combinations, and diſturbed its Uniformity.

If *Shakeſpeare* has Difficulties above other Writers,
it is to be imputed to the Nature of his Work, which
requireſ

required the Ufe of the common colloquial Language, and confequently admitted many Phrafes allufive, elliptical, and proverbial, fuch as we fpeak and hear every hour without obferving them ; and of which, being now familiar, we do not fufpect that they can ever grow uncouth, or that, being now obvious, they can ever feem remote.

Thefe are the principal Caufes of the Obfcurity of *Shakefpeare*; to which might be added the Fulnefs of Idea, which might fometimes load his Words with more Sentiment than they could conveniently convey, and that Rapidity of Imagination which might hurry him to a fecond Thought before he had fully explained the firft. But my Opinion is, that very few of his Lines were difficult to his Audience, and that he ufed fuch Expreffions as were then common, tho' the Paucity of contemporary Writers makes them now feem peculiar.

Authours are often praifed for Improvement, or blamed for Innovation, with very little Juftice, by thofe who read few other Books of the fame Age. *Addifon* himfelf has been fo unfuccefsful in enumerating the Words with which *Milton* has enriched our Language, as perhaps not to have named one of which *Milton* was the Author ; and *Bentley* has yet more unhappily praifed him as the Introducer of thofe Elifions into *Englifh* Poetry, which had been ufed from the firft Effays of Verfification among us, and which *Milton* was indeed the laft that practifed.

Another Impediment, not the leaft vexatious to the Commentator, is the Exactnefs with which *Shakefpeare* followed his Authours. Inftead of dilating his Thoughts into Generalities, and expreffing Incidents with poetical Latitude, he often combines Circumftances unneceffary to his main Defign, only becaufe he happened to find them together. Such Paffages can be illuftrated only by him who has read

the

the fame Story in the very Book which *Shakefpeare* confulted.

He that undertakes an Edition of *Shakefpeare*, has all thefe Difficulties to encounter, and all thefe Obftructions to remove.

The Corruptions of the Text will be corrected by a careful Collation of the oldeft Copies, by which it is hoped that many Reftorations may yet be made: At leaft it will be neceffary to collect and note the Variation as Materials for future Criticks; for it very often happens that a wrong Reading has Affinity to the right.

In this Part all the prefent Editions are apparently and intentionally defective. The Criticks did not fo much as wifh to facilitate the Labour of thofe that followed them. The fame Books are ftill to be compared; the Work that has been done, is to be done again; and no fingle Edition will fupply the Reader with a Text on which he can rely as the beft Copy of the Works of *Shakefpeare*.

The Edition now propofed will at leaft have this Advantage over others. It will exhibit all the obfervable Varieties of all the Copies that can be found; that, if the Reader is not fatisfied with the Editor's Determination, he may have the Means of choofing better for himfelf.

Where all the Books are evidently vitiated, and Collation can give no Affiftance, then begins the Tafk of critical Sagacity: And fome Changes may well be admitted in a Text never fettled by the Authour, and fo long expofed to Caprice and Ignorance. But nothing fhall be impofed, as in the *Oxford* Edition, without Notice of the Alteration; nor fhall Conjecture be wantonly or unneceffarily indulged.

It has been long found, that very fpecious Emendations do not equally ftrike all Minds with Conviction, nor even the fame Mind at different Times; and therefore, though perhaps many Alterations may

be

be propofed as eligible, very few will be obtruded as certain. In a Language fo ungrammatical as the *Englifh*, and fo licentious as that of *Shakefpeare*, eméndatory Criticifm is always hazardous ; nor can it be allowed to any Man who is not particularly verfed in the Writings of that Age, and particularly ftudious of his Authour's Diction. There is Danger left Peculiarities fhould be miftaken for Corruptions, and Paffages rejected as unintelligible, which a narrow Mind happens not to underftand.

All the former Criticks have been fo much employed on the Correction of the Text, that they have not fufficiently attended to the Elucidation of Paffages obfcured by Accident or Time. The Editor will endeavoured to read the Books which the Authour read, to trace his Knowledge to its Source, and compare his Copies with their Originals. If in this Part of his Defign he hopes to attain any Degree of Superiority to his Predeceffors, it muft be confidered, that he has the Advantage of their Labours ; that Part of the Work being already done, more Care is naturally beftowed on the other Part ; and that, to declare the Truth, Mr. *Rowe* and Mr. *Pope* were very ignorant of the ancient *Englifh* Literature ; Dr. *Warburton* was detained by more important Studies ; and Mr. *Theobald*, if Fame be juft to his Memory, confidered Learning only as an Inftrument of Gain, and made no further Enquiry after his Authour's Meaning, when once he had Notes fufficient to embellifh his Page with the expected Decorations.

With Regard to obfolete or peculiar Diction, the Editor may perhaps claim fome Degree of Confidence, having had more Motives to confider the whole Extent of our Language than any other Man from its firft Formation. He hopes that, by comparing the Works of *Shakefpeare* with thofe of Writers who lived at the fame Time, immediately preceded, or immediately followed him, he fhall be able to afcer-

tain

tain his Ambiguities, difentangle his Intricacies, and recover the Meaning of Words now loft in the Darknefs of Antiquity.

When therefore any Obfcurity arifes from an Allufion to fome other Book, the Paffage will be quoted. When the Diction is entangled, it will be cleared by a Paraphrafe or Interpretation. When the Senfe is broken by the Suppreffion of Part of the Sentiment in Pleafantry or Paffion, the Connexion will be fupplied. When any forgotten Cuftom is hinted, Care will be taken to retrieve and explain it. The Meaning affigned to doubtful Words will be fupported by the Authorities of other Writers, or by parallel Paffages of *Shakefpeare* himfelf.

The Obfervation of Faults and Beauties is one of the Duties of an Annotator, which fome of *Shakefpeare's* Editors have attempted, and fome have neglected. For this Part of his Tafk, and for this only, was Mr. *Pope* eminently and indifputably qualified; nor has Dr. *Warburton* followed him with lefs Diligence or lefs Succefs. But I have never obferved that Mankind was much delighted or improved by their Afterifks, Commas, or double Commas; of which the only Effect is, that they preclude the Pleafure of judging for ourfelves, teach the Young and Ignorant to decide without Principles; defeat Curiofity and Difcernment, by leaving them lefs to difcover; and at laft fhew the Opinion of the Critick, without the Reafons on which it was founded, and without affording any Light by which it may be, examined.

The Editor, though he may lefs delight his own Vanity, will probably pleafe his Reader more, by fuppofing him equally able with himfelf to judge of Beauties and Faults, which require no previous Acquifition of remote Knowledge. A Defcription of the obvious Scenes of Nature, a Reprefentation of general Life, a Sentiment of Reflection or Experience,

rience, a Deduction of conclusive Arguments, a forcible Eruption of effervescent Passion, are to be considered as proportionate to common Apprehension, unassisted by critical Officiousness; since, to convince them, nothing more is requisite than Acquaintance with the general State of the World, and those Faculties which he must almost bring with him who would read *Shakespeare*.

But when the Beauty arises from some Adaptation of the Sentiment to Customs worn out of Use, to Opinions not universally prevalent, or to any accidental or minute Particularity, which cannot be supplied by common Understanding, or common Observation, it is the Duty of a Commentator to lend his Assistance.

The Notice of Beauties and Faults thus limited, will make no distinct Part of the Design, being reducible to the Explanation of obscure Passages.

The Editor does not however intend to preclude himself from the Comparison of *Shakespeare*'s Sentiments or Expression with those of ancient or modern Authours, or from the Display of any Beauty not obvious to the Students of Poetry; for as he hopes to leave his Authour better understood, he wishes likewise to procure him more rational Approbation.

The former Editors have affected to slight their Predecessors: But in this Edition all that is valuable will be adopted from every Commentator, that Posterity may consider it as including all the rest, and exhibiting whatever is hitherto known of the great Father of the *English* Drama.

PREFACE

P R E F A C E

T O

S H A K E S P E A R E.

Publiſhed in the Year 1768.

THAT Praiſes are without Reaſon laviſhed on the Dead, and that the Honours due only to Excellence are paid to Antiquity, is a Complaint likely to be always continued by thoſe, who, being able to add nothing to Truth, hope for Eminence from the Hereſies of Paradox; or thoſe, who, being forced by Diſappointment upon conſolatory Expedients, are willing to hope from Poſterity what the preſent Age refuſes, and flatter themſelves that the Regard which is yet denied by Envy, will be at laſt beſtowed by Time.

Antiquity, like every other Quality that attracts the Notice of Mankind, has undoubtedly Votaries that reverence it, not from Reaſon, but from Prejudice. Some ſeem to admire indiſcriminately whatever has been long preſerved, without conſidering that Time has ſometimes co-operated with Chance; all perhaps are more willing to honour paſt than preſent Excellence; and the Mind contemplates Genius through the Shades of Age, as the Eye ſurveys the Sun through artificial Opacity. The great Contention of Criticiſm is to find the Faults of the Moderns, and the Beauties of the Ancients. While an Authour is yet living, we eſtimate his Powers by his worſt Performance, and when he is dead, we rate them by his beſt.

To Works, however, of which the Excellence is not abſolute and definite, but gradual and comparative;

tive ; to Works not raifed upon Principles demon-
ftrative and fcientifick, but appealing wholly to Obfervation and Experience, no other Teft can be applied than Length of Duration, and Continuance of
Efteem. What Mankind have long poffeffed, they
have often examined and compared ; and if they
perfift to value the Poffeffion, it is becaufe frequent
Comparifons have confirmed Opinion in its Favour.
As among the Works of Nature no Man can properly
call a River deep, or a Mountain high, without the
Knowledge of many Mountains and many Rivers ;
fo, in the Productions of Genius, nothing can be
ftiled excellent till it has been compared with other
Works of the fame Kind. Demonftration immediately difplays its Power, and has nothing to hope
or fear from the Flux of Years ; but Works tenta-
tive and experimental muft be eftimated by their
Proportion to the general and collective Ability of
Man, as it is difcovered in a long Succeffion of Endeavours. Of the firft Building that was raifed, it
might be with Certainty determined that it was
round or fquare ; but whether it was fpacious or
lofty muft have been referred to Time. The *Py-
thagorean* Scale of Numbers was at once difcovered
to be perfect; but the Poems of *Homer* we yet
know not to tranfcend the common Limits of human Intelligence, but by remarking, that Nation
after Nation, and Century after Century, has been
able to do little more than tranfpofe his Incidents,
new name his Characters, and paraphrafe his Sentiments.

The Reverence due to Writings that have long
fubfifted, arifes therefore not from any credulous Confidence in the fuperior Wifdom of paft Ages, or
gloomy Perfuafion of the Degeneracy of Mankind,
but is the Confequence of acknowledged and indu-
bitable Pofitions, that what has been longeft known
has

has been moſt conſidered, and what is moſt conſidered is beſt underſtood.

The Poet, of whoſe Works I have undertaken the Reviſion, may now begin to aſſume the Dignity of an Antient, and claim the Privilege of eſtabliſhed Fame and preſcriptive Veneration. He has long outlived his Century, the Term commonly fixed as the Teſt of literary Merit. Whatever Advantages he might once derive from perſonal Alluſions, local Cuſtoms, or temporary Opinions, have for many Years been loſt ; and every Topick of Merriment, or Motive of Sorrow, which the Modes of artificial Life afforded him, now only obſcure the Scenes which they once illuminated. The Effects of Favour and Competition are at an End ; the Tradition of his Friendſhips and his Enmities has periſhed ; his Works ſupport no Opinion with Arguments, nor ſupply any Faction with Invectives; they can neither indulge Vanity, nor gratify Malignity, but are read without any other Reaſon than the Deſire of Pleaſure, and are therefore praiſed only as Pleaſure is obtained ; yet, thus unaſſiſted by Intereſt or Paſſion, they have paſt through Variations of Taſte, and Changes of Manners, and, as they devolved from one Generation to another, have received new Honours at every Tranſmiſſion.

But becauſe human Judgment, though it be gradually gaining upon Certainty, never becomes infallible ; and Approbation, though long continued, may yet be only the Approbation of Prejudice or Faſhion : it is proper to inquire by what Peculiarities of Excellence *Shakeſpeare* has gained and kept the Favour of his Countrymen.

Nothing can pleaſe many, and pleaſe long, but juſt Repreſentations of general Nature. Particular Manners can be known to few, and therefore few only can judge how nearly they are copied. The irregular Combinations of fanciful Invention may delight a-while, by that Novelty of which the common Satiety of Life fends us all in queft ; but the Pleafures of fudden Wonder are foon exhaufted, and the Mind can only repofe on the Stability of Truth.

Shakefpeare is above all Writers, at leaft above all modern Writers, the Poet of Nature ; the Poet that holds up to his Readers a faithful Mirrour of Manners and of Life. His Characters are not modified by the Cuftoms of particular Places, unpractifed by the reft of the World ; by the Peculiarities of Studies or Profeffions, which can operate but upon fmall Numbers ; or by the Accidents of tranfient Fafhions, or temporary Opinions : They are the genuine Progeny of common Humanity, fuch as the World will always fupply, and Obfervation will always find. His Perfons act and fpeak by the Influence of thofe general Paffions and Principles by which all Minds are agitated, and the whole Syftem of Life is continued in Motion. In the Writings of other Poets a Character is too often an Individual ; in thofe of *Shakefpeare* it is commonly a Species.

It is from this wide Extenfion of Defign that fo much Inftruction is derived. It is this which fills the Plays of *Shakefpeare* with practical Axioms and domeftick Wifdom. It was faid of *Euripides*, that every Verfe was a Precept ; and it may be faid of *Shakefpeare*, that from his Works may be collected a Syftem of civil and œconomical Prudence. Yet his real Power is not fhown in the Splendour of particular Paffages, but by the Progrefs of his Fable, and the Tenour of his Dialogue ; and he that tries to recommend him by felect Quotations, will fucceed like the Pedant in *Hierocles*, who, when he offered his Houfe to Sale, carried a Brick in his Pocket as a Specimen.

It will not eafily be imagined how much *Shakefpeare* excells in accommodating his Sentiments to
real

real Life, but by comparing him with other Authours. It was obferved of the ancient Schools of
Declamation, that the more diligently they were frequented, the more was the Student difqualified for
the World, becaufe he found nothing there which
he fhould ever meet with in any other Place. The
fame Remark may be applied to every Stage but
that of *Shakefpeare.* The Theatre, when it is under any other Direction, is peopled by fuch Characters as were never feen, converfing in a Language
which was never heard, upon Topicks which will
never arife in the Commerce of Mankind. But the
Dialogue of this Authour is often fo evidently determined by the Incident which produces it, and is
purfued with fo much Eafe and Simplicity, that it
feems fcarcely to claim the Merit of Fiction, but to
have been gleaned by diligent Selection out of common Converfation, and common Occurrences.

Upon every other Stage the univerfal Agent is
Love, by whofe Power all Good and Evil is diftributed, and every Action quickened or retarded. To
bring a Lover, a Lady and a Rival into the Fable ;
to entangle them in contradictory Obligations, perplex them with Oppofitions of Intereft, and harrafs
them with Violence of Defires inconfiftent with each
other ; to make them meet in Rapture, and part in
Agony ; to fill their Mouths with hyperbolical Joy,
and outrageous Sorrow ; to diftrefs them as nothing human ever was diftreffed ; to deliver them as
nothing human ever was delivered, is the Bufinefs
of a modern Dramatift. For this Probability is violated, Life is mifreprefented, and Language is depraved. But Love is only one of many Paffions,
and as it has no great Influence upon the Sum of
Life, it has little Operation in the Dramas of a
Poet, who caught his Ideas from the living World,
and exhibited only what he faw before him. He

knew

knew that any other Paffion, as it was regular or exorbitant, was a Caufe of Happinefs or Calamity.

Characters thus ample and general were not eafily difcriminated and preferved, yet perhaps no Poet ever kept his Perfonages more diftinct from each other. I will not fay with *Pope*, that every Speech may be affigned to the proper Speaker, becaufe many Speeches there are which have nothing characteriftical ; but, perhaps, though fome may be equally adapted to every Perfon, it will be difficult to find any that can be properly transferred from the prefent Poffeffor to another Claimant. The Choice is right, when there is Reafon for Choice.

Other Dramatifts can only gain Attention by hyperbolical or aggravated Characters, by fabulous and unexampled Excellence or Depravity, as the Writers of barbarous Romances invigorated the Reader by a Giant and a Dwarf ; and he that fhould form his Expectations of human Affairs from the Play, or from the Tale, would be equally deceived. *Shakefpeare* has no Heroes ; his Scenes are occupied only by Men, who act and fpeak as the Reader thinks that he fhould himfelf have fpoken or acted on the fame Occafion : Even where the Agency is fupernatural, the Dialogue is level with Life. Other Writers difguife the moft natural Paffions and moft frequent Incidents ; fo that he who contemplates them in the Book will not know them in the World : *Shakefpeare* approximates the Remote, and familiarizes the Wonderful ; the Event which he reprefents will not happen, but if it were poffible, its Effect would be probably fuch as he has affigned ; and it may be faid, that he has not only fhewn human Nature as it acts in real Exigencies, but as it will be found in Trials, to which it cannot be expofed.

This therefore is the Praife of *Shakefpeare*, that his Drama is the Mirrour of Life ; that he who has

mazed

mazed his Imagination, in following the Phantoms which other Writers raife up before them, may here be cured of his delirious Extafies, by reading human Sentiments in human Language; by Scenes from which a Hermit may eftimate the Tranfactions of the World, and a Confeffor predict the Progrefs of the Paffions.

His Adherence to general Nature has expofed him to the Cenfure of Criticks, who form their Judgments upon narrower Principles. *Dennis* and *Rhymer* think his *Romans* not fufficiently *Roman*; and *Voltaire* cenfures his Kings as not completely royal. *Dennis* is offended, that *Menenius*, a Senator of *Rome*, fhould play the Buffoon; and *Voltaire* perhaps thinks Decency violated, when the *Danifh* Ufurper is reprefented as a Drunkard. But *Shakefpeare* always makes Nature predominate over Accident; and if he preferves the effential Character, is not very careful of Diftinctions fuperinduced and adventitious. His Story requires *Romans* or Kings, but he thinks only on Men. He knew that *Rome*, like every other City, had Men of all Difpofitions; and wanting a Buffoon, he went into the Senate-houfe for that which the Senate-houfe would certainly have afforded him. He was inclined to fhew an Ufurper and a Murderer not only odious, but defpicable; he therefore added Drunkennefs to his other Qualities, knowing that Kings love Wine like other Men, and that Wine exerts its natural Power upon Kings. Thefe are the petty Cavils of petty Minds; a Poet overlooks the cafual Diftinction of Country and Condition, as a Painter, fatisfied with the Figure, neglects the Drapery.

The Cenfure which he has incurred by mixing comick and tragick Scenes, as it extends to all his Works, deferves more Confideration. Let the Fact be firft ftated, and then examined.

Shake-

Shakespeare's Plays are not in the rigorous or critical Sense either Tragedies or Comedies, but Compositions of a distinct Kind; exhibiting the real State of sublunary Nature, which partakes of Good and Evil, Joy and Sorrow, mingled with endless Variety of Proportion and innumerable Modes of Combination : and expressing the Course of the World, in which the Loss of one is the Gain of another ; in which, at the same Time, the Reveller is hasting to his Wine, and the Mourner burying his Friend ; in which the Malignity of one is sometimes defeated by the Frolick of another ; and many Mischiefs and many Benefits are done and hindered without Design.

Out of this Chaos of mingled Purposes and Casualties the ancient Poets, according to the Laws which Custom had prescribed, selected some the Crimes of Men, and some their Absurdities ; some the momentous Vicissitudes of Life, and some the lighter Occurrences ; some the Terrours of Distress, and some the Gayeties of Prosperity. Thus rose the two Modes of Imitation known by the Names of *Tragedy* and *Comedy*, Compositions intended to promote different Ends by contrary Means, and considered as so little allied, that I do not recollect among the *Greeks* or *Romans* a single Writer who attempted both.

Shakespeare has united the Powers of exciting Laughter and Sorrow, not only in one Mind, but in one Composition. Almost all his Plays are divided between serious and ludicrous Characters ; and, in the successive Evolutions of the Design, sometimes produce Seriousness and Sorrow, and sometimes Levity and Laughter.

That this is a Practice contrary to the Rules of Criticism will be readily allowed ; but there is always an Appeal open from Criticism to Nature. The End of Writing is to instruct ; the End of Poetry is to instruct by pleasing. That the mingled Drama

may

may convey all the Inftruction of Tragedy or Comedy cannot be denied ; becaufe it includes both in its Alterations of Exhibition, and approaches nearer than either to the Appearance of Life, by fhewing how great Machinations and flender Defigns may promote or obviate one another, and the high and the low co-operate in the general Syftem by una- voidable Concatenation.

It is objected, that by this Change of Scenes the Paffions are interrupted in their Progreffion ; and that the principal Event, being not advanced by a due Gradation of preparatory Incidents, wants at laft the Power to move, which conftitutes the Perfection of dramatick Poetry. This Reafoning is fo fpecious, that it is received as true even by thofe who in daily Experience feel it to be falfe. The Interchanges of mingled Scenes feldom fail to produce the intended Viciffitudes of Paffion. Fiction cannot move fo much, but that the Attention may be eafily tranf- ferred ; and though it muft be allowed that pleafing Melancholy be fometimes interrupted by unwelcome Levity ; yet let it be confidered likewife, that Melan- choly is often not pleafing, and that the Difturbance of one Man may be the Relief of another ; that dif- ferent Auditors have different Habitudes ; and that, upon the Whole, all Pleafure confifts in Variety.

The Players, who in their Edition divided our Authour's Works into Comedies, Hiftories, and Tra- gedies, feem not to have diftinguifhed the three Kinds by any very exact or definitive Ideas.

An Action which ended happily to the principal Perfons, however ferious or diftrefsful through its intermediate Incidents, in their Opinion conftituted a Comedy. This Idea of a Comedy continued long amongft us, and Plays were written, which, by changing the Cataftrophe, were Tragedies to-day, and Comedies to-morrow.

H 4   Tragedy

Tragedy was not in thofe Times a Poem of more general Dignity or Elevation than Comedy; it required only a calamitous Conclufion, with which the common Criticifm of that Age was fatisfied, whatever lighter Pleafure it afforded in its Progrefs.

Hiftory was a Species of Actions, with no other than chronological Succeffion, independent of each other, and without any Tendency to introduce or regulate the Conclufion. It is not always very nicely diftinguifhed from Tragedy. There is not much nearer Approach to Unity of Action in the Tragedy of *Anthony and Cleopatra*, than in the Hiftory of *Richard the fecond*. But a Hiftory might be continued through many Plays; as it had no Plan, it had no Limits.

Through all thefe Denominations of the Drama, *Shakefpeare*'s Mode of Compofition is the fame; an Interchange of Serioufnefs and Merriment, by which the Mind is foftened at one Time, and exhilarated at another. But whatever be his Purpofe, whether to gladden or deprefs, or to conduct the Story, without Vehemence of Emotion, through Tracts of eafy and familiar Dialogue, he never fails to attain his Purpofe; as he commands us, we laugh or mourn, or fit filent with quiet Expectation, in Tranquility without Indifference.

When *Shakefpeare*'s Plan is underftood, moft of the Criticifms of *Rhymer* and *Voltaire* vanifh away. The Play of *Hamlet* is opened without Impropriety, by two Sentinels; *Iago* bellows at *Brabantio*'s Window, without Injury to the Scheme of the Play, though in Terms which a modern Audience would not eafily endure; the Character for *Polonius* is feafonable and ufeful; and the Grave-diggers themfelves may be heard with Applaufe.

Shakefpeare engaged in dramatick Poetry with the World open before him; the Rules of the Ancients were yet known to few; the publick Judgment was unformed;

unformed ; he had no Example of fuch Fame as
might force him upon Imitation, nor Criticks of
fuch Authority as might reftrain his Extravagance :
He therefore indulged his natural Difpofition, and
his Difpofition, as *Rhymer* has remarked, led him to
Comedy. In Tragedy he often writes with great
Appearance of Toil and Study, what is written at
laft with little Felicity ; but in his comic Scenes he
feems to produce without Labour, what no Labour
can improve. In Tragedy he is always ftruggling
after fome Occafion to be comick ; but in Comedy
he feems to repofe, or to luxuriate, as in a Mode of
Thinking congenial to his Nature. In his tragick
Scenes there is always fomething wanting ; but his
Comedy often furpaffes Expectation or Defire. His
Comedy pleafes by the Thoughts and the Language,
and his Tragedy for the greater Part by Incident and
Action. His Tragedy feems to be Skill, his Comedy
to be Inftinct.

The Force of his comick Scenes has fuffered little
Diminution from the Changes made by a Century
and a half in Manners or in Words. As his Perfonages act upon Principles arifing from genuine Paffion, very little modified by particular Forms, their
Pleafures and Vexations are communicable to all
Times, and to all Places ; they are natural, and
therefore durable ; the adventitious Peculiarities of
perfonal Habits are only fuperficial Dyes, bright and
pleafing for a little while, yet foon fading to a dim
Tinct, without any Remains of former Luftre, but
the Difcriminations of true Paffion and the Colours of
Nature; they pervade the whole Mafs, and can only
perifh with the Body that exhibits them. The accidental Compofitions of heterogeneous Modes are dif-
folved by the Chance which combined them ; but the
uniform Simplicity of primitive Qualities neither admits
Increafe, nor fuffers Decay. The Sand heaped by one
Flood is fcattered by another, but the Rock always
continues

I

continues in its Place. The Stream of Time, which is continually wafhing the diffoluble Fabricks of other Poets, paffes without Injury by the Adamant of *Shakefpeare*.

If there be, what I believe there is, in every Nation, a Stile which never becomes obfolete, a certain Mode of Phrafeology fo confonant and congenial to the Analogy and Principles of its refpective Language, as to remain fettled and unaltered ; this Stile is probably to be fought in the common Intercourfe of Life among thofe who fpeak only to be underftood, without Ambition of Elegance. The Polite are always catching modifh Innovations, and the Learned depart from eftablifhed Forms of Speech, in Hope of finding or making better ; thofe who wifh for Diftinction, forfake the Vulgar, when the Vulgar is right ; but there is a Converfation above Groffnefs, and below Refinement, where Propriety refides, and where this Poet feems to have gathered his Comick Dialogue. He is therefore more agreeable to the Ears of the prefent Age than any other Authour equally remote, and among his other Excellencies, deferves to be ftudied as one of the original Mafters of our Language.

Thefe Obfervations are to be confidered not as unexceptionably conftant, but as containing general and predominant Truth. *Shakefpeare*'s familiar Dialogue is affirmed to be fmooth and clear, yet not wholly without Ruggednefs or Difficulty ; as a Country may be eminently fruitful, though it has Spots unfit for Cultivation : His Characters are praifed as natural, though their Sentiments are fometimes forced and their Actions improbable ; as the Earth upon the Whole is fpherical, though its Surface is varied with Protuberances and Cavities.

Shakefpeare with his Excellencies has likewife Faults, and Faults fufficient to obfcure and overwhelm any other Merit. I fhall fhew them in the
Pro-

Proportion in which they appear to me, without envious Malignity, or superftitious Veneration. No Queftion can be more innocently difcuffed than a dead Poet's Pretenfions to Renown; and little Regard is due to that Bigotry which fets Candour higher than Truth.

His firft Defect is that to which may be imputed moft of the Evil in Books or in Men. He facrifices Virtue to Convenience, and is fo much more careful to pleafe than to inftruct, that he feems to write without any moral Purpofe. From his Writings indeed a Syftem of focial Duty may be felected, for he that thinks reafonably muft think morally; but his Precepts and Axioms drop cafually from him; he makes no juft Diftribution of Good or Evil, nor is always careful to fhew in the Virtuous a Difapprobation of the Wicked; he carries his Perfons indifferently through Right and Wrong, and at the Clofe difmiffes them without further Care, and leaves their Examples to operate by Chance. This Fault the Barbarity of his Age cannot extenuate; for it is always a Writer's Duty to make the World better; and Juftice is a Virtue independant on Time or Place.

The Plots are often fo loofely formed, that a very flight Confideration may improve them, and fo carelefsly purfued, that he feems not always fully to comprehend his own Defign. He omits Opportunities of inftructing or delighting which the Train of his Story feems to force upon him, and apparently rejects thofe Exhibitions which would be more affecting, for the Sake of thofe which are more eafy.

It may be obferved, that in many of his Plays the latter Part is evidently neglected. When he found himfelf near the End of his Work, and in View of his Reward, he fhortened the Labour, to fnatch the Profit. He therefore remits his Efforts where he fhould moft vigouroufly exert them, and
his

his Cataftrophe is improbably produced or imperfectly reprefented.

He had no Regard to Diftinction of Time or
Place, but gives to one Age or Nation, without
Scruple, the Cuftoms, Inftitutions, and Opinions
of another, at the Expence not only of Likelihood,
but of Poffibility. Thefe Faults *Pope* has endeavoured, with more Zeal than Judgment, to tranf-
fer to his imagined Interpolators. We need not
wonder to find *Hector* quoting *Ariftotle*, when we fee
the Loves of *Thefeus* and *Hippolyta* combined with
the Cothick Mythology of Fairies. *Shakefpeare* indeed was not the only Violator of Chronology,
for in the fame Age *Sydney*, who wanted not the
Advantages of Learning, has, in his *Arcadia*, confounded the Paftoral with the Feudal Times, the
Days of Innocence, Quiet and Security, with thofe
of Turbulence, Violence and Adventure.

In his Comick Scenes he is feldom very fuccefsful, when he engages his Characters in Reciproca-
tions of Smartnefs, and Contefts of Sarcafm; their
Jefts are commonly grofs, and their Pleafantry licentious; neither his Gentlemen nor his Ladies have
much Delicacy, nor are fufficiently diftinguifhed
from his Clowns by any Appearance of refined Manners. Whether he reprefented the real Converfation of his Time is not eafy to determine: The
Reign of *Elizabeth* is commonly fuppofed to have
been a Time of Statelinefs, Formality, and Referve; yet perhaps the Relaxations of that Severity
were not very elegant. There muft, however, have
been always fome Modes of Gayety preferable to
others, and a Writer ought to chufe the beft.

In Tragedy his Performance feems conftantly to be
worfe, as his Labour is more. The Effufions of
Paffion which Exigence forces out are for the moft
Part ftriking and energetick; but whenever he fo-
licits his Invention, or ftrains his Faculties, the Offspring

spring of his Throes is Tumour, Meanness, Tedioufnefs, and Obfcurity.

In Narration he affects a difproportionate Pomp of Diction, and a wearifome Train of Circumlocution, and tells the Incident imperfectly in many Words, which might have been more plainly delivered in few. Narration in dramatick Poetry is naturally tedious, as it is unanimated and inactive, and obftructs the Progrefs of the Action; it fhould therefore always be rapid, and enlivened by frequent Interruption. *Shakefpeare* found it an Encumbrance, and inftead of lightening it by Brevity, endeavoured to recommend it by Dignity and Splendour.

His Declamations or fet Speeches are commonly cold and weak, for his Power was the Power of Nature; when he endeavoured, like other tragick Writers, to catch Opportunities of Amplification, and inftead of inquiring what the Occafion demanded, to fhow how much his Stores of Knowledge could fupply, he feldom efcapes without the Pity or Refentment of his Reader.

It is incident to him to be now and then entangled with an unwieldy Sentiment, which he cannot well exprefs, and will not reject; he ftruggles with it a while, and if it continues ftubborn, comprifes it in Words fuch as occur, and leaves it to be difentangled and evolved by thofe who have more Leifure to beftow upon it.

Not that always where the Language is intricate the Thought is fubtle, or the Image always great where the Line is bulky; the Equality of Words to Things is very often neglected, and trivial Sentiments and vulgar Ideas difappoint the Attention, to which they are recommended by fonorous Epithets and fwelling Figures.

But the Admirers of this great Poet have never lefs Reafon to indulge their Hopes of fupreme Excellence, than when he feems fully refolved to fink

them

them in Dejection, and mollify them with tender Emotions by the Fall of Greatnefs, the Danger of Innocence, and the Croffes of Love. He is not long foft and pathetick, without fome idle Conceit, or contemptible Equivocation. He no fooner begins to move, than he counteracts himfelf; and Terrour and Pity, as they are rifing in the Mind, are checked and blafted by fudden Frigidity.

A Quibble is to *Shakefpeare* what luminous Vapours are to the Traveller; he follows it at all Adventures, it is fure to lead him out of his Way, and fure to entangle him in the Mire. It has fome malignant Power over his Mind, and its Fafcinations are irrefiftible. Whatever be the Dignity or Profundity of his Difquifition, whether he be enlarging Knowledge, or exalting Affection, whether he be amufing Attention with Incidents, or enchaining it in Sufpenfe, let but a Quibble fpring up before him, and he leaves his Work unfinifhed. A Quibble is the golden Apple, for which he will always turn afide from his Career, or ftoop from his Elevation. A Quibble, poor and barren as it is, gave him fuch Delight, that he was content to purchafe it by the Sacrifice of Reafon, Propriety, and Truth. A Quibble was to him the fatal *Cleopatra* for which he loft the World, and was content to lofe it.

It will be thought ftrange, that in enumerating the Defects of this Writer, I have not yet mentioned his Neglect of the Unities; his Violation of thofe Laws which have been inftituted and eftablifhed by the joint Authority of Poets and of Criticks.

For his other Deviations from the Art of Writing, I refign him to critical Juftice, without making any other Demand in his Favour, than that which muft be indulged to all human Excellence; that his Virtues be rated with his Failings: But, from the Cenfure which this Irregularity may bring upon him,

him, I shall, with due Reverence to that Learning which I must oppose, adventure to try how I can defend him.

His Histories, being neither Tragedies nor Comedies, are not subject to any of their Laws; nothing more is necessary to all the Praise which they expect, than that the Changes of Action be so prepared as to be understood, that the Incidents be various and affecting, and the Characters consistent, natural, and distinct. No other Unity is intended, and therefore none is to be sought.

In his other Works he has well enough preserved the Unity of Action. He has not, indeed, an Intrigue regularly perplexed and regularly unravelled; he does not endeavour to hide his Design only to discover it, for this is seldom the Order of real Events, and *Shakespeare* is the Poet of Nature: But his Plan has commonly what *Aristotle* requires, a Beginning, a Middle, and an End; one Event is concatenated with another, and the Conclusion follows by easy Consequence. There are perhaps some Incidents that might be spared, as in other Poets there is much Talk that only fills up Time upon the Stage; but the general System makes gradual Advances, and the End of the Play is the End of Expectation.

To the Unities of Time and Place he has shewn no Regard, and perhaps a nearer View of the Principles on which they stand will diminish their Value, and withdraw from them the Veneration which, from the Time of *Corneille*, they have very generally received, by discovering that they have given more Trouble to the Poet, than Pleasure to the Auditor.

The Necessity of observing the Unities of Time and Place arises from the supposed Necessity of making the Drama credible. The Criticks hold it impossible, that an Action of Months or Years can be possibly believed to pass in three Hours; or that the

Spectator

Spectator can suppose himself to sit in the Theatre, while Ambassadors go and return between distant Kings, while Armies are levied, and Towns besieged, while an Exile wanders and returns, or till he whom they saw courting his Mistress, shall lament the untimely Fall of his Son. The Mind revolts from evident Falshood, and Fiction loses its Force when it departs from the Resemblance of Reality.

From the narrow Limitation of Time necessarily arises the Contraction of Place. The Spectator, who knows that he saw the first Act at *Alexandria*, cannot suppose that he sees the next at *Rome*, at a Distance to which not the Dragons of *Medea* could, in so short a Time, have transported him: He knows with Certainty that he has not changed his Place; and he knows that Place cannot change itself; that what was a House cannot become a Plain; that what was *Thebes* can never be *Persepolis*.

Such is the triumphant Language with which a Critick exults over the Misery of an irregular Poet, and exults commonly without Resistance or Reply.

It is Time therefore to tell him, by the Authority of *Shakespeare*, that he assumes, as an unquestionable Principle, a Position, which, while his Breath is forming it into Words, his Understanding pronounces to be false. It is false, that any Representation is mistaken for Reality; that any dramatick Fable, in its Materiality, was ever credible, or, for a single Moment, was ever credited.

The Objection arising from the Impossibility of passing the first Hour at *Alexandria*, and the next at *Rome*, supposes, that when the Play opens, the Spectator really imagines himself at *Alexandria*, and believes that his Walk to the Theatre has been a Voyage to *Egypt*, and that he lives in the Days of *Antony* and *Cleopatra*. Surely he that imagines this, may imagine more. He that can take the Stage at

one

One Time for the Palace of the *Ptolemies*, may take it in half an Hour for the Promontory of *Actium*. Delufion, if Delufion be admitted, has no certain Limitation : If the Spectator can be once perfuaded, that his old Acquaintance are *Alexander* and *Cæsar*, that a Room illuminated with Candles is the Plain of *Pharfalia*, or the Bank of *Granicus*, he is in a State of Elevation above the Reach of Reafon, or of Truth, and from the Heights of empyrean Poetry may defpife the Circumfcriptions of terreftrial Nature. There is no Reafon why a Mind thus wandering in Extafy fhould count the Clock, or why an Hour fhould not be a Century in that Calenture of the Brains that can make the Stage a Field.

The Truth is, that the Spectators are always in their Senfes, and know, from the firft Act to the laft, that the Stage is only a Stage, and that the Players are only Players. They come to hear a certain Number of Lines recited with juft Gefture and elegant Modulation. The Lines relate to fome Action, and an Action muft be in fome Place ; but the different Actions that complete a Story may be Places very remote from each other ; and where is the Abfurdity of allowing that Space to reprefent firft *Athens*, and then *Sicily*, which was always known to be neither *Sicily* nor *Athens*, but a modern Theatre.

By Suppofition, as Place is introduced, Time may be extended: The Time required by the Fable elapfes for the moft Part between the Acts ; for, of fo much of the Action as is reprefented, the real and poetical Duration is the fame. If in the firft Act, Preparations for War againft *Mithridates* are reprefented to be made in *Rome*, the Event of the War may, without Abfurdity, be reprefented, in the Cataftrophe, as happening in *Pontus* ; we know that there is neither War, nor Preparation for War ; we know that we are neither in *Rome* nor *Pontus* ; that neither *Mithridates* nor *Lucullus* are before us. The Drama exhi-

bits

bits fucceffive Imitations of fucceffive Actions; and
why may not the fecond Imitation reprefent an Action that happened Years after the firft, if it be fo
connected with it, that nothing but Time can be
fuppofed to intervene? Time is, of all Modes of
Exiftence, moft obfequious to the Imagination; a
Lapfe of Years is as eafily conceived as a Paffage of
Hours. In Contemplation we eafily contract the
Time of real Actions, and therefore willingly permit
it to be contracted when we only fee their Imitat-
tion.

It will be afked, how the Drama moves, if it is
not credited. It is credited, with all the Credit due
to a Drama. It is credited, whenever it moves, as
a juft Picture of a real Original; as reprefenting to
the Auditor what he would himfelf feel, if he were to
do or fuffer what is there feigned to be fuffered or to
be done. The Reflection that ftrikes the Heart is
not, that the Evils before us are real Evils, but that
they are Evils to which we ourfelves may be expofed.
If there be any Fallacy, it is not that we fancy the
Players, but that we fancy ourfelves unhappy for a
Moment; but we rather lament the Poffibility, than
fuppofe the Prefence of Mifery; as a Mother weeps
over her Babe, when fhe remembers that Death may
take it from her. The Delight of Tragedy proceeds
from our Confcioufnefs of Fiction; if we thought
Murders and Treafons real, they would pleafe to
more.

Imitations produce Pain or Pleafure, not becaufe
they are miftaken for Realities, but becaufe they bring
Realities to Mind. When the Imagination is recre-
ated by a painted Landfcape, the Trees are not fuppofed capable to give us Shade, or the Fountains
Coolnefs; but we confider, how we fhould be pleafed
with fuch Fountains playing befide us, and fuch
Woods waving over us. We are agitated in reading
the Hiftory of *Henry* the Fifth, yet no Man takes his

Book

Book for the Field of *Agencourt*. A dramatick Exhibition is a Book recited with Concomitants that encrease or diminish its Effect. Familiar Comedy is often more powerful on the Theatre, than in the Page; imperial Tragedy is always less. The Humour of *Petruchio* may be heightened by Grimace; but what Voice or what Gesture can hope to add Dignity or Force to the Soliloquy of *Cato* ?

A Play read affects the Mind like a Play acted. It is therefore evident, that the Action is not supposed to be real; and it follows, that between the Acts a longer or shorter Time may be allowed to pass, and that no more Account of Space or Duration is to be taken by the Auditor of a Drama, than by the Reader of a Narrative, before whom may pass in an Hour the Life of a Hero, or the Revolutions of an Empire.

Whether *Shakespeare* knew the Unities, and rejected them by Design, or deviated from them by happy Ignorance, it is, I think, impossible to decide, and useless to enquire. We may reasonably suppose that, when he rose to Notice, he did not want the Counsels and Admonitions of Scholars and Criticks, and that he at last deliberately persisted in a Practice, which he might have begun by Chance. As nothing is essential to the Fable, but Unity of Action, and as the Unities of Time and Place arise evidently from false Assumptions, and, by circumscribing the Extent of the Drama, lessen its Variety, I cannot think it much to be lamented, that they were not known by him, or not observed: Nor, if such another Poet could arise, should I very vehemently reproach him, that his first act passed at *Venice*, and his next in *Cyprus*. Such Violations of Rules merely positive, become the comprehensive Genius of *Shakespeare*, and such Censures are suitable to the minute and slender Criticisms of *Voltaire* :

Non

Non ufque adeo permifcuit imis
Longus fumma dies, ut non, fi voce Metelli
Serventur leges, malint a Cæfare tolli.

Yet when I fpeak thus flightly of dramatick Rules,
I cannot but recollect how much Wit and Learning
may be produced againft me ; before fuch Authorities I am afraid to ftand, not that I think the prefent Queftion one of thofe that are to be decided by
mere Authority, but becaufe it is to be fufpected,
that thefe Precepts have not been fo eafily received,
but for better Reafons than I have yet been able to
find. The Refult of my Enquiries, in which it
would be ludicrous to boaft of Impartiality, is, that
the Unities of Time and Place are not effential to a
juft Drama ; that tho' they may fometimes conduce to
Pleafure, they are always to be facrificed to the no-
bler Beauties of Variety and Inftruction ; and that
a Play, written with nice Obfervation of critical
Rules, is to be contemplated as an elaborate Curiofity, as the Product of fuperfluous and oftentatious
Art, by which is fhewn rather what is poffible, than
what is neceffary.

He that, without Diminution of any other Excellence, fhall preferve all the Unities unbroken, deferves the like Applaufe with the Architect, who
fhall difplay all the Orders of Architecture in a Citadel, without any Deduction from its Strength ;
but the principal Beauty of a Citadel is to exclude
the Enemy : and the greateft Graces of a Play are
to copy Nature and inftruct Life.

Perhaps, what I have here not dogmatically, but
deliberately written, may recall the Principles of the
Drama to a new Examination. I am almoft frighted
at my own Temerity ; and when I eftimate the Fame
and the Strength of thofe that maintain the contrary
Opinion, am ready to fink down in reverential Silence ; as *Æneas* withdrew from the Defence of *Troy*,
6   when

when he faw *Neptune* fhaking the Wall, and *Juno* heading the Befiegers.

Thofe whom my Arguments cannot perfuade to give their Approbation to the Judgment of *Shake-fpeare*, will eafily, if they confider the Condition of his Life, make fome Allowance for his Ignorance.

Every Man's Performances, to be rightly eftima-ted, muft be compared with the State of the Age in which he lived, and with his own particular Oppor-tunities; and though to the Reader a Book be not worfe or better for the Circumftances of the Authour, yet as there is always a filent Reference of human Works to human Abilities, and as the Enquiry, how far Man may extend his Defigns, or how high he may rate his native Force, is of far greater Dig-nity than in what Rank we fhall place any particular Performance, Curiofity is always bufy to difcover the Inftruments, as well as to furvey the Workman-fhip, to know how much is to be afcribed to original Powers, and how much to cafual and adventitious Help. The Palaces of *Peru* or *Mexico* were cer-tainly mean and incommodious Habitations, if com-pared to the Houfes of *European* Monarchs : yet who could forbear to view them with Aftonifhment, who remembered that they were built without the Ufe of Iron ?

The *Englifh* Nation in the Time of *Shakefpeare*, was yet ftruggling to emerge from Barbarity. The Philology of *Italy* had been tranfplanted hither in the Reign of *Henry* the Eigthth : and the learned Lan-guages had been fuccefsfully cultivated by *Lilly*, *Li-nacer*, and *More*; by *Pole*, *Cheke*, and *Gardiner*; and afterwards by *Smith*, *Clerk*, *Haddon*, and *Afcham*. Greek was now now taught to Boys in the principal Schools; and thofe who united Elegance with Learn-ing, read, with great Diligence, the *Italian* and *Spa-nifh* Poets. But Literature was yet confined to pro-feffed Scholars, or to Men and Women of high

I 3

Rank.

Rank. The Publick was grofs and dark; and to be able to read and write, was an Accomplifhment ftill valued for its Rarity.

Nations, like Individuals, have their Infancy. A People newly awakened to literary Curiofity, being yet unacquainted with the true State of Things, knows not how to judge of that which is propofed as its Refemblance. Whatever is remote from common Appearances is always welcome to vulgar, as to childifh Credulity; and of a Country unenlightened by Learning, the whole People is the Vulgar. The Study of thofe who then afpired to plebeian Learning was laid out upon Adventures, Giants, Dragons, and Enchantments. *The Death of Arthur* was the favourite Volume.

The Mind, which has feafted on the luxurious Wonders of Fiction, has no Tafte of the Infipidity of Truth. A Play which imitated only the common Occurrences of the World, would, upon the Admirers of *Palmerin* and *Guy of Warwick*, have made little Impreffion; he that wrote for fuch an Audience was under the Neceffity of looking round for ftrange Events and fabulous Tranfactions, and that Incredibility, by which maturer Knowledge is offended, was the chief Recommendation of Writings, to unfkilful Curiofity.

Our Authour's Plots are generally borrowed from Novels, and it is reafonable to fuppofe, that he chofe the moft popular, fuch as were read by many, and related by more; for his Audience could not have followed him through the Intricacies of the Drama, had they not held the Thread of the Story in their Hands.

The Stories which we now find only in remoter Authours, were in his Time acceffible and familiar.

The Fable of *As you like it*, which is fuppofed to be copied from *Chaucer's Gamelyn*, was a little Pamphlet of thofe Times; and old Mr. *Cibber* remembered

bered the Tale of *Hamlet* in plain *Englifh* Profe, which the Criticks have now to feek in *Saxo Grammaticus*.

His *Englifh* Hiftories he took from *Englifh* Chronnicles and *Englifh* Ballads; and as the ancient Writers were made known to his Countrymen by Verfions, they fupplied him with new Subjects; he dilated fome of *Plutarch*'s Lives into Plays, when they had been tranflated by *North*.

His Plots, whether Hiftorical or Fabulous, are always crouded with Incidents, by which the Attention of a rude People was more eafily caught than by Sentiment or Argumentation; and fuch is the Power of the Marvellous even over thofe who defpife it, that every Man finds his Mind more ftrongly feized by the Tragedies of *Shakefpeare* than of any other Writer; others pleafe us by particular Specches, but he always make us anxious for the Event, and has perhaps excelled all but *Homer* in fecuring the firft Purpofe of a Writer, by exciting reftlefs and unquenchable Curiofity, and compelling him that reads his Work to read it through.

The Shows and Buftle with which his Plays abound have the fame Original. As Knowledge advances, Pleafure paffes from the Eye to the Ear, but returns, as it declines, from the Ear to the Eye. Thofe to whom our Authour's Labours were exhibited had more Skill in Pomps or Proceffions than in poetical Language, and perhaps wanted fome vifible and difcriminated Events, as Comments on the Dialogue. He knew how he fhould moft pleafe; and whether his Practice is more agreeable to Nature, or whether his Example has prejudiced the Nation, we ftill find that on our Stage fomething muft be done as well as faid, and inactive Declamation is very coldly heard, however mufical or elegant, paffionate or fublime.

Voltaire expreffes his Wonder, that our Authour's Extravagancies are endured by a Nation, which has feen the Tragedy of *Cato*. Let him be anfwered,

that

that *Addison* speaks the Language of Poets, and *Shake-speare* of Men. We find in *Cato* innumerable Beauties which enamour us of its Authour, but we see nothing that acquaints us with human Sentiments or human Actions; we place it with the faireft and the nobleft Progeny which Judgment propagates by Conjunction with Learning, but *Othello* is the vigorous and vivacious Offspring of Obfervation impregnated by Genius. *Cato* affords a fplendid Exhibition of artificial and fictitious Manners, and delivers juft and noble Sentiments, in Diction eafy, elevated, and harmonious; but its Hopes and Fears communicate no Vibration to the Heart; the Compofition refers us only to the Writer; we pronounce the Name of *Cato*, but we think on *Addison*.

The Work of a correct and regular Writer is a Garden accurately formed and diligently planted, varied with Shades, and fcented with Flowers; the Compofition of *Shakefpeare* is a Foreft, in which Oaks extend their Branches, and Pines tower in the Air, interfperfed fometimes with Weeds and Brambles, and fometimes giving Shelter to Myrtles and to Rofes; filling the Eye with awful Pomp, and gratifying the Mind with endlefs Diverfity. Other Poets difplay Cabinets of precious Rarities, minutely finifhed, wrought into Shape, and polifhed unto Brightnefs. *Shakefpeare* opens a Mine which contains Gold and Diamonds in inexhauftible Plenty, though clouded by Incruftations, debafed by Impurities, and mingled with a Mafs of meaner Minerals.

It has been much difputed, whether *Shakefpeare* owed his Excellence to his own native Force, or whether he had the common Helps of fcholaftick Education, the Precepts of critical Science, and the Examples of ancient Authours.

There has always prevailed a Tradition, that *Shakefpeare* wanted Learning, that he had no regular Education, nor much Skill in the dead Languages. *John-son,*

fon, his Friend, affirms, that ' he had fmall *Latin*, ' and no *Greek* ;' who, befides that he had no imaginable Temptation to Falfehoood, wrote at a Time
when the Character and Acquifitions of *Shakefpeare*
were known to Multitudes. His Evidence ought
therefore to decide the Controverfy, unlefs fome
Teftimony of equal Force could be oppofed.

Some have imagined, that they have difcovered
deep Learning in many Imitations of old Writers;
but the Examples which I have known urged, were
drawn from Books tranflated in his Time ; or were
fuch eafy Coincidencies of Thought, as will happen
to all who confider the fame Subjects ; or fuch Remarks on Life or Axioms of Morality as float in
Converfation, and are tranfmitted through the World
in proverbial Sentences.

I have found it remarked, that, in this important
Sentence, *Go before, I'll follow*, we read a Tranflation
of, *I præ fequar* I have been told, that when *Ca-
liban*, after a pleafing Dream, fays, *I cry'd to fleep
again*, the Author imitates *Anacreon*, who had, like
every other Man, the fame Wifh on the fame Occafion.

There are a few Paffages which may pafs for Imitations, but fo few, that the Exception only con-
firms the Rule ; he obtained them from accidental
Quotations, or by oral Communication, and as he
ufed what he had, would have ufed more if he had
obtained it.

The *Comedy of Errors* is confeffedly taken from
the *Menæchmi* of *Plautus* ; from the only Play of
Plautus which was then in *Englifh*. What can be
more probable, than that he who copied that, would
have copied more; but that thofe which were not
tranflated were inacceffible ?

Whether he knew the modern Languages is uncertain. That his Plays have fome *French* Scenes
proves but little ; he might eafily procure them to be
written ;

written; and probably, even though he had known the Language in the common Degree, he could not have written it without Affiftance. In the Story of *Romeo* and *Juliet* he is obferved to have followed the *Englifh* Tranflation, where it deviates from the *Italian*; but this on the other Part proves nothing againft his Knowledge of the Original. He was to copy, not what he knew himfelf, but what was known to his Audience.

It is moft likely that he had learned *Latin* fufficiently to make him acquainted with Conftruction, but that he never advanced to any eafy Perufal of the *Roman* Authours. Concerning his Skill in modern Languages, I can find no fufficient Ground of Determination; but as no Imitation of *French* or *Italian* Authours have been difcovered, though the *Italian* Poetry was then in high Efteem, I am inclined to believe, that he read little more than *Englifh*, and chofe for his Fables only fuch Tales as he found tranflated.

That much Knowledge is fcattered over his Works is very juftly obferved by *Pope*, but it is often fuch Knowledge as Books did not fupply. He that will underftand *Shakefpeare*, muft not be content to ftudy him in the Clofet, he muft look for his Meaning fometimes among the Sports of the Field, and fometimes among the Manufactures of the Shop.

There is however Proof enough that he was a very diligent Reader, nor was our Language then fo indigent of Books, but that he might very liberally indulge his Curiofity without Excurfion into foreign Literature. Many of the *Roman* Authors were tranflated, and fome of the *Greek*; the Reformation had filled the Kingdom with theological Learning; moft of the Topicks of human Difquifition had found *Englifh* Writers; and Poetry had been cultivated, not only with Diligence, but Succefs. This was a Stock of

Knowledge

Knowledge sufficient for a Mind so capable of appropriating and improving it.

But the greater Part of his Excellence was the Product of his own Genius. He found the *English* Stage in a State of the utmost Rudeness; no Essays either in Tragedy or Comedy had appeared, from which it could be discovered to what Degree of Delight either one or other might be carried. Neither Character nor Dialogue were yet understood. *Shakespeare* may be truly said to have introduced them both amongst us, and in some of his happier Scenes to have carried them both to the utmost Height.

By what Gradations of Improvement he proceeded, is not easily known: for the Chronology of his Works is yet unsettled. *Rowe* is of Opinion, that *perhaps we are not to look for his Beginning, like those of other Writers, in his least perfect Works; Art had so little, and Nature so large a Share in what he did, that for ought I know*, says he, *the Performances of his Youth, as they were the most vigorous, were the best.* But the Power of Nature, is only the Power of using to any certain Purpose the Materials which Diligence procures, or Opportunity supplies. Nature gives no Man Knowledge, and when Images are collected by Study and Experience, can only assist in combining or. applying them. *Shakespeare*, however favoured by Nature, could impart only what he had learned; and as he must increase his Ideas, like other Mortals, by gradual Acquisition, he, like them, grew wiser as he grew older, could display Life better, as he knew it more, and instruct with more Efficacy, as he was himself more amply instructed.

There is a Vigilance of Observation and Accuracy of Distinction which Books and Precepts cannot confer; from this almost all original and native Excellence proceeds. *Shakespeare* must have looked upon Mankind with Perspicacity, in the highest Degree curious and attentive. Other Writers borrow

their

their Characters from preceding Writers, and diver, fify them only by the accidental Appendages of pre-fent Manners ; the Drefs is a little varied, but the Body is the fame. Our Authour had both Matter and Form to provide ; for except the Characters of *Chaucer*, to whom I think he is not much indebted, there were no Writers in *Englifh*, and perhaps not many in other modern Languages, which fhewed Life in its native Colours.

The Conteft about the original Benevolence or Malignity of Man had not yet commenced. Spe-culation had not yet attempted to analyfe the Mind, to trace the Paffions to their Sources, to unfold the feminal Principles of Vice and Virtue, or found the Depths of the Heart for the Motives of Action. All thofe Enquiries, which from that Time that human Nature became the fafhionable Study, have been made fometimes with nice Difcernment, but often with idle Subtilty, were yet unattempted. The Tales, with which the Infancy of Learning was fatisfied, exhibited only the fuperficial Appearances of Action, related the Events but omitted the Caufes, and were formed for fuch as delighted in Wonders rather than in Truth. Mankind was not then to be ftudied in the Clofet ; he that would know the World, was under the Neceffity of glean-ing his own Remarks, by mingling as he could in its Bufinefs and Amufements.

Boyle congratulated himfelf upon his high Birth, becaufe it favoured his Curiofity, by facilitating his Accefs. *Shakefpeare* had no fuch Advantage ; he came to *London* a needy Adventurer, and lived for a Time by very mean Employments. Many Works of Genius and Learning have been performed in States of Life, that appear very little favourable to Thought or to Enquiry ; fo many, that he who confiders them is inclined to think that he fees Enterprife and Perfeverance predominating over all external Agency,

and

and bidding Help and Hindrance vanifh before them. The Genius of *Shakefpeare* was not to be depreffed by the Weight of Poverty, nor limited by the narrow Converfation to which Men in Want are inevitably condemned; the Incumbrances of his Fortune were fhaken from his Mind, *as Dewdrops from a Lion's Mane.*

Though he had fo many Difficulties to encounter, and fo little Affiftance to furmount them, he has been able to obtain an exact Knowledge of many Modes of Life, and many Cafts of native Difpofitions; to vary them with great Multiplicity; to mark them by nice Diftinctions; and to fhew them in full View by proper Combinations. In this Part of his Performances he had none to imitate, but has himfelf been imitated by all fucceeding Writers; and it may be doubted whether from all his Succeffors more Maxims of theoretical Knowledge, or more Rules of practical Prudence, can be collected, than he alone has given to his Country.

Nor was his Attention confined to the Actions of Men; he was an exact Surveyor of the inanimate World; his Defcriptious have always fome Peculiarities, gathered by contemplating Things as they really exift. It may be obferved, that the oldeft Poets of many Nations preferve their Reputation, and that the following Generations of Wit, after a fhort Celebrity, fink into Oblivion. The firft, whoever they be, muft take their Sentiments and Defcriptions immediately from Knowledge; the Refemblance is therefore juft, their Defcriptions are verified by every Eye, and their Sentiments acknowledged by every Breaft. Thofe whom their Fame invites to the fame Studies, copy partly them, and partly Nature, till the Books of one Age gain fuch Authority, as to ftand in the Place of Nature to another, and Imitation, always deviating a little, becomes at laft capricious and cafual. *Shakefpeare,* whether Life or

Nature

Nature be his Subject, shews plainly that he has seen with his own Eyes; he gives the Image which he receives. not weakened or distorted by the Intervention of any other Mind; the Ignorant feel his Representations to be just, and the Learned see that they are complete.

Perhaps it would not be easy to find any Authour, except *Homer*, who invented so much as *Shakespeare*, who so much advanced the Studies which he cultivated, or effused so much Novelty upon his Age or Country. The Form, the Characters, the Language, and the Shows of the *English* Drama are his. ' He seems, says *Dennis*, to have been 'the ' very Original of our *English* tragical Harmony, ' that is, the Harmony of Blank Verse, diversified ' often by dissyllable and trissyllable Terminations. ' For the Diversity distinguishes it from heroic ' Harmony, and, by bringing it nearer to common ' Use, makes it more proper to gain Attention, ' and more fit for Action and Dialogue. Such ' Verse we make when we are writing Profe; we ' make such Verse in common Conversation.'

I know not whether this Praise is rigorously just. The dissyllable Termination, which the Critick rightly appropriates to the Drama, is to be found, though, I think. not in *Gorboduc*, which is confessedly before our Authour; yet in *Hieronnymo*, of which the Date is not certain, but which there is Reason to believe at least as old as his earliest Plays. This however is certain, that he is the first who taught either Tragedy or Comedy to please, there being no theatrical Piece of any older Writer, of which the Name is known, except to Antiquaries and Collectors of Books, which are sought because they are scarce, and would not have been scarce, had they been much esteemed.

To him we must ascribe the Praise, unless *Spenser* may divide it with him, of having first discovered to
how

how much Smoothnefs and Harmony the *Englifh* Language could be foftened. He has Speeches, perhaps fometimes Scenes, which have all the Delicacy of *Rowe*, without his Effeminancy. He endeavours indeed commonly to ftrike by the Force and Vigour of his Dialogue, but he never executes his Purpofe better than when he tries to footh by Softnefs.

Yet it muft be at laft confeffed, that as we owe every Thing to him, he owes fomething to us; that if much of his Praife is paid by Perception and Judgment, much is likewife given by Cuftom and Veneration. We fix our Eyes upon his Graces, and turn them from his Deformities, and endure in him what we fhould in another loath or defpife. If we endured without praifing, Refpect for the Father of our Drama might excufe us; but I have feen, in the Book of fome modern Critick, a Collection of Anomalies, which fhew that he has corrupted Language by every Mode of Depravation, but which his Admirer has accumulated as a Monument of Honour.

He has Scenes of undoubted and perpetual Excellence, but perhaps not one Play, which, if it were now exhibited as the Work of a contemporary Writer, would be heard to the Conclufion. I am indeed far from thinking that his Works were wrought to his own Ideas of Perfection : when they were fuch as would fatisfy the Audience, they fatisfied the Writer. It is feldom that Authours, though more ftudious of Fame than *Shakefpeare*, rife much above the Standard of their own Age ; to add a little to what is beft will always be fufficient for prefent Praife, and thofe who find themfelves exalted into Fame, are willing to credit their Encomiafts, and to fpare the Labour of contending with themfelves:

It does not appear that *Shakefpeare* thought his Works worthy of Pofterity, that he levied any ideal Tribute upon future Times, or had any further Profpect spect than of present Popularity and present Profit. When his Plays had been acted his Hope was at an End ; he solicited no Addition of Honour from the Reader. He therefore made no Scruple to repeat the same Jests in many Dialogues, or to entangle different Plots by the same Knot of Perplexity, which may be at least forgiven him, by those who recollect, that of *Congreve's* four Comedies, two are concluded by a Marriage in a Mask, by a Deception, which perhaps never happened ; and which, whether likely or not, he did not invent.

So careless was this great Poet of future Fame, that, though he retired to Ease and Plenty, while he was yet little declined into the Vale of Years, before he could be disgusted with Fatigue, or disabled by Infirmity, he made no Collection of his Works, nor desired to rescue those that had been already published, from the Depravations that obscured them; or secure to the rest a better Destiny, by giving them to the World in their genuine State.

Of the Plays which bear the Name of *Shakespeare* in the late Editions, the greater Part were not published till about seven Years after his Death, and the few which appeared in his Life are apparently thrust into the World without the Care of the Authour, and therefore probably without his Knowledge.

Of all the Publishers, clandestine or professed, their Negligence and Unskilfulness has by the late Revisers been sufficiently shown. The Faults of all are indeed numerous and gross, and have not only corrupted many Passages, perhaps beyond Recovery, but have brought others into Suspicion, which are only obscured by obsolete Phraseology, or by the Writer's Unskilfulness and Affectation. To alter is more easy than to explain, and Temerity is a more common Quality than Diligence. Those who saw that they must employ Conjecture to a certain Degree, were willing to indulge it a little further. Had

the

the Authour publifhed his own Works, we fhould
have fat quietly down to difentangle his Intricacies,
and clear his Obfcurities ; but now we tear what we
cannot loofe, and ejeꞓt what we happen not to underftand.

The Faults are more than could have happened
without the Concurrence of many Caufes. The
Stile of *Shakefpeare* was in itfelf ungrammatical,
perplexed, and obfcure ; his Works were tranfcribed
for the Players by thofe who may be fuppofed to
have feldom underftood them ; they were tranfmitted
by Copiers equally unfkilful, who ftill multiplied Errours; they were perhaps fometimes mutilated by the
Aꞓtors, for the Sake of fhortening the Speeches ; and
were at laft printed without Correꞓtion of the Prefs.

In this State they remained, not as Dr. *Warbur-*
ton fuppofes, becaufe they were unregarded, but becaufe the Editor's Art was not yet applied to modern
Languages, and our Anceftors were accuftomed to
fo much Negligence of *Englifh* Printers, that they
could very patiently endure it. At laft an Edition
was undertaken by *Rowe* ; not becaufe a Poet was
to be publifhed by a Poet, for *Rowe* feems to have
thought very little on Correꞓtion or Explanation,
but that our Authour's Works might appear like
thofe of his Fraternity, with the Appendages of a
Life and recommendatory Preface. *Rowe* has been
clamoroufly blamed for not performing what he did
not undertake, and it is Time that Juftice be done
him, by confeffing, that though he feems to have
had no Thought of Corruption beyond the Printer's
Errours, yet he has made many Emendations, if
they were not made before, which his Succeffors
have received without Acknowledgment, and which
if they had produced them, would have filled Pages
and Pages with Cenfures of the Stupidity by which
the Faults we committed, with Difplays of the
Abfurdities, which they involved, with oftentatious

Expofitions of the new Reading, and Self-congra-tulations on the Happinefs of difcovering it.

Of *Rowe*, as of all the Editors, I have preferved the Preface, and have likewife retained the Anthour's Life, though not written with much Elegance or Spirit; it relates however what is now to be known, and therefore deferves to pafs through all fucceeding Publications.

The nation had been for many Years content enough with Mr. *Rowe*'s Performance, when Mr. *Pope* made them acquainted with the true State of *Shakefpeare*'s Text, fhewed that it was extremely corrupt, and gave Reafon to hope that there were Means of reforming it. He collated the old Copies, which none had thought to examine before, and reftored many Lines to their Integrity; but, by a very compendious Criticifm, he rejected whatever he difliked, and thought more of Amputation than of Cure.

I know not why he is commended by Dr. *War-burton* for diftinguifhing the genuine from the fpuri-ous Plays. In this Choice he exerted no Judgment of his own; the Plays which he received, were given by *Hemings* and *Condel*, the firft Editors; and thofe which he rejected, though, according to the Licen-tioufnefs of the Prefs in thofe Times, they were printed during *Shakefpeare*'s Life, with his Name, had been omitted by his Friends, and were never added to his Works before the Edition of 1664, from which they were copied by the later Printers.

This was a Work which *Pope* feems to have thought unworthy of his Abilities, bring not able to fupprefs his Contempt of *the dull Duty of an Edi-tor*. He underftood but half his Undertaking. The Duty of a Collator is indeed dull, yet, like other tedious Tafks, is very neceffary; but an emendatory Critick would ill difcharge his Duty, without Qua-lities very different from Dulnefs. In perufing a
corrupted

corrupted-Piece, he muſt have before him all Poſſibities of Meaning, with all Poſſibilities of Expreſſion. Such muſt be his Comprehenſion of Thought, and ſuch his Copiouſneſs of Language. Out of many Readings poſſible, he muſt be able to ſelect that which beſt ſuits with the State, Opinions, and Modes of Language prevailing in every Age, and with his Authour's particular Caſt of Thought, and Turn of Expreſſion. Such muſt be his Knowledge, and ſuch his Taſte. Conjectural Criticiſm demands more than Humanity poſſeſſes, and he that exerciſes it with moſt Praiſe has frequent Need of Indulgence. Let us now be told no more of the dull Duty of an Editor.

Confidence is the common Conſequence of Succeſs. They whoſe Excellence of any Kind has been loudly celebrated, are ready to conclude, that their Powers are univerſal. *Pope's* Edition fell below his own Expectations, and he was ſo much offended, when he was found to have left any Thing for others to do, that he paſſed the latter Part of his Life in a State of Hoſtility with verbal Criticiſm.

I have retained all his Notes, that no Fragment of ſo great a Writer may be loſt ; his Preface, valuable alike for Elegance of Compoſition and Juſtneſs of Remark, and containing a general Criticiſm on his Authour, ſo extenſive that little can be added, and ſo exact, that little can be diſputed, every Editor has an Intereſt to ſuppreſs, but that every Reader would demand its Inſertion.

Pope was ſucceeded by *Theobald,* a Man of narrow Comprehenſion and ſmall Acquiſitions, with no native and intrinſick Splendour of Genius, with little of the artificial Light of Learning, but zealous for minute Accuracy, and not negligent in purſuing it. He collated the ancient Copies, and rectified many Errours. A Man ſo anxiouſly ſcrupulous might have

been

been expected to do more, but what little he did was commonly right.

In his Reports of Copies and Editions he is not to be trufted, without Examination. He fpeaks fometimes indefinitely of Copies, when he has only one. In his Enumeration of Editions, he mentions the two firft Folios as of high, and the third Folio as of middle Authority ; but the Truth is, that the firft is equivalent to all others, and that the reft only deviate from it by the Printer's Negligence. Whoever has any of the Folios has all, excepting thofe Diverfities which mere Reiteration of Editions will produce. I collated them all at the Beginning, but afterwards ufed only the firft.

Of his Notes I have generally retained thofe which he retained himfelf in his fecond Edition, except when they were confuted by fubfequent Annotators, or were too minute to merit Prefervation. I have fometimes adopted his Reftoration of a Comma, without inferting the Panegyrick in which he celebrated himfelf for his Atchievement. The exuberant Excrefcence of Diction I have often lopped, his triumphant Exultations, over *Pope* and *Rowe* I have fometimes fuppreffed, and his contemptible Oftentation I have frequently concealed ; but I have in fome Places fhewn him, as he would have fhewn himfelf, for the Reader's Diverfion, that the inflated Emptinefs of fome Notes may juftify or excufe the Contraction of the reft.

Theobald, thus weak and ignorant, thus mean and faithlefs, thus petulent and oftentatious, by the good Luck of having *Pope* for his Enemy, has efcaped, and efcaped alone, with Reputation from this Undertaking. So willingly does the World fupport thofe who folicite Favour, againft thofe who command Reverence ; and fo eafily is he praifed, whom no Man can envy.

Our

Our Authour fell then into the Hands of Sir *Thomas Hanmer*, the *Oxford* Editor, a Man, in my Opinion, eminently qualified by Nature for such Studies. He had, what is the first Requisite to emendatory Criticism, that Intuition by which the Poet's Intention is immediately discovered, and that Dexterity of Intellect which dispatches its Work by the easiest Means. He had undoubtedly read much ; his Acquaintance with Customs, Opinions, and Traditions, seem to have been large; and he is often learned without Shew. He seldom passes what he does not understand, without an Attempt to find or to make a Meaning, and sometimes hastily makes what a little more Attention would have found. He is solicitous to reduce to Grammar, what he could not be sure that his Authour intended to be grammatical. *Shakespeare* regarded more the Series of Ideas, than of Words; and his Language, not being designed for the Reader's Desk, was all that he desired it to be, if it conveyed his Meaning to the Audience.

Hanmer's Care of the Metre has been too violently censured. He found the Measures reformed in so many Passages, by the silent Labours of some Editors, with the silent Acquiescence of the rest, that he thought himself allowed to extend a little further the Licence, which had already been carried so far without Reprehension ; and of his Corrections in general, it must be confessed, that they are often just, and made commonly with the least possible Violation of the Text.

But, by inserting his Emendations, whether invented or borrowed, into the Page, without any Notice of varying Copies, he has appropriated the Labour of his Predecessors, and made his own Edition of little Authority. His Confidence indeed, both in himself and others, was too great ; he supposes all to be right that was done by *Pope* and *Theobald* ;

he

he feems not to fufpect a Critick of Fallibility, and it was but reafonable that he fhould claim what he fo liberally granted.

As he never writes without careful Enquiry and diligent Confideration, I have received all his Notes, and believe that every Reader will wifh for more.

Of the laft Editor it is more difficult to fpeak. Refpect is due to high Place, Tendernefs to living Reputation, and Veneration to Genius and Learning: but he cannot be juftly offended at that Liberty of which he has himfelf fo frequently given an Example, nor very folicitous what is thought of Notes, which he ought never to have confidered as Part of his ferious Employments, and which, I fuppofe, fince the Ardour of Compofition is remitted, he no longer numbers among his happy Effufions.

The original and predominant Errour of his Commentary, is Acquiefcence in his firft Thoughts; that Precipitation which is produced by Confcioufnefs of quick Difcernment; and that Confidence which prefumes to do, by furveying the Surface, what Labour only can perform, by penetrating the Bottom. His Notes exhibit fometimes perverfe Interpretations, and fometimes improbable Conjectures; he at one Time gives the Authour more Profundity of Meaning than the Sentence admits, and at another difcovers Abfurdities, where the Senfe is plain to every other Reader. But his Emendations are likewife often happy and juft; and his Interpretation of obfcure Paffages learned and fagacious.

Of his Notes, I have commonly rejected thofe, againft which the general Voice of the Publick has exclaimed, or which their own Incongruity immediately condemns, and which, I fuppofe, the Authour himfelf would defire to be forgotten. Of the reft, to Part I have given the higheft Approbation, by

by inferting the offered Reading in the Text; Part
I have left to the Judgment of the Reader, as doubtful, though fpecious; and Part I have cenfured
without Referve, but I am fure without Bitternefs
of Malice, and, I hope, without Wantonnefs of
Infult.

It is no Pleafure to me, in revifing my Volumes,
to obferve how much Paper is wafted in Confutation.
Whoever confiders the Revolution of Learning, and
the various Queftions of greater or lefs Importance,
upon which Wit and Reafon have exercifed their
Powers, muft lament the Unfuccefsfulnefs of Enquiry, and the flow Advances of Truth, when he
reflects, that great Part of the Labour of every Writer is only the Deftruction of thofe that went before
him. The firft Care of the Builder of a new Syftem,
is to demolifh the Fabricks which are ftanding.
The chief Defire of him that comments an Authour,
is to fhew how much other Commentators have
corrupted and obfcured him. The Opinions prevalent in one Age, as Truths above the Reach of
Controverfy, are confuted and rejected in another,
and rife again to Reception in remoter Times. Thus
the human Mind is kept in Motion without Progrefs.
Thus fometimes Truth and Errour, and fometimes
Contrarieties of Errour, take each others Place by
reciprocal Invafion. The Tide of feeming Knowledge which is poured over one Generation, retires
and leaves another naked and barren; the fudden
Meteors of Intelligence which for a while appear to
fhoot their Beams into the Regions of Obfcurity, on
a Sudden withdraw their Luftre, and leave Mortals
again to grope their Way.

Thefe Elevations and Depreffions of Renown,
and the Contradictions to which all Improvers of
Knowledge muft for ever be expofed, fince they
are not efcaped by the higheft and brighteft of Mankind, may furely be endured with Patience by Cri-

ticks

ticks and Annotators, who can rank themselves but as the Satellites of their Authours. How canst thou beg for Life, says *Achilles* to his Captive, when thou knowest that thou art now to suffer only for what must another Day be suffered by *Achilles?*

Dr. *Warburton* had a Name sufficient to confer Celebrity on those who could exalt themselves into Antagonists, and his Notes have raised a Clamour too loud to be distinct. His chief Assailants are the Authours of *The Canons of Criticism,* and of *The Review of* Shakespeare's *Text*; of whom one ridicules his Errours with airy Petulance, suitable enough to the Levity of the Controversy; the other attacks them with gloomy Malignity, as if he were dragging to Justice an Assassin or Incendiary. The one stings like a Fly, sucks a little Blood, takes a gay Flutter, and returns for more; the other bites like a Viper, and would be glad to leave Inflammations and Gangrene behind him. When I think on one, with his Confederates, I remember the Danger of *Coriolanus,* who was afraid that ' Girls with Spits, ' and Boys with Stones, should slay him in puny ' Battle;' when the other crosses my Imagination, I remember the Prodigy in *Macbeth,*

' An Eagle tow'ring in his Pride of Place,
' Was by a mousing Owl hawk'd at and kill'd.'

Let me however do them Justice. One is a Wit, and one a Scholar. They have both shewn Acuteness sufficient in the Discovery of Faults, and have both advanced some probable Interpretations of obscure Passages; but when they aspire to Conjecture and Emendation, it appears how falsely we all estimate our own Abilities, and the little which they have been able to perform might have taught them more Candour to the Endeavours of others.

Before Dr. *Warburton*'s Edition, *Critical Observations on* Shakespeare had been published by Mr. *Upton*

ton, a Man fkilled in Languages, and acquainted with Books, but who feems to have had no great Vigour of Genius or Nicety of Tafte. Many of his Explanations are curious and ufeful, but he likewife, though he profeffed to oppofe the licentious Confidence of Editors, and adhere to the old Copies, is unable to reftrain the Rage of Emendation, though his Ardour is ill feconded by his Skill. Every cold Emperick, when his Heart is expanded by a fuccefsful Experiment, fwells into a Thecrift, and the laborious Collator at fome unlucky Moment frolicks in Conjecture.

Critical, Hiflorical, and Explanatoay Notes have been likewife publifhed upon *Shakefpeare* by Dr. *Grey,* whofe diligent Perufal of the old *Englifh* Writers has enabled him to make fome ufeful Obfervations. What he undertook was well enough performed, but as he neither attempts judicial nor emendatory Criticifm, he employs rather his Memory than his Sagacity. It were to be wifhed that all would endeavour to imitate his Modefty who have not been able to furpafs his Knowledge.

I can fay with great Sincerity of all my Predeceffors, what I hope will hereafter be faid of me, that not one has left *Shakefpeare* without Improvement, nor is there one to whom I have not been indebted for Affiftance and Information. Whatever I have taken from them it was my Intention to refer to its original Authour, and it is certain, that what I have not given to another, I believed when I wrote it to be my own. In fome perhaps I have been anticipated; but if I am ever found to encroach upon the Remarks of any other Commentator, I am willing that the Honour, be it more or lefs, fhould be transferred to the firft Claimant, for his Right, and his alone, ftands above Difpute; the Second can prove his Pretenfions only to himfelf, nor can him-

felf

ſelf always diſtinguiſh Invention, with ſufficient Certainty, from Recollection.

They have all been treated by me with Candour,
which they have not been careful of obſerving to one
another. It is not eaſy to diſcover from what Cauſe
the Acrimony of a Scholiaſt can naturally proceed.
The Subjects to be diſcuſſed by him are of very ſmall
Importance; they involve neither Property nor Liberty; nor favour the Intereſt of Sect or Party. The
various Readings of Copies, and different Interpretations of a Paſſage, ſeem to be Queſtions that
might exerciſe the Wit, without engaging the Paſſions. But, whether it be, that, ' ſmall Things
' make mean Men proud,' and Vanity catches ſmall
Occaſions; or that all Contrariety of Opinion, even
in thoſe that can defend it no longer, makes proud
Men angry; there is often found in Commentaries
a ſpontaneous Train of Invective and Contempt,
more eager and venomous than is vented by the moſt
furious Controvertiſt in Politicks againſt whom he is
hired to defame.

Perhaps the Lightneſs of the Matter may conduce
to the Vehemence of the Agency; when the Truth
to be inveſtigated is ſo near to Inexiſtence, as to eſcape
Attention, its Bulk is to be enlarged by Rage and
Exclamation: That to which all would be indifferent
in its original State, may attract Notice when the
Fate of a Name is appended to it. A Commentator
has indeed great Temptations to ſupply by Turbulence what he wants of Dignity, to beat his little
Gold to a ſpacious Surface, to work that to Foam
which no Art or Diligence can exalt to Spirit.

The Notes which I have borrowed or written are
either illuſtrative, by which Difficulties are explained;
or judicial, by which Faults and Beauties are remarked; or emendatory, by which Depravations are corrected.

The

The Explanations tranfcribed from others, if I do not fubjoin any other Interpretation, I fuppofe commonly to be right, at leaft I intend by Acquiefcence to confefs that I have nothing better to propofe.

After the Labours of all the Editors, I found many Paffages which appeared to me likely to obftruct the greater Number of Readers, and thought it my Duty to facilitate their Paffage. It is impoffible for an Expofitor not to write too little for fome, and too much for others. He can only judge what is neceffary by his own Experience ; and how long foever he may deliberate, will at laft explain many Lines which the Learned will think impoffible to be miftaken, and omit many for which the Ignorant will want his Help. Thefe are Cenfures merely relative, and muft be quietly endured. I have endeavoured to be neither fuperfluoufly copious, nor fcrupuloufly referved, and hope that I have made my Authour's Meaning acceffible to many who before were frighted from perufing him, and contributed fomething to the Publick, by diffufing innocent and rational Pleafure.

The complete Explanation of an Authour not fyftematick and confequential, but defultory and vagrant, abounding in cafual Allufions and light Hints, is not to be expected from any fingle Scholiaft. All perfonal Reflections, when Names are fuppreffed, muft be in a few Years irrecoverably obliterated; and Cuftoms, too minute to attract the Notice of Law, fuch as Modes of Drefs, Formalities of Converfation, Rules of Vifits, Difpofition of Furniture, and Practices of Ceremony, which naturally find Places in familiar Dialogue, are fo fugitive and unfubftantial, that they are not eafily retained or recovered. What can be known, will be collected by Chance, from the Receffes of obfcure and obfolete Papers, perufed commonly with fome other View.

Of

Of this Knowledge every Man has some, and none has much ; but when an Authour has engaged the publick Attention, those who can add any Thing to his Illuftration, communicate their Difcoveries, and Time produces what had eluded Diligence.

To Time I have been obliged to refign many Paffages, which, though I did not underftand them, will perhaps hereafter be explained; having, I hope, illuftrated fome, which others have neglected or miftaken, fometimes by fhort Remarks, or marginal Directions, fuch as every Editor has added at his Will, and often by Comments more laborious than the Matter will feem to deferve ; but that which is moft difficult is not always moft important, and to an Editor nothing is a Trifle by which his Authour is obfcured.

The poetical Beauties or Defects I have not been very diligent to obferve. Some Plays have more, and fome fewer judicial Obfervations, not in Proportion to their Difference of Merit, but becaufe I gave this Part of my Defign to Chance and to Caprice. The Reader, I believe, is feldom pleafed to find his Opinion anticipated ; it is natural to delight more in what we find or make, than in what we receive. Judgment, like other Faculties, is improved by Practice, and its Advancement is hindered by Submiffion to dictatorial Decifions, as the Memory grows torpid by the Ufe of a Table-book. Some Initiation is however neceffary ; of all Skill Part is infufed by Precept, and Part is obtained by Habit ; I have therefore fhewn fo much as may enable the Candidate of Criticifm to difcover the reft.

To the End of moft Plays I have added fhort Strictures, containing a general Cenfure of Faults, or Praife of Excellence ; in which I know not how much I have concurred with the current Opinion ; but I have not, by any Affectation of Singularity, deviated from it. Nothing is minutely and particu

larly

larly examined, and therefore it is to be fuppofed, that in the Plays which are condemned there is much to be praifed, and in thofe which are praifed much to be condemned.

The Part of Criticifm in which the whole Suc-ceffion of Editors has laboured with the greateft Di-ligence, which has occafioned the moft arrogant Oftentation, and excited the keeneft Acrimony, is the Emendation of corrupted Paffages, to which the publick Attention having been firft drawn by the Violence of the Contention between *Pope* and *Theo-bald*, has been continued by the Perfecution, which, with a Kind of Confpiracy, has been fince raifed againft all the Publifhers of *Shakefpeare*.

That many Paffages have paffed in a State of De-pravation through all the Editions, is indubitably cer-tain ; of thefe the Reftoration is only to be attempted by Collation of Copies, or Sagacity of Conjecture. The Collator's Province is fafe and eafy, the Con-jecturer's perilous and difficult. Yet, as the greater Part of the Plays are extant only in one Copy, the Peril muft not be avoided, nor the Difficulty re-fufed.

Of the Readings which this Emulation of Amend-ment has hitherto produced, fome from the Labours of every Publifher I have advanced into the Text ; thofe are to be confidered as in my Opinion fuffi-ciently fupported : Some I have rejected without Mention, as evidently erroneous ; fome I have left in the Notes without Cenfure or Approbation, as refting in Equipoife between Objection and De-fence; and fome, which feemed fpecious, but not right, I have inferted with a fubfequent Animad-verfion.

Having claffed the Obfervations of others, I was at laft to try what I could fubftitute for their Mif-takes, and how I could fupply their Omiffions. I collated fuch Copies as I could procure, and wifhed
for

for more ; but have not found the Collectors of thefe
Rarities very communicative. Of the Editions which
Chance or Kindnefs put into my Hands, I have given
an Enumeration, that I may not be blamed for neg-
lecting what I had not the Power to do.

By examining the old Copies, I foon found that
the late Publifhers, with all their Boafts of Diligence,
fuffered many Paffages to ftand unauthorifed, and
contented themfelves with *Rowe*'s Regulation of the
Text, even where they knew it to be arbitrary, and
with a little Confideration might have found it to be
wrong. Some of thefe Alterations are only the Ejec-
tion of a Word for one that appeared to him more
elegant, or more intelligible. Thefe Corruptions I
have often filently rectified ; for the Hiftory of our
Language, and the true Force of our Words, can
only be preferved by keeping the Text of Authours
free from Adulteration. Others, and thofe very frequent, fmoothed the Cadence, or regulated the Meafure ; on thefe I have not exercifed the fame Rigour ;
if only a Word was tranfpofed, or a Particle inferted
or omitted, I have fometimes fuffered the Line to
ftand ; for the Inconftancy of the Copies is fuch, as
that fome Liberties may be eafily permitted. But
this Practice I have not fuffered to proceed far, having reftored the primitive Diction wherever it could
for any Reafon be preferred.

The Emendations, which Comparifon of Copies
fupplied, I have inferted in the Text ; fometimes
where the Improvement was flight, without Notice ;
and fometimes with an Account of the Reafons of
the Change.

Conjecture, though it is fometimes unavoidable,
I have not wantonly not licentioufly indulged. It
has been my fettled Principle, that the Reading of
the ancient Books is probably true ; and therefore is
not to be difturbed for the Sake of Elegance, Perfpicuity, or mere Improvement of the Senfe. For,
though

though much Credit is not due to the Fidelity, nor any to the Judgment of the firſt Publiſhers ; yet they who had the Copy before their Eyes were more likely to read it right, than we who only read it by Imagination. But it is evident that they have often made ſtrange Miſtakes by Ignorance or Negligence ; and that therefore ſomething may be properly attempted by Criticiſm, keeping the middle Way between Preſumption and Timidity.

Such Criticiſm I have attempted to practiſe ; and, where any Paſſage appeared inextricably perplexed, have endeavoured to diſcover how it may be recalled to Senſe with leaſt Violence. But my firſt Labour is, always to turn the old Text on every Side, and try if there be any Interſtice, though which Light can find its Way ; nor would *Huetius* himſelf condemn me, as refuſing the Trouble of Reſearch, for the Ambition of Alteration. In this modeſt Induſtry I have not been unſucceſsful. I have reſcued many Lines from the Violation of Temerity, and ſecured many Scenes from the Inroads of Correction. I have adopted the *Roman* Sentiment, that it is more honourable to ſave a Citizen, than to kill an Enemy, and have been more careful to protect than to attack.

I have preſerved the common Diſtribution of the Plays into Acts, though I believe it to be in almoſt all the Plays void of Authority. Some of thoſe which are divided in the later Editions have no Diviſion in the firſt Folio, and ſome that are divided in the Folio have no Diviſion in the preceding Copies. The ſettled Mode of the Theatre requires four Intervals in the Play ; but few, if any, of our Authour's Compoſitions can be properly diſtributed in that Manner. An Act is ſo much of the Drama as paſſes without Intervention of Time, or Change of Place. A Pauſe makes a new Act. In every real, and therefore in every imitative Action, the Intervals may be

more

more or fewer, the Reftriction of five Acts being accidental and arbitrary. This *Shakefpeare* knew, and this he practifed: His Plays were written, and at firft printed, in one broken Continuity, and ought now to be exhibited with fhort Paufes, interpofed as often as the Scene is changed, or any confiderable Time is required to pafs. This Method would at once quell a thoufand Abfurdities.

In reftoring the Author's Works to their Integrity, I have confidered the Punctuation as wholly in my Power: For what could be their Care of Colons and Commas, who corrupted Words and Sentences; Whatever could be done by adjufting Points is therefore filently performed, in fome Plays with much Diligence, in others with lefs: It is hard to keep a bufy Eye ftedfaftly fixed upon evanefcent Atoms, or a difcurfive Mind upon evanefcent Truth.

The fame Liberty has been taken with a few Particles, or other Words of flight Effect. I have fometimes inferted or omitted them without Notice. I have done that fometimes, which the other Editors have done always, and which indeed the State of the Text may fufficiently juftify.

The greater Part of Readers, inftead of blaming us for paffing Trifles, will wonder that on mere Trifles fo much Labour is expended, with fuch Importance of Debate, and fuch Solemnity of Diction. To thefe I anfwer with Confidence, that they are judging of an Art which they do not underftand; yet cannot much reproach them with their Ignorance, nor promife that they would become in general, by learning Criticifm, more ufeful, happier, or wifer.

As I practifed Conjecture more, I learned to truft it lefs; and after I had printed a few Plays, refolved to infert none of my own Readings in the Text. Upon this Caution I now congratulate myfelf, for every Day encreafes my Doubt of my Emendations.

Since

Since I have confined my Imagination to the Margin, it muſt not be conſidered as very reprehenſible, if I have ſuffered it to play ſome Freaks in its own Dominion. There is no Danger in Conjecture, if it be propoſed as Conjecture ; and while the Text remains uninjured, thoſe Changes may be ſafely offered, which are not conſidered, even by him that offers them, as neceſſary or ſafe.

If my Readings are of little Value, they have not been oſtentatiouſly diſplayed, or importunately obtruded. I could have written longer Notes, for the Art of writing Notes is not of difficult Attainment. The Work is performed firſt, by railling at the Stupidity, Negligence, Ignorance, and aſinine Taſteleſſneſs of the former Editors, and ſhewing, from all that goes before, and all that follows, the Inelegance and Abſurdity of the old Reading; then by propoſing ſomething, which, to ſuperficial Readers, would ſeem ſpecious, but which, the Editor rejects with Indignation ; then by producing the true Reading, with a long Paraphraſe, and concluding with loud Acclamations on the Diſcovery, and a ſober Wiſh for the Advancement and Proſperity of genuine Criticiſm.

All this may be done, and perhaps done ſometimes without Impropriety. But I have always ſuſpected that the Reading is right, which requires many Words to prove it wrong ; and the Emendation wrong, that cannot, without ſo much Labour, appear to be right. The Juſtneſs of a happy Reſtoration ſtrikes at once, and the moral Precept may be well applied to Criticiſm, *quod dubitas ne feceris.*

To dread the Shore which he ſees ſpread with Wrecks, is natural to the Sailor. I had before my Eye ſo many critical Adventures ended in Miſcarriage, that Caution was forced upon me. I encountered in every Page Wit ſtruggling with its own Sophiſtry, and Learning coufuſed by the Multiplicity of its Views. I was forced to cenſure thoſe whom I admired, and could not but reflect, while I was difpoffeffing their Emendations, how foon the fame Fate might happen to my own, and how many of the Readings which I have corrected may be, by fome other Editor, defended and eftablifhed.

‘ Criticks, I faw, that other's Names efface,
‘ And fix their own, with Labour, in the Place.;
‘ Their own, like others, foon the Place refign'd,
‘ Or difappear'd, and left the firft behind.'

POPE.

That a conjectural Critick fhould often be miftaken cannot be wonderful, either to others or to himfelf, if it be confidered, that in his Art there is no Syftem, no principal and axiomatical Truth, that regulates fubordinate Pofitions. His Chance of Errour is renewed at every Attempt; an oblique View of the Paffage, a flight Mifapprehenfion of a Phrafe, a cafual Inattention to the Parts connected, is fufficient to make him not only fail, but fail ridiculoufly; and when he fucceeds beft, he produces perhaps but one Reading of many probable; and he that fuggefts another will always be able to difpute his Claims.

It is an unhappy State in which Danger is hid under Pleafure. The Allurements of Emendation are fcarcely refiftible. Conjecture has all the Joy and all the Pride of Invention, and he that has once ftarted a happy Change is too much delighted to confider what Objections may rife againft it.

Yet conjectural Criticifm has been of great Ufe in the learned World; nor is it my Intention to depreciate a Study, that has exercifed fo many mighty Minds, from the Revival of Learning to our own Age, from the Bifhop of *Aleria* to *Englifh Bentley*. The Criticks on ancient Authours have, in the Exercife of their Sagacity, many Affiftances which the Editor of *Shakefpeare* is condemned to want. They

are

are employed upon grammatical and settled Languages, whose Construction contributes so much to Pespicuity, that *Homer* has fewer Passages unintelligible than *Chaucer*. The Words have not only a known Regimen, but invariable Quantities, which direct and confine the Choice. There are commonly more Manuscripts than one; and they do not often conspire in the same Mistakes. Yet *Scaliger* could confess to *Salmasius* how little Satisfaction his Emendations gave him. *Illudunt nobis conjecturæ nostræ, quarum nos pudet, posteaquam in meliores codices incidimus.* And *Lipsius* could complain, that Criticks were making Faults, by trying to remove them: *Ut olim vitiis, ita nunc remediis laboratur.* And indeed, where mere Conjecture is to be used, the Emendations of *Scaliger* and *Lipsius*, notwithstanding their wonderful Sagacity and Erudition, are often vague and disputable, like mine or *Theobald's*.

Perhaps I may not be more censured for doing wrong, than for doing little; for raising in the Puplick Expectations, which at last I have not answered. The Expectation of Ignorance is indefinite, and that of Knowledge is often tyrannical. It is hard to satisfy those who know not what to demand, or those who demand by Design what they think impossible to be done. I have indeed disappointed no Opinion more than my own; yet I have endeavoured to perform my Task with no slight Solicitude. Not a single Passage in the whole Work has appeared to me corrupt, which I have not attempted to restore; or obscure, which I have not endeavoured to illustrate. In many I have failed like others; and from many, after all my Efforts, I have retreated, and confessed the Repulse. I have not passed over, with affected Superiority, what is equally difficult to the Reader and to myself, but where I could not instruct him, have owned my Ignorance. I might easily have accumulated a Mass

of

of feeming Learning upon eafy Scenes ; but it ought not to be imputed to Negligence, that, where nothing was neceffary, nothing has been done ; or that, where others have faid enough, I have faid no more.

Notes are often neceffary, but they are neceffary Evils. Let him that is yet unacquainted with the Powers of *Shakefpeare*, and who defires to feel the higheft Pleafure that the Drama can give, read every Play, from the firft Scene to the laft, with utter Negligence of all his Commentators. When his Fancy is once on the Wing, let it not ftoop at Correction or Explanation. When his Attention is ftrongly engaged, let it difdain alike to turn afide to the Name of *Theobald* and *Pope*. Let him read on through Brightnefs and Obfcurity, through Integrity and Corruption ; let him preferve his Comprehenfion of the Dialogue, and his Intereft in the Fable ; and when the Pleafures of Novelty have ceafed, let him attempt Exactnefs, and read the Commentators.

Particular Paffages are cleared by Notes, but the general Effect of the Work is weakened. The Mind is refrigerated by Interruption ; the Thoughts are diverted from the principal Subject, the Reader is weary, he fufpects not why, and at laft throws away the Book, which he has too diligently ftudied.

Parts are not to be examined till the Whole has been furveyed ; there is a Kind of intellectual Remotenefs neceffary for the Comprehenfion of any great Work, in its full Defign and its true Proportions ; a clofe Approach fhews the fmaller Niceties, but the Beauty of the Whole is difcerned no longer.

It is not very grateful to confider how little the Succeffion of Editors has added to this Authour's Power of pleafing. He was read, admired, ftudied, and imitated, while he was yet deformed with all the Improprieties which Ignorance and Neglect could

accumulate

accumulate upon him ; while the Reading was yet
not rectified, nor his Allusions understood ; yet then
did *Dryden* pronounce, that ' *Shakespeare* was the
' Man, who, of all modern, and perhaps ancient
' Poets, had the largest and most comprehensive
' Soul. All the Images of Nature were still pre-
' sent to him, and he drew them not laboriously, but
' luckily: When he describes any Thing, you more
' than see it, you feel it too. Those who accuse
' him to have wanted Learning, give him the greater
' Commendation : He was naturally learned: He
' needed not the Spectacles of Books to read Na-
' ture ; he looked inwards, and found her there.
' I cannot say he is every where alike ; were he so
' I should do him Injury to compare him with the
' Greatest of Mankind. He is many times flat and
' insipid; his comick Wit degenerating into Clenches,
' his serious Swelling into Bombast. But he is al-
' ways great when some great Occasion is presented
' to him : No Man can say he ever had a fit Sub-
' ject for his Wit, and did not then raise himself as
' high above the Rest of Poets,

    ' *Quantum lenta solent inter viburna cupressi.*'

It is to be lamented that such a Writer should
want a Comentary ; that his Language should become obsolete, or his Sentiments obscure. But it is
vain to carry Wishes beyond the Condition of human Things ; that which must happen to all, has
happened to *Shakespeare*, by Accident and Time ;
and more than has been suffered by any other Writer
since the Use of Types, has been suffered by him
through his own Negligence of Fame, or perhaps
by that Superiority of Mind which despised its own
Performances, when it compared them with its
Powers, and judged those Works unworthy to be
preserved, which the Criticks of following Ages were
to contend for the Fame of restoring and explaining.

L 3   Among

Among thefe Candidates of inferiour Fame, I am now to ftand the Judgment of the Publick, and wifh that I could confidently produce my Commentary as equal to the Encouragement which I have had the Honour of receiving. Every Work of this Kind is by its Nature deficient ; and I fhould feel litt e Solicitude about the Sentence, were it to be pronounced only by the Skilful and the Learned.

PREFACE

TO THE

ARTIST's CATALOGUE

For 1762.

THE public may juftly require to be informed
of the Nature and Extent of every Defign, for
which the Favour of the Publick is openly folicited.
The Artifts, who were themfelves the firft Projectors
of an Exhibition in this Nation, and who have now
contributed to the following Catalogue, think it
therefore neceffary to explain their Purpofe, and juftify their Conduct. An Exhibition of the Works of
Art, being a Spectacle new in this Kingdom, has
raifed various Opinions and Conjectures among
thofe who are unacquainted with the Practice in foreign Nations. Thofe who fet out their Performances
to general View, have been too often confidered as
the Rivals of each other, as Men actuated, if not by
Avarice, at leaft by Vanity, and contending for Superiority of Fame, though not for a pecuniary Prize.
It cannot be denied or doubted, that all who offer
themfelves to Criticifm are defirous of Praife ; this
Defire is not only innocent, but virtuous, while it is
undebafed by Artifice, and unpolluted by Envy ; and
of Envy or Artifice thefe Men can never be accufed,
who, already enjoying all the Honours and Profits of
their Profeffion, are content to ftand Candidates for
public Notice, with Genius yet unexperienced, and
Diligence yet unrewarded ; who, without any Hope
of increafing their own Reputation or Intereft, ex-
pofe their Names and their Works only that they
may furnifh an Opportunity of Appearance to the

Young.

Young, the Diffident, and the Neglected. The Purpose of this Exhibition is not to enrich the Artists, but to advance the Art; the Eminent are not flattered with Preference, nor the Obscure insulted with Contempt, whoever hopes to deserve public Favour, is here invited to display his Merit.

Of the Price put upon this Exhibition some Account may be demanded. Whoever sets his Work to be shewn, naturally desires a Multitude of Spectators; but his Desire defeats its own End, when Spectators assemble in such Numbers as to obstruct one another. Though we are far from wishing to diminish the Pleasures, or depreciate the Sentiments of any Class of the Community, we know, however, what every one knows, that all cannot be Judges or Purchasers of Works of Art: yet we have already found by Experience, that all are desirous to see an Exhibition. When the Terms of Admission were low, our Room was thronged with such Multitudes as made Access dangerous, and frightened away those whose Approbation was most desired.

Yet, because it is seldom believed that Money is got but for the Love of Money, we shall tell the Use which we intend to make of our expected Profits.

Many Artists of great Abilities are unable to sell their Works for their due Price; to remove this Inconvenience, an annual Sale will be appointed, to which every Man must send his Works, and send them if he will without his Name. These Works will be reviewed by the Committee that conduct the Exhibition. A Price will be secretly set on every Piece, and registered by the Secretary. If the Piece exposed is sold for more, the whole Price shall be the Artist's; but if the Purchaser's Value it at less than the Committee, the Artist shall be paid the Deficiency from the Profits of the Exhibition.

PRELI.

PRELIMINARY DISCOURSE

TO THE

LONDON CHRONICLE,

In which is delineated what a NEWS-PAPER may and ought to be.

IT has always been lamented, that of the little Time allotted to Man, much muſt be ſpent upon Superfluities. Every Proſpect has its Obſtructions which we muſt break to enlarge our View : Every Step of our Progreſs finds Impediments, which however eager to go forward we muſt ſtop to remove. Even thoſe who profeſs to teach the Way to Happineſs, have multiplied our Incumbrances, and the Authour of almoſt every Book retards his Inſtructions by a Preface.

The Writers of the Chronicle hope to be eaſily forgiven, though they ſhould not be free from an Infection that has ſeized the whole Fraternity, and inſtead of falling immediately to their Subjects, ſhould detain the Reader for a Time with an Account of the Importance of their Deſign, the Extent of their Plan, and the Accuracy of the Method which they intend to proſecute. Such Premonitions, though not always neceſſary when the Reader has the Book complete in his Hand, and may find by his own Eyes whatever can be found in it, yet may more eaſily be allowed to Works publiſhed

gradually

gradually in fucceffive Parts, of which the Scheme can only be fo far known, as the Authour fhall think fit to difcover it.

The Paper which we now invite the Public to add to the Papers with which it is already rather wearied than fatisfied, confifts of many Parts; fome of which it has in common with other periodical Sheets, and fome peculiar to itfelf.

The firft Demand made by the Reader of a Journal is, that he fhould find an accurate Account of foreign Tranfactions and domeftic Incidents. This is always expected, but this is very rarely performed. Of thofe Writers who have taken upon themfelves the Tafk of Intelligence, fome have given and others have fold their Abilities, whether fmall or great, to one or other of the Parties that divide us; and without a Wifh for Truth or Thought of Decency, without Care of any other Reputation than that of a ftubborn Adherence to their Abettors, carry on the fame Tenor of Reprefentation through all the Viciffitudes of Right and Wrong, neither depreffed by Detection, nor abafhed by Confutation, proud of the hourly Increafe of Infamy, and ready to boaft of all the Contumelies that Falfchood and Slander may bring upon them, as new Proofs of their Zeal and Fidelity.

With thefe Heroes we have no Ambition to be numbered, we leave to the Confeffors of Faction the Merit of their Sufferings, and are defirous to fhelter ourfelves under the Protection of Truth. That all our Facts will be authentic, or all our Remarks juft, we dare not venture to promife: We can relate but what we hear, we can point out but what we fee. Of remote Tranfactions, the firft Accounts are always confufed, and commonly exaggerated; and in domeftic Affairs, if the Power to conceal is lefs, the Intereft to mifreprefent is often greater; and what is fufficiently vexatious, Truth feems to

fly

fly from Curiofity, and as many Enquirers produce many Narratives, whatever engages the public Attention is immediately difguifed by the Embellifhments of Fiction. We pretend to no peculiar Power of difentangling Contradiction or denuding Forgery, we have no fettled Correfpondence with the Antipodes, nor maintain any Spies in the Cabinets of Princes. But as we fhall always be confcious that our Miftakes are involuntary, we fhall watch the gradual Difcoveries of Time, and retract what we have haftily and erroneoufly advanced.

In the Narratives of the daily Writers every Reader perceives fomewhat of Neatnefs and Purity wanting, which at the firft View it feems eafy to fupply; but it muft be confidered, that thofe Paffages muft be written in Hafte, and that there is often no other Choice, but that they muft want either Novelty or Accuracy; and that as Life is very uniform, the Affairs of one Week are fo like thofe of another, that by any Attempt after Variety of Expreffion, Invention would foon be wearied, and Language exhaufted. Some Improvements however we hope to make; and for the reft we think that when we commit only common Faults, we fhall not be excluded from common Indulgence. The Accounts of Prices of Corn and Stocks are to moft of our Readers of more Importance than Narratives of greater Sound, and as Exactnefs is here within the Reach of Diligence, our Readers may juftly require it from us.

Memorials of a private and perfonal Kind, which relate Deaths, Marriages, and Preferments, muft always be imperfect by Omiffion, and often erroneous by Mifinformation; but even in thefe there fhall not be wanting Care to avoid Miftakes, or to rectify them whenever they fhall be found.

That Part of our Work, by which it is diftinguifhed from all others, is the literary Journal, or
Account

Account of the Labours and Productions of the Learned. This was for a long Time among the Deficiencies of *English* Literature, but as the Caprice of Man is always ftarting from too little to too much, we have now amongft other Difturbers of human Quiet, a numerous Body of Reviewers and Remarkers.

Every Art is improved by the Emulation of Competitors ; thofe who make no Advances towards Excellence, may ftand as Warnings againft Faults. We fhall endeavour to avoid that Petulance which treats with Contempt whatever has hitherto been reputed facred.

We fhall reprefs that Elation of Malignity, which wantons in the Cruelties of Criticifm, and not only murders Reputation, but murders it by Torture. Whenever we feel ourfelves ignorant we fhall at leaft be modeft. Our Intention is not to pre-occupy Judgment by Praife or Cenfure, but to gratify Curiofity by early Intelligence, and to tell rather what our Authours have attempted, than what they have performed. The Titles of Books are neceffarily fhort, and therefore difclofe but imperfectly the Contents ; they are fometimes fraudulent and intended to raife falfe Expectations. In our account this Brevity will be extended, and thefe Frauds whenever they are detected will be expofed ; for though we write without Intention to injure, we fhall not fuffer ourfelves to be made Parties to Deceit.

If any Authour fhall tranfmit a Summary of his Work, we fhall willingly receive it ; if any literary Anecdote, or curious Obfervation fhall be communicated to us, we fhall carefully infert it. Many Facts are known and forgotten, many Obfervations are made and fuppreffed ; and Entertainment and Inftruction are frequently loft, for want of a Repofitory pository in which they may be conveniently preferved.

No Man can modeftly promife what he cannot afcertain: we hope for the Praife of Knowledge and Difcernment, but we claim only that of Diligence and Candour.

INTRODUC-

INTRODUCTION

TO THE

Proceedings of the Committee appointed to manage the Contributions begun at *London*, *Dec.* 18, 1758, for Cloathing *French* Prifoners of War.

THE Committee intrufted with the Money contributed to the Relief of the Subjects of *France*, now Prifoners in the *Britifh* Dominions, here lay before the Public an exact Account of all the Sums received and expended, that the Donors may judge how properly their Benefactions have been applied.

Charity would lofe its Name, were it influenced by fo mean a Motive as human Praife : It is therefore not intended to celebrate by any particular Memorial, the Liberality of fingle Perfons, or diftinct Societies ; it is fufficient that their Works praife them.

Yet he who is far from feeking Honour, may very juftly obviate Cenfure. If a good Example has been fet, it may lofe its Influence by Mifreprefentation; and to free Charity from Reproach, is itfelf a charitable Action.

Againft the Relief of the *French* only one Argument has been brought ; but that one is fo popular and fpecious, that if it were to remain unexamined, it would by many be thought irrefragable. It has been urged that Charity, like other Virtues, may be improperly and unfeafonably exerted ; that while we are relieving *Frenchmen*, there remain many *Englifhmen* unrelieved ; that while we lavifh Pity on our Enemies, we forget the Mifery of our Friends.

Grant

Grant this Argument all it can prove, and what is the Conclusion?—That to relieve the *French* is a good Action, but that a better may be conceived: This is all the Result, and this All is very little. To do the best can seldom be the Lot of Man; it is sufficient if, when Opportunities are presented, he is ready to do Good. How little Virtue could be practised, if Beneficence were to wait always for the most proper Objects, and the noblest Occasions; Occasions that may never happen, and Objects that may never be found?

It is far from certain, that a single *Englishman* will suffer by the Charity to the *French*. New Scenes of Misery make new Impressions; and much of the Charity which produced these Donations, may be supposed to have been generated by a Species of Calamity never known among us before. Some imagine that the Laws have provided all necessary Relief in common Cases, and remit the Poor to the Care of the Public; some have been deceived by fictitious Misery, and are afraid of encouraging Imposture; many have observed Want to be the Effect of Vice, and consider casual Almsgivers as Patrons of Idleness. But all these Difficulties vanish in the present Case: We know that for the Prisoners of War there is no legal Provision; we see their Distress, and are certain of its Cause; we know that they are poor and naked, and poor and naked without a Crime.

But it is not necessary to make any Concessions. The Opponents of this Charity must allow it to be good, and will not easily prove it not to be the best. That Charity is best, of which the Consequences are most extensive: The Relief of Enemies has a Tendency to unite Mankind in fraternal Affection; to soften the Acrimony of adverse Nations, and dispose them to Peace and Amity: In the mean Time, it alleviates Captivity, and takes away something from

the

the Miseries of War. The Rage of War, however mitigated, will always fill the World with Calamity and Horror: Let it not then be unnecessarily extended; let Animosity and Hostility cease together; and no Man be longer deemed an Enemy, than while his Sword is drawn against us.

The Effects of these Contributions may, perhaps, reach still further. Truth is best supported by Virtue: We may hope from those who feel or who see our Charity, that they shall no longer detest as Heresy that Religion, which makes its Professors the Followers of Him, who has commanded us to 'do good 'to them that hate us.'

S O M E

Thoughts on Agriculture;

B O T H

ANCIENT and MODERN:

With an Account of the Honour that is due to an
English Farmer.

AGRICULTURE, in the primeval Ages,
was the common Parent of Traffick; for the
Opulence of Mankind then confifted in Cattle, and
the Product of Tillage; which are now very eflen-
tial for the Promotion of Trade in general, but
more particularly fo to fuch Nations as are moft
abundant in Cattle, Corn, and Fruits. The Labour of the Farmer gives Employment to the Manufacturer, and yields a Support for the other Parts of
a Community: It is now the Spring which fets
the whole grand Machine of Commerce in Motion;
and the Sail could not be fpread without the Affiftance of the Plough. But, though the Farmers are
of fuch Utility in a State, we find them in general
too much difregarded among the politer Kind of
People in the prefent Age: While we cannot help
obferving the Honour that Antiquity has always paid
to the Profeffion of the Hufbandman: Which na-

turally leads us into fome Reflections upon that Occafion.

Though Mines of Gold and Silver fhould be exhaufted, and the Species made of them loft; though Diamonds and Pearls fhould remain concealed in the Bowels of the Earth, and the Womb of the Sea; though Commerce with Strangers be prohibited; though all Arts, which have no other Object than Splendor and Embellifhment, fhould be abolifhed; yet, the Fertility of the Earth alone would afford an abundant Supply for the Occafions of an induftrious People, by furnifhing Subfiftence for them, and fuch Armics as fhould be muftered in their Defence. We, therefore, ought not to be furprized, that Agriculture was in fo much Honour among the Ancients: For it ought rather to feem wonderful that it fhould ever ceafe to be fo, and that the moft neceffary and moft indifpenfible of all Profeffions fhould have fallen into any Contempt.

Agriculture was in no Part of the World in higher Confideration than *Egypt,* where it was the particular Object of Government and Policy: Nor was any Country ever better peopled, richer, or more powerful. The *Satrapæ,* among the *Affyrians* and *Perfians,* were rewarded, if the Lands in their Governments were well cultivated; but were punifhed, if that Part of their Duty was neglected. *Africa* abounded in Corn; but the moft famous Countries were *Thrace, Sardinia,* and *Sicily.*

Cato, the Cenfor, has juftly called *Sicily* the Magazine and nurfing Mother of the *Roman* People, who were fupplied from thence with almoft all their Corn, both for the Ufe of the City, and the Subfiftence of her Armies: Though we alfo find in *Livy,* that the *Romans* received no inconfiderable Quantities of Corn from *Sardinia.* But, when *Rome* had made herfelf Miftrefs of *Carthage* and *Alexandria, Africa* and *Egypt* became her Store-houfes: For
those

thofe Cities fent fuch numerous Fleets every Year, freighted with Corn to *Rome*, that *Alexandria* alone annually fupplied twenty Millions of Bufhels: And, when the Harveft happened to fail in one of thefe Provinces, the other came in to its Aid, and fupported the Metropolis of the World ; which, without this Supply, would have been in Danger of perifhing by Famine. *Rome* actually faw herfelf reduced to this Condition under *Auguftus* ; for there remained only three Days Provifion of Corn in the City: And that Prince was fo full of Tendernefs for the People, that he had refolved to poifon himfelf, if the expected Fleets did not arrive before the Expiration of that Time ; but they came ; and the Prefervation of the *Romans* was attributed to the good Fortune of their Emperor: But wife Precautions were taken to avoid the like Danger for the future.

When the Seat of Empire was tranfplanted to *Conflantinople*, that City was fupplied in the fame Manner: And when the Emperor *Septimus Severus* died, there was Corn in the publick Magazines for feven Years, expending daily 75,000 Bufhels in Bread, for 600,000 Men.

The Ancients were no lefs induftrious in the Cultivation of the Vine than in that of Corn, though they applied themfelves to it later : For *Noah* planted it by Order, and difcovered the Ufe that might be made of the Fruit, by prefling out, and preferving the Juice. The Vine was carried by the Offspring of *Noah* into the feveral Countries of the World : But *Afia* was the firft to experience the Sweets of this Gift ; from whence it was imparted to *Europe* and *Africa*. *Greece* and *Italy*, which were diftinguifhed in fo many other Refpects, were particularly fo by the Excellency of their Wines. *Greece* was moft celebrated for the Wines of *Cyprus*, *Lefbos*, and *Chio* ; the former of which is in great Efteem at prefent: Though the Cultivation of the Vine has

been

been generally fuppreffed in the *Turkifh* Dominions.
As the *Romans* were indebted to the *Grecians* for the
Arts and Sciences, fo were they likewife for the Improvement of their Wines; the beft of which were
produced in the Country of *Capua*, and were called
the *Maffic*, *Calenian*, *Formian*, *Cæcuban*, and *Faler-
nian*, fo much celebrated by *Horace*. *Domitian* paffed
an Edict for deftroying all the Vines, and that no
more fhould be planted throughout the greateft Part
of the Weft; which continued almoft two hundred
Years afterwards, when the Emperor *Probus* employed his Soldiers in planting Vines in *Europe*, in
the fame Manner as *Hannibal* had formerly employed
his Troops in planting Olive-trees in *Africa*. Some
of the Ancients have endeavoured to prove, that the
Cultivation of Vines is more beneficial than any
other Kind of Hufbandry: But, if this was thought
fo in the Time of *Columella*, it is very different at
prefent; nor were all the Ancients of his Opinion,
for feveral gave the Preference to pafture Lands.

The Breeding of Cattle has always been confidered as an important Part of Agriculture. The
Riches of *Abraham*, *Laban*, and *Job*, confifted in
their Flocks and Herds. We alfo find from *Latinus*
in *Virgil*, and *Ulyffes* in *Homer*, that the Wealth of
thofe Princes confifted in Cattle. It was likewife
the fame among the *Romans*, till the Introduction of
Money, which put a Value upon Commodities, and
eftablifhed a new Kind of Barter. *Varro* has not
difdained to give an extenfive Account of all the
Beafts that are of any Ufe to the Country, either for
Tillage, Breed, Carriage, or other Conveniencies
of Man. And *Cato*, the Cenfor, was of Opinion,
that the Feeding of Cattle was the moft certain and
fpeedy Method of enriching a Country.

Luxury, Avarice, Injuftice, Violence, and Ambition, take up their ordinary Refidence in populous
Cities: While the hard and laborious Life of the

Hufbandman

Husbandman will not admit of these Vices. The honest Farmer lives in a wise and happy State, which inclines him to Justice, Temperance, Sobriety, Sincerity, and every Virtue that can dignify the human Nature. This gave Room for the Poets to feign, that *Astraa*, the Goddess of Justice, had her last Residence among Husbandmen, before she quitted the Earth. *Hesiod* and *Virgil* have brought the Assistance of the Muses in Praise of Agriculture. Kings, Generals, and Philosophers, have not thought it unworthy their Birth, Rank, and Genius, to leave Precepts to Posterity upon the Utility of the Husbandman's Profession. *Hiero*, *Attalus*, and *Archelaus*, Kings of *Syracuse*, *Pergamus*, and *Cappadocia*, have composed Books for supporting and augmenting the Fertility of their different Countries. The *Carthaginian* General, *Mago*, wrote twenty-eight Volumes upon this Subject; and *Cato*, the Censor, followed his Example. Nor have *Plato*, *Xenophon*, and *Aristotle*, omitted this Article, which makes an essential Part of their Politicks. And *Cicero*, speaking of the Writings of *Xenophon*, says, ' How fully and ' excellently does he, in that Book called his *Oecono-* ' *mics*, set out the Advantages of Husbandry, and a ' country Life?'

When *Britain* was subject to the *Romans*, she annually supplied them with great Quantities of Corn; and the *Isle of Anglesea* was then looked upon as the Grainary for the *Western* Provinces: But the *Britons*, both under the *Romans* and *Saxons*, were employed like Slaves at the Plough. On the Intermixture of the *Danes* and *Normans*, Possessions were better regulated, and the State of Vassalage gradually declined, till it was entirely wore off under the Reigns of *Henry* VII. and *Edward* VI. for they hurt the old Nobility by favouring the Commons, who grew rich by Trade, and purchased Estates.

The

The Wines of *France*, *Portugal*, and *Spain*, are now the beft; while *Italy* can only boaft of the Wine made in *Tufcany*. The Breeding of Cattle is now chiefly confined to *Denmark* and *Ireland*. The Corn of *Sicily* is ftill in great Efteem, as well as what is produced in the Northern Countries: But *England* is the happieft Spot in the Univerfe for all the principal Kinds of Agriculture, and efpecially its great Produce of Corn.

The Improvement of our landed Eftates, is the Enrichment of the Kingdom: For, without this, how could we carry on our Manufactures, or profecute our Commerce? We fhould look upon the *Englifh* Farmer as the moft ufeful Member of Society. His arable Grounds not only fupply his Fellow-fubjects with all Kinds of the beft Grain, but his Induftry enables him to Export great Quantities to other Kingdoms, which might otherwife ftarve; particularly *Spain* and *Portugal:* For, in one Year, there have been exported 51,520 Quarters of Barley, 219,781 of Malt, 1920 of Oatmeal, 1329 of Rye, and 153,343 of Wheat; the Bounty on which amounted to 72,433 Pounds. What a Fund of Treafure arifes from his pafture Lands, which breed fuch innumerable Flocks of Sheep, and afford fuch fine Herds of Cattle, to feed *Britons*, and cloath Mankind? He rears Flax and Hemp for the making of Linen; while his Plantations of Apples and Hops fupply him with generous Kinds of Liquors.

The Land-tax, when at four Shillings in the Pound, produces 2,000,000 Pounds a Year. This arifes from the Labour of the Hufbandman: It is a great Sum: But how greatly is it increafed by the Means it furnifhes for Trade? Without the Induftry of the Farmer, the Manufacturer could have no Goods to fupply the Merchant, nor the Merchant find any Employment for the Mariners: Trade would

would be ftagnated ; Riches whould be of no Advantage to the Great ; and Labour of no Service to the
Poor.

The *Romans*, as Hiftorians all allow,
Sought, in extreme Diftrefs, the rural Plough ;
Io Triumphe ! for the village Swain
Retir'd to be a * Nobleman again.

* *Cincinnatus.*

M 4 INTRO.

INTRODUCTION

TO THE

WORLD DISPLAYED.

NAVIGATION, like other Arts, has been perfected by Degrees. It is not easy to conceive that any Age or Nation was without some Vessel, in which Rivers might be passed by Travellers, or Lakes frequented by Fishermen ; but we have no Knowledge of any Ship that could endure the Violence of the Ocean, before the Ark of *Noah*.

As the Tradition of the Deluge has been transmitted to almost all the Nations of the Earth ; it must be supposed that the Memory of the Means by which *Noah* and his Family were preserved, would be continued long among their Descendants, and that the Possibility of passing the Seas could never be doubted.

What Men know to be practicable, a thousand Motives will incite them to try ; and there is Reason to believe, that from the Time that the Generations of the postdiluvian Race spread to the Sea Shores, there were always Navigators that ventured upon the Sea, though, perhaps, not willingly beyond the Sight of Land.

Of the ancient Voyages little certain is known, and it is not necessary to lay before the Reader such Conjectures as learned Men have offered to the World. The *Romans* by conquering *Carthage*, put a Stop to a great Part of the Trade of distant Nations with one another, and because they thought only on War and Conquest, as their Empire encreased, creafed, Commerce was difcouraged; till under the latter Emperors, Ships feem to have been of little other Ufe than to tranfport Soldiers.

Navigation could not be carried to any great Degree of Certainty, without the Compafs; which was unknown to the Ancients. The wonderful Quality by which a Needle, or fmall Bar of Steel, touched with a Loadftone or Magnet, and turning freely by Equilibration on a Point, always preferves the Meridian, and directs its two Ends North and South, was difcovered according to the common Opinion in 1299, by *John Gola* of *Amalphi*, a Town in *Italy*.

From this Time it is reafonable to fuppofe that Navigation made continual, though flow, Improvements, which the Confufion and Barbarity of the Times, and the Want of Communication between Orders of Men fo diftant as Sailors and Monks, hindered from being diftinctly and fucceffively recorded.

It feems, however, that the Sailors ftill wanted either Knowledge or Courage, for they continued for two Centuries to creep along the Coaft, and confidered every Headland as unpaffable, which ran far into the Sea, and againft which the Waves broke with uncommon Agitation.

The Firft who is known to have formed the Defign of new Difcoveries, or the Firft who had Power to execute his Purpofes, was Don *Henry* the Fifth, Son of *John* the Firft, King of *Portugal*, and *Philippina*, Sifter of *Henry* the Fourth of *England*. Don *Henry* having attended his Father to the Conqueft of *Ceuta*, obtained by Converfation with the Inhabitants of the Continent, fome Accounts of the interior Kingdoms and fouthern Coaft of *Africa*; which, though rude and indiftinct, were fufficient to raife his Curiofity, and convince him that there were Countries yet unknown and worthy of Difcovery.

He

He therefore equipped fome fmall Veffels, and commanded that they fhould pafs as far as they could along that Coaft of *Africa*, which looked upon the great *Atlantick Ocean*, the Immenfity of which ftruck the grofs and unfkilful Navigators of thefe Times, with Terror and Amazement. He was not able to communicate his own Ardour to his Seamen, who proceeded very flowly in the new Attempt; each was afraid to venture much further than he that went before him, and ten Years were fpent before they had advanced beyond *Cape Bajador*, fo called from its long Progreffion into the Ocean, and the Circuit by which it muft be doubled. The Oppofition of this Promontory to the Courfe of the Sea, produced a violent Current and high Waves, into which they durft not venture, and which they had not yet Knowledge enough to avoid by ftanding off from the Land into the open Sea.

The Prince was defirous to know fomething of the Countries that lay beyond this formidable Cape, and fent two Commanders, named *John Gonzales Zarco*, and *Trifiran Vaz*, (1418) to pafs beyond *Bajador*, and furvey the Coaft behind it. They were caught by a Tempeft, which drove them out into the unknown Ocean, where they expected to perifh by the Violence of the Wind, or perhaps to wander for ever in the boundlefs Deep. At laft, in the Midft of their Defpair, they found a fmall Ifland, where they fheltered themfelves, and which the Senfe of their Deliverance difpofed them to call *Puerto Santo*, or the *Holy Haven*.

When they returned with an Account of this new Ifland, *Henry* performed a publick Act of Thankfgiving, and fent them again with Seeds and Cattle; and we are told by the *Spanifh* Hiftorian, that they fet two Rabbits on Shore, which encreafed fo much in a few Years, that they drove away the Inhabitants,

tants, by deftroying their Corn and Plants, and were fuffered to enjoy the Ifland without Oppofition.

In the fecond. or third Voyage to *Puerto Santo*, for Authours do not well agree, a third Captain called *Perello*, was joined to the two former. As they looked round the Ifland upon the Ocean, they faw at a Diftance fomething which they took for a Cloud, till they perceived that it did not change its Place. They directed their Courfe towards it, and (1419) difcovered another Ifland covered with Trees, which they therefore called *Madera*, or the *Ifle of Wood.*

Madera was given to *Vaz* or *Zarco*, who fet Fire to the Woods, which are reported by *Scuza*, to have burnt for feven Years together, and to have been wafted, till Want of Wood was the greateft Inconvenience of the Place. But green Wood is not very apt to burn, and the heavy Rains which fall in thefe Countries muft furely have extinguifhed the Conflagration, were it ever fo violent.

There was yet little Progrefs made upon the Southern Coaft, and *Henry*'s Project was treated as chimerical by many of his Countrymen. At laft *Gilianes* (1433) paffed the dreadful Cape, to which he gave the Name of *Bajador*, and came back, to the Wonder of the Nation.

In two Voyages more, made in the two following Years, they paffed forty-two Leagues further, and in the latter, two Men with Horfes being fet on Shore, wandered over the Country, and found nineteen Men, whom according to the favage Manners of that Age they attacked, the Natives having Javelins, wounded one of the *Portuguefe*, and received fome Wounds from them. At the Mouth of a River they found Sea-wolves in great Numbers, and brought home many of their Skins, which were much efteemed.

Antonio

Antonio Gonzales, who had been one of the Affociates of *Gilianes*, was fent again (1440) to bring
back a Cargo of the Skins of Sea-wolves. He was
followed in another Ship by *Nunno Triflam*. They
were now of Strength fufficient to venture upon Violence, they therefore landed, and without either
Right or Provocation, made all whom they feized
their Prifoners, and brought them to *Portugal*, with
great Commendations both from the Prince and the
Nation.

Henry now began to pleafe himfelf with the Succefs of his Projects, and as one of his Purpofes was
the Converfion of Infidels, thought it neceffary to
impart his Undertaking to the Pope, and to obtain
the Sanctions of Ecclefiaftical Authority. To this
End *Fernando Lopez d'Azevedo* was difpatched to
Rome, who related to the Pope and Cardinals the
great Defigns of *Henry*, and magnified his Zeal for
the Propagation of Religion. The Pope was pleafed
with the Narrative, and by a formal Bull conferred
upon the Crown of *Portugal*, all the Countries which
fhould be difcovered as far as *India*, together with
India itfelf, and granted feveral Privileges and Indul-
gences to the Churches, which *Henry* had built in
his new Regions, and to the Men engaged in the
Navigation for Difcovery. By this Bull all other
Princes are forbidden to encroach upon the Conquefts of the *Portuguefe*, on Pain of the Cenfures incurred by the Crime of Ufurpation.

The Approbation of the Pope, the Sight of Men
whofe Manners and Appearance were fo different
from thofe of *Europeans*, and the Hope of Gain from
golden Regions, which has been always the great
Incentive of Hazard and Difcovery, now began to
operate with full Force. The Defire of Riches and
of Dominion, which is yet more pleafing to the
Fancy, filled the Courts of the *Portuguefe* Prince
with innumerable Adventurers from very diftant Parts
; of

of *Europe*. Some wanted to be employed in the Search after new Countries, and some to be settled in those which had been already found.

Communities now began to be seized with the Infection of Enterprise, and many Associations were formed for the Equipment of Ships, and the Acquisition of the Riches of distant Regions, which perhaps were always supposed to be more wealthy, as more remote. These Undertakers agreed to pay the Prince a fifth Part of the Profit, sometimes a greater Share, and sent out the Armament at their own Expence.

The City of *Lagos* was the first that carried on this Design by Contribution. The Inhabitants fitted out six Vessels, under the Command of *Luçarot*, one of the Prince's Houshold, and soon after fourteen more were furnished for the same Purpose, under the same Commander; to those were added many belonging to private Men, so that in a short Time, twenty-six Ships put to Sea in quest of whatever Fortune should present.

The Ships of *Lagos* were soon separated by foul Weather, and the rest, taking each its own Course, stopped at different Parts of the *African* Coast, from *Cape Blanco* to *Cape Verd*. Some of them, in 1444, anchored at *Gomera*, one of the *Canaries*, where they were kindly treated by the Inhabitants, who took them into their Service, against the People of the Isle of *Palma*, with whom they were at War; but the *Portuguese* at their Return to *Gomera*, not being made so rich as they expected, fell upon their Friends, in contempt of all the Laws of Hospitality, and Stipulations of Alliance, and, making several of them Prisoners and Slaves, set sail for *Lisbon*.

The *Canaries* are supposed to have been known, however imperfectly, to the Antients, but in the Confusion of the subsequent Ages, they were lost and forgotten, till about the Year 1340, the *Biscay-*

neers

neers found *Luçarot*, and invading it, for to find a
new Country and invade it has always been the same,
brought away seventy Captives, and some Commodities of the Place. *Louis de la Cerda*, Count of
Clermont, of the Blood Royal both of *France* and
Spain, Nephew of *John de la Cerda*, who called himself the Prince of Fortune, had once a Mind to settle
in those Islands, and applying himself first to the
King of *Arragon*, and then to *Clement* VI. was by
the Pope crowned at *Avignon*, King of the *Canaries*,
on Condition that he should reduce them to the true
Religion; but the Prince altered his Mind, and
went into *France* to serve against the *English*. The
Kings both of *Castile* and *Portugal*, though they did
not oppose the papal Grant, yet complained of it,
as made without their Knowledge, and in Contra-
vention of their Rights.

The first Settlement in the *Canaries* was made
by *John de Betancour*, a *French* Gentleman, for
whom his Kinsman *Robin de Braquement*, Admiral
of *France*, begged them, with the Title of King,
from *Henry the Magnificent of Castile*, to whom
he had done eminent Services. *John* made himself Master of some of the Isles, but could never
conquer the *Grand Canary*, and having spent all
that he had, went back to *Europe*, leaving his Nephew *Maffiot de Betancour*, to take Care of his new
Dominion. *Maffiot* had a Quarrel with the Vicar-
General, and was likewise disgusted by the long
Absence of his Uncle, whom the *French* King detained in his Service, and being able to keep his
Ground no longer, he transferred his Rights to Don
Henry, in Exchange for some Districts in the *Madera*, where he settled his Family.

Don *Henry*, when he had purchased those Islands,
sent thither in 1424, two thousand five hundred
Foot, and an hundred and twenty Horse; but the
Army was too numerous to be maintained by the
Country.

Country. The King of *Castile* afterwards claimed them, as conquered by his Subjects under *Betancour*, and held under the Crown of *Castile* by Fealty and Homage; his Claim was allowed, and the *Canaries* were resigned.

It was the constant Practice of *Henry's* Navigators, when they stopped at a desert Island, to land Cattle upon it, and leave them to breed, where neither wanting Room nor Food, they multiplied very fast, and furnished a very commodious Supply to those who came afterwards to the same Place. This was imitated in some Degree by *Anson*, at the Isle of *Juan Fernandez*.

The Islands of *Madera* he not only filled with Inhabitants, assisted by Artificers of every Kind, but procured such Plants as seemed likely to flourish in that Climate, and introduced the Sugar Canes and Vines, which afterwards produced a very large Revenue.

The Trade of *Africa* now began to be gainful, but a great Part of the Gain arose from the Sale of Slaves, who were annually brought into *Portugal* by Hundreds, as *Lafitau* relates, and relates without any Appearance of Indignation or Compassion; they likewise imported Gold Dust in such Quantities, that *Alphonsus* V. coined it into a new Species of Money called *Crusades*, which is still continued in *Portugal*.

In Time they made their Way along the South Coast of *Africa*, Eastward to the Country of the Negroes, whom they found living in Tents, without any political Institutions, supporting Life with very little Labour by the Milk of their Kine, and Millet, to which those who inhabited the Coast added Fish dried in the Sun. Having never seen the Natives or heard of the Arts of *Europe*, they gazed with Astonishment on the Ships when they approached their Coasts, sometimes thinking them Birds, and sometimes Fishes, according as their

5

Sails were spread or lowered ; and sometimes conceiving them to be only Phantoms, which played to and fro in the Ocean. Such is the Account given by the Historian, perhaps with too much Prejudice against a Negroe's Underftanding ; who tho' he might well wonder at the Bulk and Swiftnefs of the first Ship, would scarcely conceive it to be either a Bird or a Fish ; but having seen many Bodies floating in this Water, would think it what it really is, a large Boat ; and if he had no knowledge of any Means by which feparate Pieces of Timber may be joined together, would form very wild Notions concerning its Construction, or perhaps suppose it to be a hollow Trunk of a Tree, from some Country where Trees grow to a much greater Height and Thicknefs than in his own.

When the *Portugueze* came to land, they encreafed the Aftonishment of the poor Inhabitants, who faw Men clad in Iron, with Thunder and Lightning in their Hands. They did not understand each other, and Signs are a very imperfect Mode of Communication even to Men of more Knowledge than the Negroes, fo that they could not eafily negotiate or traffick : At last the *Portugueze* laid Hands on some of them to carry them home for a Sample ; and their Dread and Amazement was raifed, fays *Lafitau*, to the highest Pitch, when the *Europeans* fired their Cannons and Muskets among them, and they faw their Companions fall dead at their Feet without any Enemy at Hand, or any visible Caufe of their Deftruction.

On what Occafion, or for what Purpose, Cannons and Muskets were difcharged among a People harmlefs and fecure, by Strangers who without any Right vifited their Coaft ; it is not thought neceffary to inform us. The *Portugueze* could fear nothing from them, and had therefore no adequate Provocation ; nor is there any Reafon to believe but that they murdered

dered

dered the Negroes in wanton Merriment, perhaps only to try how many a Volley would deftroy, or what would be the Confternation of thofe that fhould efcape. We are openly told, that they had the lefs Scruple concerning their Treatment of the favage People, becaufe they fcarcely confidered them as diftinct from Beafts; and indeed the Practice of all the *European* Nations, and among others of the *Englifh* Barbarians that cultivate the fouthern Iflands of *America* proves, that this Opinion, however abfurd and foolifh, however wicked and injurious, ftill continues to prevail. Intereft and Pride harden the Heart, and it is vain to difpute againft Avarice and Power.

By thefe Practices the firft Difcoverers alienated the Natives from them; and whenever a Ship appeared, every one that could fly betook himfelf to the Mountains and the Woods, fo that nothing was to be got more than they could fteal: They fometimes furprifed a few Fifhers, and made them Slaves, and did what they could to offend the Negroes, and enrich themfelves. This Practice of Robbery continued till fome of the Negroes who had been enflaved learned the Language of *Portugal*, fo as to be able to interpret for their Countrymen, and one *John Fernandez* applied himfelf to the Negroe Tongue.

From this Time began fomething like a regular Traffick, fuch as can fubfift between Nations where all the Power is on one Side; and a Factory was fettled in the Ifle of *Arguin*, under the Protection of a Fort. The Profit of this new Trade was affigned for a certain Term to *Ferdinando Gomez*; which feems to be the common Method of eftablifhing a Trade that is yet too fmall to engage the Care of a Nation, and can only be enlarged by that Attention which is beftowed by private Men upon private Advantage. *Gomez* continued the Difcoveries to *Cape Catharine*, two Degrees and a half beyond the Line.

In the latter Part of the Reign of *Alphonſo* V. the Ardour of Diſcovery was ſomewhat intermitted, and all commercial Enterpriſes were interrupted by the Wars, in which he was engaged with various Succeſs. But *John* II. who ſucceeded, being fully convinced both of the Honour and Advantage of extending his Dominions in Countries hitherto unknown, proſecuted the Deſigns of Prince *Henry* with the utmoſt Vigour, and in a ſhort Time added to his other Titles, that of King of *Guinea* and of the Coaſt of *Africa*.

In 1463, in the third Year of the Reign of *John* II. died Prince *Henry*, the firſt Encourager of remote Navigation, by whoſe Incitement, Patronage, and Example, diſtant Nations have been made acquainted with each other, unknown Countries have been brought into general View, and the Power of *Europe* has been extended to the remoteſt Parts of the World. What Mankind has loſt and gained by the Genius and Deſigns of this Prince, it would be long to compare, and very difficult to eſtimate. Much Knowledge has been acquired, and much Cruelty been committed, the Belief of Religion has been very little propagated, and its Laws have been outrageouſly and enormouſly violated. The *Europeans* have ſcarcely viſited any Coaſt, but to gratify Avarice, and extend Corruption; to arrogate Dominion without Right, and practiſe Cruelty without Incentive. Happy had it then been for the Oppreſſed, if the Deſigns of *Henry* had ſlept in his Boſom, and ſurely more happy for the Oppreſſors. But there is Reaſon to hope that out of much Evil Good may be ſometimes produced; and that the Light of the Goſpel will at laſt illuminate the Sands of *Africa*, and the Deſarts of *America*, though its Progreſs cannot but be ſlow, when it is ſo much obſtructed by the Lives of Chriſtians.

The

The Death of *Henry* did not interrupt the Progrefs of King *John*, who was very diligent in his Injunctions, not only to make Difcoveries, but to fecure Poffeffion of the Countries that were found. The Practice of the firft Navigators was only to raife a Crofs upon the Coaft, and to carve upon Trees the Device of Don *Henry*, the Name which they thought it proper to give to the new Coaft, and any other Information, for thofe that might happen to follow them; but now they began to erect Piles of Stone, with a Crofs on the Top, and engraved on the Stone, the Arms of *Portugal*, the Name of the King, and of the Commander of the Ship, with the Day and Year of the Difcovery. This was accounted fufficient to prove their Claim to the new Lands; which might be pleaded with Juftice enough againft any other *Europeans*, and the Rights of the original Inhabitants were never taken into Notice. Of thefe Stone Records, nine more were erected in the Reign of King *John*, along the Coaft of *Africa*, as far as the Cape of *Good Hope*.

The Fortrefs in the Ifle of *Arguin* was finifhed, and it was thought neceffary to build another at *S. Georgio de la Mina*, a few Degrees North of the Line, to fecure the Trade of Gold Duft, which was chiefly carried on at that Place. For this Purpofe a Fleet was fitted out, of ten large, and three fmaller Veffels, freighted with Materials for building the Fort, and with Provifions and Ammunition for Six hundred Men, of whom One hundred were Workmen and Labourers. Father *Lafitau* relates, in very particular Terms, that thefe Ships carried hewn Stones, Bricks, and Timber, for the Fort, fo that nothing remained but barely to erect it. He does not feem to confider how fmall a Fort could be made out of the Lading of ten Ships.

.The Command of the Fleet was given to Don *Diego d'Azambue*, who fet fail *Dec.* 11, 1481, and

reaching

reaching *La Mina Jan.* 19, 1482, gave immediate Notice of his Arrival to *Caramanfa*, a petty Prince of that Part of the Country, whom he very earneftly invited to an immediate Conference.

Having received a Meffage of Civility from the Negro Chief, he landed, and chofe a rifing Ground, proper for his intended Fortrefs, on which he planted a Banner, with the Arms of *Portugal*, and took Poffeffion in the Name of his Mafter. He then raifed an Altar at the Foot of a great Tree, on which Mafs was celebrated, the whole Affembly, fays *Lafitau*, breaking out into Tears of Devotion at the Profpect of inviting thefe barbarous Nations to the Profeffion of the true Faith. Being fecure of the Goodnefs of the End, they had no Scruple about the Means, nor ever confidered how differently from the primitive Martyrs and Apoftles they were attempting to make Profelytes. The firft Propagators of Chriftianity recommended their Doctrines by their Sufferings and Virtues; they entered no defencelefs Territories with Swords in their Hands; they built no Forts upon Ground to which they had no Right, nor polluted the Purity of Religion with the Avarice of Trade, or Infolence of Power.

What may ftill raife higher the Indignation of a Chriftian Mind, this Purpofe of propagating Truth appears never to have been ferioufly purfued by any *European* Nation; no Means, whether lawful or unlawful, have been practifed with Diligence and Perfeverance for the Converfion of Savages. When a Fort is built, and a Factory eftablifhed, there remains no other Care than to grow rich. It is foon found that Ignorance is moft eafily kept in Subjection, and that by enlightening the Mind with Truth, Fraud and Ufurpation would be made lefs practicable, and lefs fecure.

In a few Days an Interview was appointed between *Caramanfa* and *Azambue*. The *Portuguefe* uttered

tered by his Interpreter a pompous Speech, in which
he made the Negroe Prince large Offers of his Master's Friendship, exhorted him to embrace the Religion of his new Ally, and told him, that as they
came to form a League of Friendship with him, it
was neceffary that they should build a Fort, which
might serve as a Retreat from their common Enemies, and in which the *Portuguese* might be always
at hand to lend him Affiftance.

The Negroe, who feemed very well to understand
what the Admiral intended, after a short Paufe, returned an Anfwer full of Refpect to the King of *Portugal*,
but appeared a little doubtful what to determine with
relation to the Fort. The Commander faw his
Diffidence, and ufed all his Art of Perfuafion to
overcome it. *Caramanfa*, either induced by Hope,
or conftrained by Fear, either defirous to make them
Friends, or not daring to make them Enemies, con-
fented, with a Shew of Joy, to that which it was
not in his Power to refufe, and the new Comers began next Day to break the Ground for the Foundation of a Fort.

Within the Limit of their intended Fortification
were fome Spots appropriated to fuperftitious Practices; which the Negroes no fooner perceived in
Danger of Violation by the Spade and Pickax, than
they ran to Arms, and began to interrupt the Work.
The *Portuguese* perfifted in their Purpofe, and there
had foon been Tumult and Bloodfhed, had not the
Admiral, who was at a Diftance, to fuperintend the
unlading the Materials for the Edifice, been informed of the Danger. He was told at the fame
Time, that the Support of their Superftition was
only a Pretence, and that all their Rage might be ap-
peifed by the Prefents which the Prince expected,
and of which he had been offended by the Delay.

The *Portuguese* Admiral immediately ran to his
Men, prohibited all Violence, and ftopped the Commotion;

motion; he then brought out the Prefents, and
fpread them with great Pomp before the Prince; if
they were of no great Value, they were rare, for the
Negroes had never feen fuch Wonders before, they
were therefore received with Extafy, and perhaps
the *Portuguefe* derided them for their Fondnefs of
Trifles, without confidering how many Things derive their Value only from their Scarcity; and that
Gold and Rubies would be Trifles, if Nature had
fcattered them with lefs Frugality.

The Work was now peaceably continued, and
fuch was the Diligence with which the Strangers
haftened to fecure the Poffeffion of the Country, that
in twenty Days they had fufficiently fortified themfelves againft the Hoftility of Negroes. They then
proceeded to complete their Defign. A Church was
built in the Place where the firft Altar had been
raifed, on which a Mafs was eftablifhed to be celebrated for ever, once a Day, for the Repofe of the
Soul of *Henry*, the firft Mover of thefe Difcoveries.

In this Fort the Admiral remained, with fixty
Soldiers, and fent back the Reft in the Ships, with
Gold, Slaves, and other Commodities. It may be
obferved that Slaves were never forgotten, and that
wherever they went, they gratified their Pride, if not
their Avarice, and brought fome of the Natives,
when it happened that they brought nothing elfe.

The *Portuguefe* endeavoured to extend their Dominions ftill farther. They had gained fome Knowledge of the *Jaloffs*, a Nation inhabiting the Coaft
of *Guinea*, between the *Gambia* and *Senegal*. The
King of the *Jaloffs* being vicious and luxurious, remitted the Care of the Government to *Bemoin*, his
Brother by the Mother's Side, in Preference to two
other Brothers by his Father. *Bemoin*, who wanted
neither Bravery nor Prudence, knew that his Station
was invidious and dangerous, and therefore made
an Alliance with the *Portuguefe*, and retained them
in

in his Defence by Liberality and Kindnefs.   At laft the King was killed, by the Contrivance of his Brothers, and *Bemoin* was to lofe his Power, or maintain it by War.

He had Recourfe in this Exigence to his great Al-ly, the King of *Portugal*, who promifed to fupport him, on Condition that he fhould become a Chriftian, and fent an Ambaffador, accompanied with Miffiona-ries. *Bemoin* promifed all that was requefted, objecting only that the Time of a Civil War was not a pro-per Seafon for a Change of Religion, which would alienate his Adherents ; but faid, that when he was once peaceably eftablifhed, he would not only em-brace the true Religion himfelf, but would endeavour the Converfion of the Kingdom.

This Excufe was admitted, and *Bemoin* delayed his Converfion for a Year, renewing his Promife from Time to Time. But the War was unfuc-cefsful, Trade was at a Stand, and *Bemoin* was not able to pay the Money which he had borrowed of the *Portuguefe* Merchants, who fent Intelligence to *Lifbon* of his Delays, and received an Order from the King, commanding them, under fevere Penalties, to return Home.

Bemoin here faw his Ruin approaching, and hoping that Money would pacify all Refentment, borrowed of his Friends a Sum fufficient to difcharge his Debts ; and finding that even this Enticement would not delay the Departure of the *Portuguefe*, he em-barked his Nephew in their Ships, with an hundred Slaves, whom he prefented to the King of *Portugal*, to folicit his Affiftance. The Effect of this Em-baffy he could not ftay to know ; for being foon after depofed, he fought Shelter in the Fortrefs of *Arguin*, whence he took Shipping for *Portugal*, with twenty-five of his principal Followers.

The King of *Portugal* pleafed his own Vanity and that of his Subjects, by receiving him with

N 4   great

great State and Magnificence, as a mighty Monarch who had fled to an Ally for Succour in Misfortune. All the Lords and Ladies of the Court were assembled, and *Bemoin* was conducted with a splendid Attendance into the Hall of Audience, where the King rose from his Throne to welcome him. *Bemoin* then made a Speech with great Ease and Dignity, representing his unhappy State, and imploring the Favour of this powerful Ally. The King was touched with his Affliction and struck by his Wisdom.

The Conversion of *Bemoin* was much desired by the King, and it was therefore immediately proposed to him that he should become a Christian. Ecclesiasticks were sent to instruct him, and having now no more Obstacles from Interest, he was easily persuaded to declare himself whatever would please those on whom he now depended. He was baptized on the third Day of *December* 1489, in the Palace of the Queen with great Magnificence, and named *John* after the King.

Some Time was spent in Feasts and Sports on this great Occasion, and the Negroes signalized themselves by many Feats of Agility, far surpassing the Power of *Europeans*, who having more Helps of Art, are less diligent to cultivate the Qualities of Nature. In the mean Time twenty large Ships were fitted out, well manned, stored with Ammunition, and laden with the Materials necessary for the Erection of a Fort. With this powerful Armament were sent a great Number of Missionaries under the Direction of *Alvarez* the King's Confessor. The Command of this Force, which filled the Coast of *Africa* with Terror, was given to *Pedro Vaz d'Acugna* surnamed *Bisagu*; who soon after they had landed, not being well pleased with his Expedition, put an End to its Inconveniences by stabbing *Bemoin* suddenly to the Heart. The King heard of
this

this Outrage with great Sorrow, but did not attempt to punish the Murderer.

The King's Concern for the Restoration of *Bemoin* was not the mere Effect of amicable Kindness, he hoped by his Help to facilitate greater Designs. He now began to form Hopes of finding a Way to the *East-Indies*, and of enriching his Country by that gainful Commerce : This he was encouraged to believe practicable, by a Map which the Moors had given to Prince *Henry*, and which subsequent Discoveries have shewn to be sufficiently near to Exactness, where a Passage round the South-east Part of *Africa*, was evidently described.

The King had another Scheme yet more likely to engage Curiosity, and not irreconcileable with his Interest. The World had for some Time been filled with the Report of a powerful Christian Prince called *Prester John*, whose Country was unknown, and whom some, after *Paulus Venetus*, supposed to reign in the Midst of *Asia*, and others in the Depth of *Ethiopia*, between the Ocean and Red-sea. The Account of the *African* Christians was confirmed by some *Abissinians* who had travelled into *Spain*, and by some Friars that had visited the Holy Land ; and the King was extremely desirous of their Correspondence and Alliance.

Some obscure Intelligence had been obtained, which made it seem probable that a Way might be found from the Countries lately discovered, to those of this far famed Monarch. In 1486, an Ambassador came from the King of *Bemin*, to desire that Preachers might be sent to instruct him and his Subjects in the true Religion. He related that in the inland Country, three hundred and fifty Leagues Eastward from *Bemin*, was a mighty Monarch called *Ogane*, who had Jurisdiction both spiritual and temporal over other Kings; that the King of *Bemin* and his Neighbours at their Accession, fion, fent Ambaffadors to him with rich Prefents, and received from him the Inveftiture of their Dominions, and the Marks of Sovereignity, which were a Kind of Scepter, a Helmet, and a Latten Crofs, without which they could not be confidered as lawful Kings; that this great Prince was never feen, but on the Day of Audience, and then held out one of his Feet to the Ambaffador, who kiffed it with great Reverence, and who at his Departure had a Crofs of Latten hung on his Neck, which ennobled him thenceforward, and exempted him from all fervile Offices.

Bemoin had likewife told the King that to the Eaft of the Kingdom of *Tembut,* there was among other Princes, one that was neither Mahometan nor Idolater, but who feemed to profefs a Religion nearly refembling the Chriftian. Thefe Informations compared with each other, and with the current Accounts of *Prefter John,* induced the King to an Opinion, which though formed fomewhat at hazard, is ftill believed to be right, that by paffing up the River *Senegal* his Dominions would be found. It was therefore ordered that when the Fortrefs was finifhed, an Attempt fhould be made to pafs upward to the Source of the River. The Defign failed then, and has never yet fucceeded.

Other Ways likewife were tried of penetrating to the Kingdom of *Prefter John,* for the King refolved to leave neither Sea or Land unfearched till he fhould be found. The two Meffengers who were fent firft on this Defign, went to *Jerufalem* and then returned, being perfuaded that for Want of underftanding the Language of the Country, it would be vain or impoffible to travel farther. Two more were then difpatched, one of whom was *Pedro de Covillan,* the other *Alphonfo de Paiva;* they paffed from *Naples* to *Alexandria,* and then travelled to *Cairo,* from whence they went to *Aden,* a Town of of *Arabia*, on the Read Sea near its Mouth. From *Aden*, *Paiva* set Sail for *Ethiopia*, and *Covillan* for the *Indies*. *Covillan* visited *Canavar*, *Calicut*, and *Goa* in the *Indies*, and *Sofula* in the eastern *Africa*, thence he returned to *Aden*, and then to *Cairo*, where he had agreed to meet *Paiva*. At *Cairo* he was informed that *Paiva* was dead, but he met with two *Portugueze Jews*, one of whom had given the King an Account of the Situation and Trade of *Ormus*: They brought Orders to *Covillan*, that he should send one of them home with the Journal of his Travels, and go to *Ormus* with the other.

Covillan obeyed the Orders, sending an exact Account of his Adventures to *Lisbon*, and proceeding with the other Messenger to *Ormus*; where having made sufficient Enquiry, he sent his Companion homewards with the Caravans that were going to *Aleppo*, and embarking once more on the Red Sea, arrived in Time at *Abissinia*, and found the Prince whom he had sought so long with so much Danger.

Two Ships were sent out upon the same Search, of which *Bartholomew Diaz* had the chief Command; they were attended by a smaller Vessel laden with Provisions, that they might not return upon Pretence of Want either felt or feared.

Navigation was now brought nearer to Perfection. The *Portugueze* claim the Honour of many Inventions by which the Sailor is assisted, and which enable him to leave Sight of Land, and commit himself to the boundless Ocean. *Diaz* had Orders to proceed beyond the *River Zaire*, where *Diego Can* had stopped, to build Monuments of his Discoveries, and to leave upon the Coasts Negroe Men and Women well instructed, who might Enquire after *Prester John*, and fill the Natives with Reverence for the *Portuguese*.

Diaz

Diaz with much Oppofition from his Crew, whofe Mutinies he repreffed partly by Softnefs and partly by Steadinefs, failed on till he reached the utmoft Point of *Africa*, which from the bad Weather that he met there, he called *Cabo Tormentofo*, or *The Cape of Storms*. He would have gone forward, but his Crew forced him to return. In his Way he met the Victualler, from which he had been parted nine Months before: of the nine Men which were in it at the Separation, fix had been killed by the Negroes, and of the three remaining, one died for Joy at the Sight of his Friends. *Diaz* returned to *Lifbon* in *December* 1487, and gave an Account of his Voyage to the King, who ordered the *Cape of Storms* to be called thenceforward *Cabo de buena Efperanza*, or *The Cape of Good Hope*.

Some Time before the Expedition of *Diaz*, the River *Zaire* and the Kingdom of *Congo* had been difcovered by *Diego Can*, who found a Nation of Negroes who fpoke a Language which thofe that were in his Ships could not underftand. He landed, and the Natives whom he expected to fly like the other Inhabitants of the Coaft, met them with Confidence, and treated them with Kindnefs; but *Diego*, finding that they could not underftand each other, feized fome of their Chiefs, and carried them to *Portugal*, leaving fome of his own People in their Room to learn the Language of *Congo*.

The Negroes were foon pacificed, and the *Portuguefe* left to their Mercy were well treated, and as they by Degrees grew able to make themfelves underftood, recommended themfelves, their Nation, and their Religion. The King of *Portugal* fent *Diego* back in a very fhort Time with the Negroes whom he had forced away; and when they were fet fafe on Shore, the King of *Congo* conceived fo

much

much Efteem for *Diego*, that he fent one of thofe who had returned, back again in his Ship to *Lifbon*, with two young Men difpatched as Ambaffadors, to defire Inftructors to be fent for the Converfion of his Kingdom.

The Ambaffadors were honourably received, and baptized with great Pomp, and a Fleet was immediately fitted out for *Congo*, under the Command of *Gonfalvo Sorza*, who dying in his Paffage, was fucceeded in Authority by his Nephew *Roderigo*.

When they came to Land, the King's Uncle, who commanded the Province, immediately requefted to be folemnly initiated in the Chriftian Religion, which was granted to him and his young Son, on *Eafter* Day 1491. The Father was named *Manuel*, and the Son *Antonio*. Soon afterward the King, Queen, and eldeft Prince received at the Font, the Names of *John*, *Eleanor*, and *Alphonfo*; and a War breaking out, the whole Army was admitted to the Rites of Chriftianity, and then fent againft the Enemy. They returned victorious, but foon forgot their Faith, and formed a Confpiracy to reftore Paganifm; a powerful Oppofition was raifed by Infidels and Apoftates, headed by one of the King's younger Sons; and the Miffionaries had been deftroyed had not *Alphonfo* pleaded for them and for Chriftianity.

The Enemies of Religion now became the Enemies of *Alphonfo*, whom they accufed to his Father of Difloyalty. His Mother, the Queen *Eleanor*, gained Time by one Artifice after another, till the King was calmed; he then heard the Caufe again, declared his Son innocent, and punifhed his Accufers with Death.

The King died foon after, and the Throne was difputed by *Alphonfo*, fupported by the Chriftians, and *Aquitimo* his Brother, followed by the Infidels.

Infidels. A Battle was fought, *Aquitino* was taken and put to Death, and Chriſtianity was for a Time eſtabliſhed at *Congo*: but the Nation has relapſed into its former Follies.

Such was the State of the *Portugueze* Navigation, when in 1492, *Columbus* made the daring and proſperous Voyage, which gave a new World to *European* Curioſity and *European* Cruelty. He had offered his Propoſal, and declared his Expectations to King *John* of *Portugal*, who had ſlighted him as a fanciful and raſh Projector, that promiſed what he had no reaſonable Hopes to perform. *Columbus* had ſolicited other Princes, and had been repulſed with the ſame Indignity; at laſt *Iſabella* of *Arragon*, furniſhed him with ſhips, and having found *America*, he entered the Mouth of the *Tagus* in his Return, and ſhewed the Natives of the new Country. When he was admitted to the King's Preſence, he acted and talked with ſo much Haughtineſs, and reflected on the Neglect which he had undergone with ſo much Acrimony, that the Courtiers who ſaw their Prince inſulted, offered to deſtroy him; but the King who knew that he deſerved the Reproaches that had been uſed, and who now ſincerely regretted his Incredulity, would ſuffer no Violence to be offered him, but diſmiſſed him with Preſents and with Honours.

The *Portugueze* and *Spaniards* became now jealous of each others Claim to Countries, which neither had yet ſeen; and the Pope, to whom they appealed, divided the new World between them by a Line drawn from North to South, a hunrded Leagues weſtward from *Cape Verd* and the *Azores*, giving all that lies weſt from that Line to the *Spaniards*, and all that lies eaſt to the *Portugueze*. This was no very ſatisfactory Diviſion, for the eaſt and weſt muſt meet at laſt, but that Time was then at great Diſtance.

According

According to this Grant, the *Portuguese* continued their Discoveries eastward, and became Masters of much of the Coast both of *Africa* and the *Indies*, but they seized much more than they could occupy, and while they were under the Dominion of *Spain*, lost the greater Part of their *Indian* Territories.

A DIS-

A

DISSERTATION

ON THE

EPITAPHS

WRITTEN BY POPE.

EVERY Art is beft taught by Example. Nothing contributes more to the Cultivation of
Propriety than Remarks on the Works of thofe who
have moft excelled. I fhall therefore endeavour, at
this Vifit, to entertain the young Students in Poetry,
with an Examination of *Pope's* Epitaphs.

To define an Epitaph is ufelefs ; every one knows
that it is an Infcription on a Tomb. An Epitaph,
therefore, implies no particular Character of Writing, but may be compofed in Verfe or Profe. It is
indeed commonly Panegyrical ; becaufe we are feldom
diftinguifhed with a Stone, but by our Friends;
but it has no Rule to reftrain or modify it, except
this, that it ought not to be longer than common
Beholders may be expected to have Leifure and Patience to perufe.

I.

On CHARLES *Earl of* DORSET, *in the Church of*
Wythyham *in* Suffex.

' *DORSET*, the Grace of Courts, the Mufes Pride,
' Patron of Arts, and Judge of Nature, dy'd.

' The

' The Scourge of Pride, tho' fanctify'd or great,
' Of Fops in Learning, and of Knaves in State ;
' Yet foft his Nature, tho' fevere his Lay,
' His Anger moral, and his Wifdom gay.
' Bleft Satyrift ! who touch'd the Mean fo true,
' As fhow'd, Vice had his Hate and Pity too.
' Bleft Courtier ! who could King and Country pleafe,
' Yet facred keep his Friendfhips, and his Eafe.
' Bleft Peer ! his great Forefathers ev'ry Grace
' Reflecting, and reflected on his Race ;
' Where other *Buckhurfts*, other *Dorfets* fhine,
' And Patriots ftill, or Poets, deck the Line.'

The firft Diftich of this Epitaph contains a Kind of Information which few would want, that the Man, for whom the Tomb was erected, *died.* There are indeed fome Qualities worthy of Praife afcribed to the Dead, but none that were likely to exempt him from the Lot of Man, or incline us much to wonder that he fhould die. What is meant by *Judge of Nature*, is not eafy to fay. Nature is not the Object of human Judgment, for it is vain to judge where we cannot alter. If by Nature is meant, what is commonly called *Nature* by the Criticks, a juft Reprefentation of Things really exifting and Actions really performed, Nature cannot be properly oppofed to *Art* ; Nature being, in this Senfe, only the beft Effect of *Art*.

The Scourge of Pride———

Of this Couplet, the fecond Line is not, what is intended, an Illuftration of the former. Pride, in the Great, is indeed well enough connected with Knaves in State, though Knaves is a Word rather too ludicrous and light ; but the mention of *fanctified* Pride will not lead the Thoughts to *Fops in Learning*, but rather to fome Species of Tyranny or Oppreffion, fomething more gloomy and more formidable than Foppery.

Yet soft his Nature——

This is a high Compliment, but was not first bestowed on *Dorset* by *Pope.* The next Verse is extremely beautiful.

Blest Satyrist !——

In this Distich is another Line of which *Pope* was not the Authour. I do not mean to blame these Imitations with much Harshness ; in long Performances they are scarcely to be avoided, and in slender they may be indulged, because the Train of the Composition may naturally involve them, or the Scantiness of the Subject allow little Choice. However, what is borrowed is not to be enjoyed as our own, and it is the Business of critical Justice to give every Bird of the Muses his proper Feather.

Blest Courtier !——

Whether a Courtier can be properly commended for keeping his *Ease sacred* may perhaps be disputable. To please King and Country, without sacrificing Friendship to any Change of Times, was a very uncommon Instance of Prudence or Felicity, and deserved to be kept separate from so poor a Commendation as Care of this Ease. I wish our Poets would attend a little more accurately to the Use of the Word *sacred,* which surely should never be applied in a serious Composition, but where some Reference may be made to a higher Being, or where some Duty is exacted or implied. A man may keep his Friendship *sacred,* because Promises of Friendship are very awful Ties ; but methinks he cannot, but in a burlesque Sense, be said to keep his Ease *sacred.*

Blest Peer !——

The Blessing ascribed to the *Peer* has no Connection with his Peerage ; they might happen to any other Man, whose Ancestors were remembered, or whose Posterity were likely to be regarded.

I know not whether this Epitaph be worthy either of the Writer, or of the Man entombed.

II. *On*

II.

On Sir WILLIAM TRUMBUL, *One of the Principal Secretaries of State to King* WILLIAM III. *who having refigned his Place, died in his Retirement at* Eafthamfted, *in* Berkfhire, 1716.

' A pleafing Form, a firm, yet cautious Mind,
' Sincere, tho' prudent ; conftant, yet refign'd ;
' Honour unchang'd, a Principle profeft,
' Fix'd to one Side, but mod'rate to the reft :
' An honeft Courtier, yet a Patriot too,
' Juft to his Prince, and to his Country true.
' Fill'd with the Senfe of Age, the Fire of Youth,
' A Scorn of Wrangling, yet a Zeal for Truth ;
' A gen'rous Faith, from Superftition free ;
' A Love to Peace, and Hate of Tyranny ;
' Such this Man was ; who now, from Earth remov'd,
' At length enjoys that Liberty he lov'd.

In this Epitaph, as in many others, there appears, at the firft View, a Fault which I think fcarcely any Beauty can compenfate. The Name is omitted. The End of an Epitaph is to convey fome Account of the Dead, and to what Purpofe is any Thing told of him whofe Name is concealed? An Epitaph, and a Hiftory, of a namelefs Hero, are equally abfurd, fince the Virtues and Qualities fo recounted in either, are fcattered at the Mercy of Fortune to be appropriated by Guefs. The Name, it is true, may be read upon the Stone, but what Obligation has it to the Poet, whofe Verfes wander over the Earth, and leave their Subject behind them, and who is forced, like an unfkilful Painter, to make his Purpofe known by adventitious Help?

This Epitaph is wholly without Elevation, and contains nothing ftriking or particular ; but the Poet is not to be blamed for the Defects of his Subject. He faid perhaps the beft that could be faid.   There

are however fome Defects which were not made neceffary by the Character in which he was employed.
There is no Oppofition between an *honeft Courtier*
and a *Patriot*, for an *honeft Courtier* cannot but be a
Patriot.

It was unfuitable to the Nicety required in fhort
Compofitions, to clofe his Verfe with the Word *too*;
every Rhyme fhould be a Word of Emphafis, nor
can this Rule be fafely neglected, except where the
Length of the Poem makes flight Inaccuracies ex-
cufable, or allows Room for Beauties fufficient to
overpower the Effects of petty Faults.

At the Beginning of the feventh Line the Word
filled is weak and profaic, having no particular Adaptation to any of the Words that follow it.

The Thought in the laft Line is Impertinent,
having no Connection with the foregoing Character,
nor with the Condition of the Man defcribed.   Had
the Epitaph been written on the poor Confpirator
who died lately in Prifon, after a Confinement of
more than forty Years, without any Crime proved
againft him, the Sentiment had been juft and pathe-
tical ; but why fhould *Trumbul* be congratulated upon his Liberty, who had never known Reftraint ?

III.

On the Hon. SIMON HARCOURT, *only Son of the Lord
Chancellor* HARCOURT ; *at the Church of* Stanton-
Harcourt *in* Oxfordfhire, 1720.

‘ To this fad Shrine, whoe’er thou art ! draw near,
‘ Here lies the Friend moft lov’d, the Son moft dear :
‘ Who ne’er knew Joy, but Friendfhip might divide,
‘ Or gave his Father Grief but when he dy’d.
    ‘ How vain is Reafon, Eloquence how weak !
‘ If *Pope* muft tell what *Harcourt* cannot fpeak.
‘ Oh, let thy once-lov’d Friend infcribe thy Stone,
‘ And, with a Father’s Sorrows, mix his own !’

This

This Epitaph is principally remarkable for the artful Introduction of the Name, which is inserted with a peculiar Felicity, to which Chance must concur with Genius, which no Man can hope to attain twice; and which cannot be copied but with servile Imitation.

I cannot but wish that, of this Inscription, the two last Lines had been omitted, as they take away from the Energy what they do not add to the Sense.

IV.

On JAMES CRAGGS, *Esq. in* Westminster-Abbey.

'JACOBUS CRAGGS,
'REGI MAGNÆ BRITANNIÆ A SECRETIS
'ET CONSILIIS SANCTIORIBUS,
'PRINCIPIS PARITER AC POPULI AMOR ET
DELICIÆ:
'VIXIT TITULIS ET INVIDIA MAJOR,
'ANNOS HEU PAUCOS, XXXV.
'OB. FEB. XVI. MDCCXX.'

'Statesman, yet Friend to Truth! of Soul sincere,
'In Action faithful, and in Honour clear!
'Who broke no Promise, serv'd no private End,
'Who gain'd no Title, and who lost no Friend,
'Ennobled by himself, by all approv'd,
'Prais'd, wept, and honour'd, by the Muse he lov'd.'

The Lines on *Craggs* were not originally intended for an Epitaph; and therefore some Faults are to be imputed to the Violence with which they are torn from the Poem that first contained them. We may, however, observe some Defects. There is a Redundancy of Words in the first Couplet: It is superfluous to tell of him, who was *sincere, true,* and *faithful,* that he was *in honour clear.*

There seems to be an Opposition intended in the fourth Line, which is not very obvious: Where is

the

the Wonder, that he who *gained no Title*, should *lose no Friend?*

It may be proper here to remark the Abfurdity of joining, in the fame Infcription, *Latin* and *Englifh*, or Verfe and Profe. If either Language be preferable to the other, let that only be ufed: For no Reafon can be given why Part of the Information fhould be given in one Tongue, and Part in another, on a Tomb, more than in any other Place, on any other Occafion; and to tell all that can be conveniently told in Verfe, and then to call in the Help of Profe, has always the Appearance of a very artlefs Expedient, or of an Attempt unaccomplifhed. Such an Epitaph refembles the Converfation of a Foreigner, who tells Part of his Meaning by Words, and conveys Part by Signs.

V.

Intended for Mr. ROWE. *In* Weftminfter-Abbey.

‘ Thy Reliques, *Rowe*, to this fair Urn we truft,
‘ And facred, place by *Dryden*'s awful Duft:
‘ Beneath a rude and namelefs Stone he lies,
‘ To which thy Tomb fhall guide inquiring Eyes.
‘ Peace to thy gentle Shade, and endlefs Reft;
‘ Bleft in thy Genius, in thy Love too bleft!
‘ One grateful Woman to thy Fame fupplies
♦ What a whole Thanklefs Land to his denies.’

Of this Infcription the chief Fault is, that it belongs lefs to *Rowe*, for whom it was written, than to *Dryden*, who was buried near him; and indeed gives very little Information concerning either.

To wifh, *Peace to thy Shade*, is too mythological to be admitted into a Chriftian Temple: The ancient Worfhip has infected almoft all our other Compofitions, and might therefore be contented to fpare our Epitaphs. Let Fiction, at leaft, ceafe with Life, and let us be ferious over the Grave.

3

VI. *On*

VI.

On Mrs. CORBET, *who died of a Cancer in her Breast.*

' Here rests a Woman, good without Pretence,
' Blest with plain Reason, and with sober Sense:
' No Conquests She, but o'er herself desir'd ;
' No Arts essay'd, but not to be admir'd.
' Passion and Pride were to her Soul unknown,
' Convinc'd that Virtue only is our own.
' So unaffected, so compos'd a Mind,
' So firm, yet soft, so strong, yet so refin'd,
' Heav'n, as its purest Gold, by Tortures try'd,
' The Saint sustain'd it, but the Woman dy'd.

I have always considered this as the most valuable
of all *Pope's* Epitaphs ; the Subject of it is a Character not discriminated by any shining or eminent
Peculiarities ; yet that which really makes, though
not the Splendor, the Felicity of Life, and that which
every wise Man will choose for his final and lasting
Companion in the Languor of Age, in the Quiet of
Privacy, when he departs weary and disgusted from
the Ostentatious, the Volatile, and the Vain. Of
such a Character, which the Dull overlook, and the
Gay despise, it was fit that the Value should be made
known, and the Dignity established. Domestic Virtue, as it is exerted without great Occasions, or conspicuous Consequences, in an even unnoted Tenor,
required the Genius of *Pope* to display it in such a
Manner as might attract Regard, and enforce Reverence. Who can forbear to lament that this amiable
Woman has no Name in the Verses?

If the particular Lines of this Inscription be examined, it will appear less faulty than the rest. There
is scarce one Line taken from Common Places, unless
it be that in which *only Virtue* is said to be *our own.*
I once heard a Lady of great Beauty and Elegance
object to the fourth Line, that it contained an unna-

tural

tural and incredible Panegyrick. Of this let the
Ladies judge.

VII.

On the Monument of the Hon. ROBERT DIGBY,
and of his Sifter Mary, *erected by their Father the*
Lord DIGBY, *in the Church of* Sherborne *in Dor-*
fetfhire, 1727.

  ' Go! fair Example of untainted Youth,
' Of modeft Wifdom, and pacifick Truth:
' Compos'd in Suff'rings, and in Joy fedate,
' Good without Noife, without Pretenfion great.
' Juft of thy Word, in ev'ry Thought fincere,
' Who knew no Wifh but what the World might hear:
' Of fofteft Manners, unaffected Mind,
' Lover of Peace, and Friend of human Kind:
' Go, live! for Heav'n's eternal Year is thine,
' Go, and exalt thy Moral to Divine.
  ' And thou, bleft Maid! Attendant on his Doom,
' Penfive haft follow'd to the filent Tomb,
' Steer'd the fame Courfe to the fame quiet Shore,
' Not parted long, and now to part no more!
' Go, then, where only Blifs fincere is known!
' Go, where to love and to enjoy are one!
  ' Yet take thefe Tears, Mortality's Relief,
' And till we fhare your Joys, forgive our Grief:
' Thefe little Rites, a Stone, a Verfe receive,
' 'Tis all a Father, all a Friend can give!'

  This Epitaph contains of the Brother, only a
general indifcriminate Character, and of the Sifter
tells nothing, but that fhe died. The Difficulty in
writing Epitaphs is to give a particular and appropriate Praife. This, however, is not always to be
performed, whatever be the Diligence or Ability
of the Writer; for the greater Part of Mankind
have no Character at all, have little that diftinguifhes
them from others equally good or bad, and therefore
                          nothing

nothing can be faid of them which may not be applied with equal Propriety to a thoufand more. It
is indeed no great Panegyrick, that there is inclofed
in this Tomb one who was born in one Year, and
died in another ; yet many ufeful and amiable Lives
have been fpent which yet leave little Materials for
any other Memorial. Thefe are however not the
proper Subjeĉts of Poetry ; and whenever Friendfhip, or any other Motive, obliges a Poet to write
on fuch Subjeĉts, he muft be forgiven if he fometimes wanders in Generalities, and utters the fame
Praifes over different Tombs.

The Scantinefs of human Praifes can fcarcely be
made more apparent, than by remarking how often
Pope has, in the few *Epitaphs* which he compofed,
found it neceffary to borrow from himfelf. The fourteen *Epitaphs*, which he has written, comprife about an
hundred and forty Lines, in which there are more
Repetitions than will eafily be found in all the reft
of his Works. In the eight Lines which make the
Charaĉter of *Digby*, there is fcarce any Thought,
or Word, which may not be found in the other
Epitaphs.

The ninth Line, which is far the ftrongeft and
moft elegant, is borrowed. The Conclufion is the
fame with that on *Harcourt*, but is here more elegant and better connecĺed.

VIII.

On Sir GODFREY KNELLER. *In* Weftminfter-
Abbey, 1723.

' KNELLER, by Heav'n, and not a Mafter taught,
' Whofe Art was Nature, and whofe Piĉtures
   ' thought ;
' Now for two Ages, having fnatch'd from Fate
' Whate'er was beauteous, or whate'er was great,
' Lies crown'd with Princes Honours, Poets Lays,
' Due to his Merit, and brave Thirft of Praife.
        ' Living,

‘ Living, great Nature fear'd he might outvie
‘ Her Works ; and, dying fears herself may die.’

Of this Epitaph the first Couplet is good, the second not bad, the third is deformed with a broken Metaphor, the Word *crowned* not being applicable to the *Honours* or the *Lays*, and the fourth wants grammatical Construction, the Word *dying* being no Substantive.

IX.

On General HENRY WITHERS. *In* Westminster-Abbey, 1729.

‘ Here, *WITHERS*, rest! thou bravest, gentlest
‘ Mind,
‘ Thy Country's Friend, but more of human Kind,
‘ O! born to Arms! O! Worth in Youth approv'd!
‘ O! soft Humanity in Age belov'd!
‘ For thee the hardy Vet'ran drops a Tear,
‘ And the gay Courtier feels the Sigh sincere.
‘ *WITHERS*, adieu! yet not with thee remove
‘ Thy martial Spirit, or thy social Love!
‘ Amidst Corruption, Luxury, and Rage,
‘ Still leave some ancient Virtues to our Age:
‘ Nor let us say, (those *English* Glories gone)
‘ The last true *Briton* lies beneath this Stone.’

The Epitaph on *Withers* affords another Instance of Common Places, though somewhat diversified, by mingled Qualities, and the Peculiarity of a Profession.

The second Couplet is abrupt, general, and unpleasing; Exclamation seldom succeeds in our Language; and, I think it may be observed, that the Particle O! used at the Beginning of a Sentence, always offends.

The third Couplet is more happy; the Value express'd for him, by different Sorts of Men, raises him

him to Efteem ; there is yet fomething of the common Cant of fuperficial Satirifts, who fuppofe that the Infincerity of a Courtier deftroys all his Senfations, and that he is equally a Diffembler to the Living and the Dead.

At the third Couplet I fhould wifh the *Epitaph* to clofe, but that I fhould be unwilling to lofe the two next Lines, which yet are dearly bought if they cannot be retained without the four that follow them.

X.

On Mr. ELIJAH FENTON. *At* Eafthamfted *in* Berkfhire, 1730.

' This modeft Stone, what few vain Marbles can,
' May truly fay, Here lies an honeft Man :
' A Poet, bleft beyond the Poet's Fate,
' Whom heav'n kept facred from the Proud and Great:
• Foe to loud Praife, and Friend to learned Eafe,
' Content with Science in the Vale of Peace.
' Calmly he look'd on either Life, and here
' Saw nothing to regret, or there to fear ;
' From Nature's temp'rate Feaft rofe fatisfy'd,
' Thank'd Heav'n that he had liv'd, and that he dy'd.,

The firft Couplet of this Epitaph is borrowed. The four next Lines contain a Species of Praife peculiar, original, and juft. Here, therefore, the Infcription fhould have ended, the latter Part containing nothing but what is common to every Man who is wife and good. The Character of *Fenton* was fo amiable, that I cannot forbear to wifh' for fome Poet or Biographer to difplay it more fully for the Advantage of Pofterity. If he did not ftand in the firft Rank of Genius he may claim a Place in the fecond ; and, whatever Criticifm may object to his Writings, Cenfure could find very little to blame in his Life.

XI. *On*

XI.

On Mr. GAY. *In* Weſtminſter-Abbey, 1732.

' Of Manners gentle, of Affections mild;
' In Wit, a Man; Simplicity, a Child:
' With native Humour temp'ring virtuous Rage,
' F rm'd to delight at once and laſh the Age:
' Above Temptation, in a low Eſtate,
' And uncorrupted, even among the Great:
' A ſafe Companion, and an eaſy Friend,
' Unblam'd thro' Life, lamented in thy End.
' Theſe are thy Honours! not that here thy Buſt
' Is mix'd with Heroes, or with Kings thy Duſt;
' But that the Worthy and the Good ſhall ſay,
' Striking their penſive Boſoms—*Here lies* GAY.'

As *Gay* was the Favourite of our Authour, this Epitaph was probably written with an uncommon Degree of Attention; yet it is not more happily executed than the reſt, for it does not always happen that the Succeſs of a Poet is proportionate to his Labour. The ſame Obſervation may be extended to all Works of Imagination, which are often influenced by Cauſes wholly out of the Performer's Power, by Hints of which he perceives not the Origin, by ſudden Elevations of Mind which he cannot produce in himſelf, and which ſometimes riſe when he expects them leaſt.

The two Parts of the firſt Line are only Echoes of each other, *gentle Manners* and *mild Affections*, if they mean any Thing, muſt mean the ſame.

That *Gay* was a *Man in Wit* is a very frigid Commendation; to have the Wit of a Man is not much for a Poet. The *Wit of Man*, and the *Simplicity of a Child*, make a poor and vulgar Contraſt, and raiſe no Ideas of Excellence, either Intellectual or Moral.

In the next Couplet *Rage* is leſs properly introduced after the Mention of *Mildneſs* and *Gentleneſs*,

which

which are made the Conſtituents of his Charaѐer,
for a Man ſo *mild* and *gentle* to *temper* his *Rage* was
not difficult.

The next Line is unharmonious in its Sound,
and mean in its Conception, the Oppoſition is obvious, and the Word *laſh* uſed abſolutely, and without any Modification, is groſs and improper.

To be *above Temptation* in Poverty, and *free from
Corruption among the Great*, is indeed ſuch a Peculiarity as deſerved Notice. But to be a *ſafe Companion* is Praiſe merely negative, ariſing not from the
Poſſeſſion of Virtue, but the Abſence of a Vice, and
that one of the moſt odious.

As little can be added to his Charaѐer, by aſſert-
ing that he was *lamented in his End*. Every Man
that dies is at leaſt, by the Writer of his Epitaph,
ſuppoſed to be lamented, and therefore this general
Lamentation does no Honour to *Gay*.

The eight firſt Lines have no Grammar, the Ad-
jeѐives are without any Subſtantive, and the Epithets without a Subjeѐ.

The Thought in the laſt Line, that *Gay* is buried
in the Boſoms of the *Worthy* and the *Good*, who are
diſtinguiſhed only to lengthen the Line, is ſo dark
that few underſtand it; and ſo harſh, when it is explained, that ſtill fewer approve.

XII.

Intended for Sir Isaac Newton. *In* Weſtminſter-
Abbey.

'ISAACUS NEWTONIUS:
' Quem Immortalem
' Teſtantur, *Tempus, Natura, Cœlum:*
' Mortalem
' Hoc marmor fatetur.

' Nature, and Nature's Laws, lay hid in Night:
' God ſaid, *Let Newton be!* And all was Light.'

Of

Of this Epitaph, fhort as it is, the Faults feem not to be very few, Why Part fhould be *Latin* and Part *English*, it is not eafy to difcover. In the *Latin*, the Oppofition of *Immortalis* and *Mortalis*, is a mere Sound, or a mere Quibble, he is not *Immortal* in any Senfe contrary to that in which he is *Mortal*.

In the Verfes the Thought is obvious, and the Words *Night* and *Light* are too nearly allied.

XIII.

On EDMUND *Duke of* Buckingham, *who died in the* 19*th Year of his Age*, 1735.

. ‘ If modeft Youth, with cool Reflection crown'd,
‘ And ev'ry opening Virtue blooming round,
‘ Could fave a Parent's juftft Pride from **Fate,**
‘ Or add one Patriot to a finking State ;
‘ This weeping Marble had **not** afk'd thy Tear,
‘ Or fadly told, how many Hopes lie here !
‘ The living Virtue now had fhone approv'd,
‘ The Senate heard him, and his Country lov'd.
‘ Yet fofter Honours, and lefs noify Fame
‘ Attend the Shade of gentle *Buckingham :*
‘ In whom a Race, for Courage fam'd and **Art,**
‘ Ends in the milder Merit of the Heart ;
‘ And Chiefs or Sages long to *Britain* giv'n,
‘ Pays the laft Tribute of a Saint to Heav'n.’

This Epitaph Mr. *Warburton* prefers to the reft, but I know not for what Reafon. To *Crown* with *Reflection* is furely a Mode of Speech approaching to Nonfenfe. *Opening Virtues blooming round*, is fomething like Tautology ; the fix following Lines are Poor and Profaic. *Art* is in another Couplet ufed for *Arts*, that a Rhyme may be had to *Heart*. The fix laft Lines are the beft, but not excellent.

The

The reft of his fepulchral Performances hardly
deferve the Notice of Criticifm.   The contemptible
Dialogue between HE and SHE, fhould have been
fuppreffed for the Author's Sake.

In his laft Epitaph on himfelf, in which he attempts to be jocular upon one of the few Things
that make wife Men ferious, he confounds the living
Man with the Dead:

' Under this Stone, or under this Sill,
' Or under this Turf, &c.'

When a Man is once buried, the Queftion, under what he is buried, is eafily decided.   He forgot
that though he wrote the Epitaph in a State of Uncertainty, yet it could not be laid over him till his
Grave was made.   Such is the Folly of Wit when
it is ill employed.

THE

THE

L I F E

OF THAT

EMINENT PHYSICIAN

HERMAN BOERHAAVE.

HERMAN BOERHAAVE was born on the laſt Day of *December*, 1668, about One in the Morning, at *Voorhout*, a Village two Miles diſtant from *Leyden*. His Father, *James Boerhaave*, was Miniſter of *Voorhout*, of whom his Son, in a ſmall Account of his own Life, has given a very amiable Character, for the Simplicity and Openneſs of his Behaviour, for his exact Frugality, in the Management of a narrow Fortune, and the Prudence, Tenderneſs, and Diligence with which he educated a numerous Family of nine Children. He was eminently ſkilled in Hiſtory and Genealogy, and well verſed in the *Latin*, *Greek*, and *Hebrew* Languages.

His Mother was *Hagar Daelder*, a Tradeſman's Daughter of *Amſterdam*, from whom he might perhaps derive an hereditary Inclination to the Study of Phyſic; in which ſhe was very inquiſitive, and had obtained a Knowledge of it, not common in female Students.

This Knowledge, however, ſhe did not live to communicate to her Son; for ſhe died in 1673, ten Years after her Marriage.

His Father finding himſelf incumbered with the Care of ſeven Children, thought it neceſſary to take

a ſecond

a fecond Wife, and in *July*, 1674, was married to *Eve du Bois*, Daughter of a Minifter of *Leyden*, who, by her prudent and impartial Conduct, fo endeared herfelf to her Hufband's Children, that they all regarded her as their own Mother.

Herman Boerhaave was always defigned by his Father for the Miniftry, and with that View inftructed by him in grammatical Learning, and the firft Elements of Languages ; in which he made fuch a Proficiency, that he was, at the Age of eleven Years, not only Mafter of the Rules of Grammar, but capable of tranflating, with tolerable Accuracy ; and not wholly ignorant of critical Niceties.

At Intervals, to recreate his Mind, and ftrengthen his Conftitution, it was his Father's Cuftom to fend him into the Fields, and employ him in Agriculture, and fuch Kind of rural Occupations, which he continued through all his Life to love and practife ; and by this Viciffitude of Study and Exercife, preferved himfelf, in a great Meafure, from thofe Diftempers and Depreffions, which are frequently the Confequences of indifcreet Diligence, and uninterrupted Application ; and from which Students, not well acquainted with the Conftitution of the human Body, fometimes fly for Relief to Wine, inftead of Exercife, and purchafe temporary Eafe, at the Hazard of chronical Diftempers.

The Studies of young *Boerhaave* were about this Time interrupted by an Accident, which deferves a particular Mention, as it firft inclined him to that Science, to which he was by Nature fo well adapted, and which he afterwards carried to fo great Perfection.

In the twelfth Year of his Age a ftubborn painful, and malignant Ulcer hroke out upon his left Thigh, which, for near five Years, defeated all the Art of the Surgeons and Phyficians, and not only afflicted him with the moft excruciating Pains, but expofed him to fuch fharp and tormenting Applications, that the Difeafe and Remedies were equally infufferable. Then it was that his own Anguifh taught him to compaffionate that of others; and his Experience of the Ineflicacy of the Methods then in Ufe, incited him to attempt the Difcovery of others more certain.

He began to practife at leaft honeftly, for he began upon himfelf, and his firft Eflay was a Prelude to his future Succefs; for having laid afide all the Prefcriptions of his Phyficians, and all the Applications of his Surgeons, he at laft, by fomenting the Part with Salt and Urine, effected a Cure.

That he might on this Occafion obtain the Affiftance of Surgeons with lefs Inconvenience and Expence, he was brought by his Father, at Fourteen, to *Leyden*, and placed in the fourth Clafs of the public School, after having been examined by the Mafter: Here his Application and Abilities were equally confpicuous. In fix Months, by gaining the firft Prize in the fourth Clafs, he was raifed to the Fifth; and in fix Months more, upon the fame Proof of the Superiority of his Genius, rewarded with another Prize, and tranflated to the Sixth; from whence it is ufual, in fix Months more, to be removed to the Univerfity.

Thus did our young Student advance in Learning and Reputation, when, as he was within View of the Univerfity, a fudden and unexpected Blow threatened to defeat all his Expectations.

On the 12th of *November*, 1682, his Father died, and left behind him a very flender Provifion for his Widow and nine Children, of which the Eldeft was not feventeen Years old.

This was a moft afflicting Lofs to the young Scholar, whofe Fortune was by no means fufficient to bear the Expences of a learned Education, and who therefore now feemed to be fummoned by Ne-

I   ceffity

ceffity, to fome Way of Life more immediately and certainly lucrative ; but with a Refolution equal to his Abilities, and a Spirit not to be depreffed or fhaken, he determined to break through the Obfta-cles of Poverty, and fupply by Diligence the Want of Fortune.

He therefore afked and obtained the Confent of his Guardian, to profecute his Studies as long as his Patrimony would fupport him ; and, continuing his wonted Induftry, gained another Prize.

He was now to quit the School for the Univer-fity ; but, on Account of the Weaknefs yet remain-ing in his Thigh, was, at his own Intreaty, conti-nued fix Months longer, under the Care of his Maf-ter the learned Wynfchoton, where he once more was honoured with the Prize.

At his Removal to the Univerfity, the fame Ge-nius and Induftry met with the fame Encouragement and Applaufe. The learned *Triglandius*, one of his Father's Friends, made foon after Profeffor of Divi-nity of *Leyden*, diftinguifhed him in a particular Manner, and recommended him to the Friendfhip of Mr. *Van Apphen*, in whom he found a generous and conftant Patron.

He became now a diligent Hearer of the moft cele-brated Profeffors, and made great Advances in all the Sciences, ftill regulating his Studies with a View principally to Divinity, for which he was originally intended by his Father ; and for that Reafon he ex-erted his utmoft Application to attain an exact Know-ledge of the Hebrew Tongue.

Being convinced of the Neceffity of mathematical Learning, he began to ftudy thofe Sciences in 1687, but without that intenfe Induftry with which the Pleafure he found in that Kind of Knowledge in-duced him afterwards to cultivate them.

In 1690, having performed the Exercifes of the Univerfity with uncommon Reputation, he took his

Degree

Degree in Philofophy ; and on that Occafion difcuffed
the important and arduous Queftion of the diftinct
Natures of the Soul and Body, with fuch Accuracy,
Perfpicuity, and Subtilty, that he entirely confuted
all the Sophiftry of *Epicurus*, *Hobbes*, and *Spinofa*,
and equally raifed the Character of his Piety and
Erudition.

Divinity was ftill his great Employment, and the
chief Aim of all his Studies. He read the Scriptures
in their original Languages ; and when Difficulties
occurred, confulted the Interpretations of the moft
ancient Fathers, whom he read in order of Time,
beginning with *Clemens Romanus.*

In the Perufal of thofe early Writers, he was ftruck
with the profoundeft Veneration for the Simplicity
and Purity of their Doctrine, the Holinefs of their
Lives, and the Sanctity of the Difcipline practifed
by them ; but as he defcended to the lower Ages, he
found the Peace of Chriftianity broken by ufelefs
Controverfics, and its Doctrines fophifticated by the
Subtilties of the Schools. He found the Holy Writers interpreted according to the Notions of Philofophers, and the Chimeras of Metaphyficians adopted
as Articles of Faith. He found Difficulties raifed by
idle Curiofity, and fomented to Bitternefs and Ran-
cour. He faw the Simplicity of the Chriftian Doctrine corrupted by the private Notions of particular
Parties, of which each adhered to its own Philofophy,
and Orthodoxy was confined to the Sect in Power.

Having now exhaufted his Fortune in the Purfuit
of his Studies, he found the Neceffity of applying to
fome Profeffion, that, without engroffing all his
Time, might enable him to fupport himfelf: and
having obtained a very uncommon Knowledge of the
Mathematicks, he read Lectures in thofe Sciences to
a felect Number of young Gentlemen in the Univerfity.

At

At length his Propenfion to the Study of Phyfic grew too violent to be refifted ; and though he ftill intended to make Divinity the great Employment of his Life, he could not deny himfelf the Satisfaction of fpending fome Time upon the medicinal Writers, for the perufal of which he was fo well qualified by his Acquaintance with the Mathematics and Philofophy.

But this Science correfponded fo much with his natural Genius, that he could not forbear making that his Bufinefs, which he intended only as his Diverfion ; and ftill growing more eager, as he advanced further, he at length determined wholly to mafter that Profeffion, and to take his Degree in Phyfic, before he engaged in the Duties of the Miniftry.

It is, I believe, a very juft Obfervation, that Mens Ambition is generally proportioned to their Capacity. Providence feldom fends any into the World with an Inclination to attempt great Things, who have not Abilities likewife to perform them. To have formed the Defign of gaining a competent Knowledge in Medicine by way of Digreffion from theological Studies, would have been little lefs than Madnefs in moft Men, and would have expofed them to Ridicule and Contempt : But *Boerhaave* was one of thofe mighty Capacities to whom fcarce any Thing appears impoffible, and who think nothing worthy of their Efforts but what appears infurmountable to common Underftandings.

He began this new Courfe of Study by a diligent Perufal of *Verfalius, Bartholine,* and *Fallopius* ; and to acquaint himfelf more fully with the Structure of Bodies, was a conftant Attendant upon *Nuck's* public Diffections in the Theatre, and himfelf very accurately infpected the Bodies of different Animals.

Having furnifhed himfelf with this preparatory Knowledge, he began to read the ancient Phyficians in the Order of Time, purfuing his Inquiries down-

P 3

wards

wards from *Hippocrates* through all the *Greek* and *Latin* Writers.

Finding, as he tells himfelf, that *Hippocrates* was the original Source of all medicinal Knowledge, atid that all the later Writers were little more than Tranfcribers from him, he returned to him with more Attention, and fpent much Time in making Extracts from him, digefting his Treatifes into Method, and fixing them in his Memory.

He then defcended to the Moderns, among whom none engaged him longer, or improved him more, than Sydenham, to whofe Merits he has left this Atteftation ; that he frequently perufed him, and always with greater ragernefs.

His infatiable Curiofity after Knowledge engaged him now in the Practice of Chymiftry, which he profecuted with all the Ardor of a Philofopher, whofe Induftry was not to be wearied, and whofe Love of Truth was too ftrong to fuffer him to acquiefce in the Reports of others.

Yet did he not fuffer one Branch of Science to withdraw his Attention from others ; Anatomy did not withold him from the Profecution of Chymiftry, nor Chymiftry, enchanting as it is, from the Study of Botany. He was not only a careful Examiner of all the Plants in the Garden of the Univerfity, but made Excurfions, for his further Improvement, into the Woods and Fields, and left no Place unvifited where any Increafe of botanical Knowledge could be reafonably hoped for.

In Conjunction with all thefe Enquiries, he ftill purfued his theological Studies ; and ftill, as we are informed by himfelf, propofed, when he had made himfelf Mafter of the whole Art of Phyfic, and obtained the Honor of a Degree in that Science, to petition regularly for a Licence to preach, and to engage in the Cure of Souls ; and intended, in his theological Exercifes, to difcufs this Queftion ; ' Why fo
' many

' many were formerly converted to Chriftianity
' by illiterate Perfons, and fo few at prefent by Men
' of Learning.'

In Purfuance of their Plan he went to *Hardwick*,
in order to take the Degree of Doctor in Phyfic,
which he obtained in *July* 1693, having performed
a public Difputation, *De Utilitate explorandorum ex-
crementorum in Ægris, ut Signorum.*

Then returning to *Leyden* full of his pious Defign
of undertaking the Miniftry, he found, to his Surprize unexpected Obftacles thrown in his Way,
and an Infinuation difperfed through the Univerfity,
that made him fufpected, not of any flight Deviation from received Opinions, not of any pertinacious
Adherence to his own Notions in doubtful and dif-
putable Matters, but of no lefs than Spinofifm; or
in plainer Terms, of Atheifm itfelf.

How fo injurious a Report came to be raifed,
circulated and credited, will be doubtlefs very ea-
gerly inquired, and an exact Relation of the Affair
will not only fatisfy the Curiofity of Mankind, but
fhew that no Merit, however exalted, is exempt
from being not only attacked, but wounded, by
the moft contemptible Whifpers. Thofe who cannot ftrike with Force, can however poifon their
Weapon, and weak as they are give mortal Wounds,
and bring a Hero to the Grave: fo true is that Obfervation, that many are able to do Hurt, but few
to do Good.

This deteftable Calumny owed its Rife to an Incident from which no Confequence of Importance
could be reafonably apprehended. As *Boerhaave*
was fitting in a common Boat, there arofe a Converfation among the Paffengers upon the impious
and pernicious Doctrine of *Spinofa*, which as they
all agreed tends to the utter Overthrow of all Religion. *Boerhaave* fat and filently attended to this
Difcourfe for fome Time, till one of the Company,
willing to diftinguifh himfelf by his Zeal, inftead

P 4   of

of confuting the Pofitions of *Spinofa* by Argument, began to give a Loofe to contumelious Language and virulent Invectives, with which *Boerhaave* was fo little pleafed, that at laft he could not forbear afking him, " Whether he had ever read the Author againft whom he declaimed?"

The Orator not being able to make much Anfwer, was check'd in the Midft of his Invectives, but not without feeling a fecret Refentment againft him who at once interrupted his Harangue and expofed his Ignorance.

This was obferved by a Stranger who was in the Eeat with them: he inquired of his Neighbour the Name of the young Man, whofe Queftion had put an End to the Difcourfe; and having learned it, fet it down in his Pocket Book, as it foon appeared with a malicious Defign; for in a few Days, it was the common Converfation at *Leyden*, that *Boerhaave* had revolted to *Spinofa*.

It was in vain that his Advocates and Friends pleaded his learned and unanfwerable Confutation of all atheiftical Opinions, and particularly of the Syftem of *Spinofa*, in his Difcourfe of the Diftruction between Soul and Body; fuch Calumnies are not eafily fuppreffed, when they are once become general: They are kept alive and fupported by the Malice of bad, and fometimes by the Zeal of good Men: who, though they do not abfolutely believe them, think it yet the fureft Method, to keep not only guilty, but fufpected Men out of public Employments, upon this Principle, that the Safety of many is to be preferred before the Advantage of a few.

Boerhaave finding this formidable Oppofition raifed againft his Pretenfions to ecclefiaftical Honours and Preferments, and even againft his Defign of affuming the Character of a Divine, thought it neither neceffary nor prudent to ftruggle with the Torrent

rent of popular Prejudice, as he was equally qualified for a Profeffion, not indeed of equal Dignity
or Importance, but which muft undoubtedly claim
the facred Place among thofe which are of the
greateft Benefit to Mankind.

He therefore applied himfelf to his medicinal Studies with frefh Ardour and Alacrity, reviewed all his
former Obfervations and Inquiries, and was continually employed in making new Acquifitions.

Having now qualified himfe'f for the Practice of
Phyfic, he began to vifit Patients, but without
that Encouragement which others, not equally deferving, have fometimes met with : His Bufinefs
was at firft not great, and his Circumftances by no
Means eafy ; but, ftill fuperior to any Difcouragement, he continued his Search after Knowledge,
and determined, that Profperity, if ever he was to
enjoy it, fhould be the Confequence, not of mean
Art or difingenuous Solicitations, but of real Merit and folid Learning.

His fteady Adherence to his Refolutions appears
yet more plainly from this Circumftance : He was,
while yet he remained in this unpleafing Situation,
invited by one of the firft Favourites of King
William the Third, to fettle at the *Hague* upon very advantageous Conditions, but declined the Offer:
For having no Ambition but after Knowledge, he
was defirous of living at Liberty, without any Reftraint upon his Looks, his Thoughts, or his
Tongue, and at the utmoft Diftance from all Con-
tentions and ftate Parties. His Time was wholly
taken up in vifiting the Sick, ftudying, making
chymical Experiments, fearching into every Part of
Medicine, with the utmoft Diligence, teaching the
Mathematicks, and reading the Scriptures and
thofe Authours who profefs to teach a certain Method of loving God.

This was his Method of living to the Year 1701,
when he was recommended by Mr. *Vanberg* to the
University,

University, as a proper Person to succeed *Drelin-court* in the Office of Lecturer on the Institutes of Physic, and elected without any Solicitation on his Part, and almost without his Consent on the 18th of *May*.

On this Occasion having observed, with Grief, that *Hippocrates*, whom he regarded not only as the Father, but as the Prince of Physicians, was not sufficiently read or esteemed by young Students, he pronounced an Oration, *De commendando Studio Hippocratico*; by which he restored that great Author to his just and antient Reputation.

He now began to read public Lectures with great Applause, and was prevailed upon by his Audience to enlarge his original Design, and instruct them in Chymistry.

This he undertook not only to the great Advantage of his Pupils, but to the great Improvement of the Art itself, which had hitherto been treated only in a confused and irregular Manner, and was little more than a History of Particular Experiments, not reduced to certain Principles nor connected one with another. This vast Chaos he reduced to Order, and made that clear and easy, which was before to the last Degree perplexed and obscure.

His Reputation began now to bear some Proportion to his Merit, and extended itself to distant Universities; so that in 1703 the Professorship of Physic being vacant at *Groningen*, he was invited thither, but he chose to continue his present Course of Life, and therefore refused to quit *Leyden*.

This Invitation and Refusal being related to the Governors of the University of *Leyden*, they had so grateful a Sense of his Regard for them, that they immediately voted an honorary Increase of his Salary, and promised him the first Professorship that should be vacant.

On this Occasion he pronounced an Oration upon the Use of Mechanics in the Science of Physic;

fic; in which he endeavoured to recommend a rational and mathematical Inquiry into the Caufes of Difeafes and the Structure of Bodies; and to fhew the Folly and Weaknefs of the Jargon introduced by *Paracelfus*, *Helmont*, and other chymical Enthufiafts, who have obtruded idle Dreams upon the World, and inftead of enlightening their Readers with explicating of Nature, have darkened the plaineft Appearances, and bewildered Mankind in Error and Obfcurity.

Boerhaave had now for nine Years read Phyfical Lectures, but without the Title or Dignity of a Profeffor, when, by the Death of Profeffor *Hotten*, the Profefforfhip of Phyfic and Botany fell to him of Courfe.

On this Occafion he afferted the Simplicity and Facility of the Science of Phyfic, in Oppofition to thofe who think that Obfcurity contributes to the Dignity of Learning, and that to be admired it is neceffary not to be underftood.

His Profeffion of Botany made it a Part of his Duty to fuperintend the phyfical Garden, which he improved fo much by the immenfe Number of new Plants which he procured, that it was inlarged to twice its original Extent.

In 1714 he was defervedly advanced to the higheft Dignities of the Univerfity, and in the fame Year made Phyfician of St. *Auguftine's* Hofpital in *Leyden*, into which the Students are admitted twice a Week to learn the Practice of Phyfic.

This was of equal Advantage to the Sick and to the Students, for the Succefs of his Practice was the beft Demonftration of the Soundnefs of his Principles.

When he laid down his Office of Governor of the Univerfity, in 1715, he made an Oration upon the Subject " of Attaining to Certainty in Natural Philofophy;" in which he declares himfelf, in the ftrongeft Terms, a Favourer of Experimental Knowledge,

ledge, and reflects with juſt Severity upon thoſe arrogant Philoſophers who are too eaſily diſguſted with
the ſlow Methods of obtaining true Notions by frequent Experiments, and who, poſſeſſed with too high
an Opinion of their own Abilities, rather chuſe to
conſult their own Imaginations, than inquire into
Nature ; and are better pleaſed with the delightful
Amuſements of forming Hypotheſes, than the toil-
ſome Drudgery of amaſſing Obſervations.

The Emptineſs and Uncertainty of all thoſe Syſtems, whether venerable for their Antiquity, or
agreeable for their Novelty, he has evidently ſhewn ;
and not only declared, but proved, that we are entirely Ignorant of the Principles of Things ; and that
all the Knowledge we have is of ſuch Qualities alone
as are diſcoverable by Experience, or ſuch as may be
deduced from them by Mathematical Demonſtration.

This Diſcourſe, filled as it was with Piety, and a
true Senſe of the Greatneſs of the Supreme Being,
and the Incomprehenſibility of his Works, gave ſuch
Offence to a Profeſſor of *Franker*, who having long
entertained a high Eſteem for *Deſcartes*, conſidered
his Principles as the Bulwark of Orthodoxy, that
he appeared in Vindication of his darling Authour,
and complained of the Injury done him with the
greateſt Vehemence, declaring little leſs than that
the *Carteſian* Syſtem and the Chriſtian muſt inevitably ſtand and fall together; and that to ſay we
were Ignorant of the Principles of Things, was not
only to enliſt among the Scepticks, but to ſink into
Atheiſm itſelf. So far can Prejudice darken the Underſtanding, as to make it conſider precarious and
uncertain Syſtems as the chief Support of ſacred and
unvariable Truth.

This Treatment of *Boerhaave* was ſo far reſented
by the Governors of his Univerſity, that they procured from *Franker* a Recantation of the Invective
that had been thrown out againſt him. This was

not

not only complied with, but Offers were made him
of more ample Satisfaction, to which he returned an
Anſwer not leſs to his Honour than the Victory he
gained: 'That he ſhould think himſelf ſufficiently
' compenſated, if his warned Adverſary received no
' farther Moleſtation on his Account.'

So far was this weak and injudicious Attack from
ſhaking a Reputation, not caſually raiſed by Faſhion
or Caprice, but founded upon ſolid Merit, that the
ſame Year his Correſpondence was deſired upon Botany and Natural Philoſophy, by the Academy of
Sciences at *Paris*, of which he was, upon the Death
of Count *Marſigli*, in the Year 1728, elected a
Member.

Nor were the *French* the only Nation by which
this great Man was courted and diſtinguiſhed; for
two Years after he was elected Fellow of our Royal
Society.

It cannot be doubted, but thus careſſed and honoured with the higheſt and moſt publick Marks of
Eſteem by other Nations, he became more celebrated in his own Univerſity; for *Boerhaave* was not
one of thoſe learned Men, of whom the World has
ſeen too many, that diſgrace their Studies by their
Vices, and by unaccountable Weakneſſes make themſelves ridiculous at home, while their Writings procure them the Veneration of diſtant Countries where
their Learning is known, but not their Follies.

Not that his Countrymen can be charged with
being inſenſible of his Excellencies, till other Nations taught them to admire him; for in 1718 he
was choſen to ſucceed *de Mort* in the Profeſſorſhip of
Chymiſtry, on which Occaſion he pronounced an
Oration, *de Chymia errores ſuos expurgante*; in which
he treated that Science with an Elegance of Style not
often to be found in Chymical Writers, who ſeem
generally to have affected not only a barbarous, but
unintelligible Phraſe, and, like the *Pythagoreans* of
old,

old, to have wrapt up their Secrets in Symbols and Enigmatical Expreſſions, either becauſe they believed that Mankind would reverence moſt what they leaſt underſtood, or becauſe they wrote not from Benevolence, but Vanity, and were deſirous to be praiſed for their Knowledge, though they could not prevail upon themſelves to communicate it.

In 1722 his Courſe both of Lectures and Practice was interrupted by the Gout, which, as he relates it in his Speech after his Recovery, he brought upon himſelf by an imprudent Confidence in the Strength of his own Conſtitution; and by tranſgreſſing thoſe Rules which he had a thouſand Times inculcated to his Pupils and Acquaintance. Riſing in the Morning before Day, he went immediately, hot and ſweating, from his Bed into the open Air, and expoſed himſelf to the cold Dews.

The Hiſtory of his Illneſs can hardly be read without Horror: He was for five Months confined to his Bed, where he lay upon his Back without daring to attempt the leaſt Motion, becauſe any Effort renewed his Torments, which were ſo exquiſite that he was at length not only deprived of Motion, but of Senſe. Here Art was at a Stand, nothing could be attempted, becauſe nothing could be propoſed with the leaſt Proſpect of Succeſs; at length having, in the ſixth Month of his Illneſs, obtained ſome Remiſſion, he took ſimple Medicines in large Quantities, and at length wonderfully recovered.

Succos preſſos bibit noſter herbarum Cichoreæ, Endiviæ, Fumariæ, naſturtij aquatici, Veronicæ, aquaticæ latifoliæ, copia ingenti: Simul diglutiens abundantiſſime gummi ferulacea Aſiatica.

His Recovery ſo much deſired, and ſo unexpected, was celebrated on *January* 11, 1723, when he opened his School again with general Joy and publick Illuminations.

It

It would be an Injury to the Memory of *Boer-haave* not to mention what was related by himfelf to one of his Friends, ' that when he lay whole Days ' and Nights without Sleep, he found no Method of ' diverting his Thoughts fo effectual as Meditation ' upon his Studies, and that he often relieved and ' mitigated the Senfe of his Torments, by the Re-' collection of what he had read, and by reviewing ' thofe Stores of Knowledge which he had repofited ' in his Memory.'

This is perhaps an Inftance of Fortitude and fteady Compofure of Mind which would have been for ever the Boaft of the Stoick Schools, and increafed the Re-putation of *Seneca* or *Cato*. The Patience of *Boer-haave*, as it was more rational, was more lafting than theirs : It was that *Patientia Chriftiana*, which *Lip-fius* the great Mafter of the Stoical Philofophy, beg-ged of God in his laft Hours, it was founded on Religion not Vanity, not on vain Reafonings, but on Confidence in God.

In 1727 he was feized with a violent burning Fe-ver, which continued fo long that he was once more given up by his Friends.

From this Time he was frequently afflicted with Returns of his Diftemper, which yet did not fo far fubdue him, as to make him lay afide his Studies or his Lectures, till in 1729 he found himfelf fo worn out, that it was improper for him to continue any longer the Profefforfhips of Botany and Chymiftry, which he therefore refigned *April* 28 ; and upon his Refignation he fpoke a *Sermo Academicus*, or Oration, in which he afferts the Power and Wifdom of the Creator, from the wonderful Fabrick of the human Body ; and confutes all thofe idle Reafoners who pretend to explain the Formation of Parts, or the animal Operations, to which he proves, that Art can produce nothing equal, nor any Thing parallel. One Inftance I fhall mention produced by him of

the

the Vanity of any Attempt to rival the Works of God. Nothing is more boafted by the Admirers of Chymiftry than that they can, by artificial Heat and Digeftion, imitate the Productions of Nature. ' Let ' all thefe Heroes of Science meet together,' fays *Boerhaave*, ' let them take Bread and Wine, the ' Food that forms the Blood of Man, and by Affi- ' milation contributes to the Growth of the Body: ' Let them try all their Arts, they fhall not be able ' from thefe Materials to produce a fingle Drop of ' Blood.' So much is the moft common Act of Nature beyond the utmoft Efforts of the moft ex- tended Science.

From this Time *Boerhaave* lived with lefs publick Employment indeed, but not an idle or a ufelefs Life; for befides his Hours fpent in inftructing his Scholars, a great Part of his Time was taken up by Patients, who came when the Diftemper would admit it, from all Parts of *Europe* to confult him, or did it by Letters, which in more urgent Cafes, were continually fent to inquire his Opinion, and afk his Advice.

Of the Sagacity and the wonderful Penetration with which he often difcovered and defcribed at the firft Sight of a Patient, fuch Diftempers as betray themfelves by no Symptoms to common Eyes, fuch wonderful Relations have been fpread over the World, as, though attefted beyond doubt, can fcarely be credited. I mention none of them, be- caufe I have no Opportunity of collecting Teftimo- nies, or diftinguifhing between thofe Accounts which are well proved, and thofe which owe their rife to Fiction and Credulity.

Yet I cannot but implore with the greateft Ear- neftnefs fuch as have been converfant with this great Man, that they will not fo far neglect the common Intereft of Mankind, as to fuffer any of thefe Cir- cumftances to be loft to Pofterity. Men are generally idle,

idle, and ready to fatisfy themfelves, and intimidate the Induftry of others, by calling that impoffible which is only difficult. The Skill to which *Boerhaave* attained by a long and unwearied Obfervation of Nature, ought therefore to be tranfmitted in all its Particulars to future Ages, that his Succeffors may be afhamed to fall below him, and that none may hereafter excufe his Ignorance, by pleading the Impoffibility of clearer Knowledge.

Yet fo far was this great Mafter from prefumptuous Confidence in his Abilities, that in his Examination of the Sick he was remarkably Circumftantial and Particular. He well knew that the Originals of Diftempers are often at a Diftance from their vifible Effects; that to acquiefce in Conjecture, where Certainty may be obtained, is either Vanity or Negligence; and that Life is not to be facrificed either to an Affectation of quick Difcernment, or of crouded Practice, but may be required, if trifled away, at the Hand of the Phyfician.

About the Middle of the Year 1737 he felt the firft Approaches of that fatal Illnefs that brought him to the Grave; of which we have inferted an Account, written by himfelf, *September* 1738, to a Friend at *London*; which deferves not only to be preferved, as an hiftorical Relation of the Difeafe which deprived us of fo great a Man, but as a Proof of his Piety and Refignation to the Divine Will.

Ætas, labor, corporifque opima pinguetudo, effecerant ante annum, ut inertibus refertum, grave, hebes, plenitudine turgens corpus, anhelum ad motus, minimos, cum fenfu fuffocationis, pulfu mirifice anomalo, ineptum evaderet ad ullum motum. Urgebat præcipue fubfiftens prorfus et intercepte refpiratio ad primi fomni initia: unde fomnus prorfus prohibebatur cum formidabili ftrangulationis moleftia. Hinc hydrops pedum, crurum, femorum, fcroti, præputii & abdominis. Quæ

VOL. II.   Q   *tamen*

tamen omnia fublata. Sed dolor manet in abdomine cum anxietate fumma anhelitu fuffocante, & debilitate incredibili. Somno pauco, eoque vago. Per fomnia turbatiffimo. Animus vero rebus ageridis impar. Cum tris lector feffus, neque emergo. Patienter expectans Dei juffa, quibus refigno data, quæ fola amo, et honoro unice.

In this laft Illnefs, which was to the laft Degree lingering, painful, and afflictive, his Conftancy and Firmnefs did not forfake him. He neither intermitted the neceffary Cares of Life, nor forgot the proper Preparations for Death. Though Dejection and Lownefs of Spirit was, as he himfelf tells us, Part of his Diftemper, yet even this, in fome Meafure, gave way to that Vigour which the Soul receives from a Confcioufnefs of Innocence.

About three Weeks before his Death he received a Vifit at his Country-houfe from the Rev. Mr. *Schultens*, his intimate Friend, who found him fitting without Doors, with his Wife, Sifter, and Daughter. After the Compliments of Form, the Ladies withdrew, and left them to private Converfation; when *Boerhaave* took Occafion to tell him what had been, during his Illnefs, the chief Subject of his Thoughts. He had never doubted of the fpiritual and immaterial Nature of the Soul, but declared, that he had lately had a Kind of experimental Certainty of the Diftinction between corporeal and thinking Subftances, which mere Reafon and Philofophy cannot afford; and Opportunities of contemplating the wonderful and inexplicable Union of Soul and Body, which nothing but long Sicknefs can give. This he illuftrated by a Defcription of the Effects which the Infirmities of his Body had upon his Faculties, which yet they did not fo opprefs or vanquifh, but his Soul was always Mafter

of

of itfelf, and always refigned to the Pleafure of its Maker.

He related with great Concern, that once his Patience fo far gave Way to Extremity of Pain, that after having laid fifteen Hours in exquifite Tortures, he prayed to God that he might be fet free by Death.

Mr. *Schultens*, by Way of Confolation, anfwered, that he thought fuch Wifhes, when forced by continued and exceffive Torments, unavoidable in the prefent State of human Nature; that the beft of Men, even *Job* himfelf, were not able to refrain from fuch Starts of Impatience: This he did not deny, but faid, ' He that loves God ought to think ' nothing defirable, but what is moft pleafing to the ' Supreme Goodnefs.'

Such were his Sentiments, and fuch his Conduct, in this State of Weaknefs and Pain: As Death approached nearer, he was fo far from Terror and Confufion, that he feemed even lefs fenfible of Pain, and more chearful under his Torments, which continued till the 23d Day of *September*, 1738, on which he died, between Four and Five in the Morning, in the 70th Year of his Age.

Thus died *Boerhaave*, a Man formed by Nature for great Defigns, and guided by Religion in the Exertion of his Abilities: He was of a robuft and athletic Conftitution of Body, fo hardened by early Severities, and wholefome Fatigue, that he was infenfible of any Sharpnefs of Air, or Inclemency of Weather. He was tall, and remarkable for extraordinary Strength: there was in his Air and Motion fomething rough and artlefs, but fo majeftic and great at the fame Time, that no Man ever looked upon him without Veneration, and a Kind of tacit Submiffion to the Superiority of his Genius.

. The Vigour and Activity of his Mind fparkled vifibly in his Eyes; nor was it obferved that any Change of his Fortune, or Alteration in his Af-

fairs,

fairs, whether happy or unfortunate, affected his Countenance.

He was always chearful, and defirous of promoting Mirth by a facetious and humourous Converfation. He was never foured by Calumny and Detraction; nor ever thought it neceffary to confute them; for ' they are Sparks,' faid he, ' which, if ' you do not blow them, will go out of themfelves.'

Yet he took Care never to provoke Enemies by Severity of Cenfure; for he never dwelt on the Faults or Defects of others; and was fo far from inflaming the Envy of his Rivals, by dwelling on his own Excellencies, that he rarely mentioned himfelf or his Writings.

He was not to be overawed or depreffed by the Prefence, Frowns, or Infolence of great Men; but perfifted on all Occafions in the right, with a Refolution always prefent, and always calm. He was modeft, but not timorous; and firm without Rudenefs.

He could, with uncommon Readinefs and Certainty, make a Conjecture of Men's Inclinations and Capacity, by their Afpect.

His Method of Life was to ftudy in the Morning and Evening, and to allot the Middle of the Day to his publick Bufinefs. He rofe at Four in the Summer, and Five in the Winter. His ufual Exercife was Riding, till, in his latter Years, his Diftempers made it more proper for him to walk. When he was weary, he amufed himfelf by playing on the Violin.

His greateft Pleafure was to retire to his Houfe in the Country, where he had a Garden of eight Acres, ftored with all the Herbs and Trees which the Climate would bear. Here he ufed to enjoy his Hours unmolefted, and profecute his Studies without Interruption.

The

The Diligence with which he purfued his Studies is fufficiently evident from his fuccefs. Statefmen and Generals may grow great by unexpected Accidents, and a fortunate Concurrence of Circumftances, neither procured nor forefeen by themfelves. But Reputation in the learned World muft be the Effect of Induftry and Capacity. *Boerhaave* loft none of his Hours; but, when he had attained one Science, attempted another. He added Phyfick to Divinity, Chymiftry to the Mathematicks, and Botany to Anatomy. He examined Syftems by Experiments, and formed Experiments into Syftems. He neither neglected the Obfervations of others, nor blindly fubmitted to celebrated Names. He neither thought fo highly of himfelf as to imagine he could receive no Light from Books, nor fo meanly as to believe he could difcover nothing but what was to be learned from them. He examined the Obfervations of other Men, but trufted only to his own.

Nor was he unacquainted with the Art of recommending Truth by Elegance, and of embellifhing Philofophy by polite Literature: He knew that but a fmall Part of Mankind will facrifice their Pleafure to their Improvement; and thofe Authors who would find many Readers, muft endeavour to pleafe while they inftruct.

He knew the Importance of his own Writings to Mankind; and left he might, by a Roughnefs and Barbarity of Stile, too frequent among Men of great Learning, difappoint his own Intentions, and make his Labours lefs ufeful, he did not neglect the Arts of Eloquence and Poetry: Thus was his Learning at once various and exact, profound and agreeable.

He was not only fkilled in the learned Languages, and the Tongues in which the Old Teftament was written, but was able to converfe in many of the modern Languages, and to read others, which he could not fpeak.

Q 3

But

But his Knowledge, however uncommon, holds in his Character but the second Place; his Virtue was yet much more uncommon than his Learning. He was an admirable Example of Temperance, Fortitude, Humility, and Devotion. His Piety and a religious Sense of a Dependence on God, was the Basis of all his Virtues, and the Principles of his whole Conduct. He was too sensible of his Weakness to ascribe any thing to himself, or to conceive that he could subdue Passion, or withstand Temptation by his own natural Power: He attributed every good Thought and every laudable Action to the Father of Goodness. Being once asked by a Friend who had often admired his Patience under great Provocations, whether he knew what it was to be angry, and by what Means he had so entirely suppressed that impetuous and ungovernable Passion; he answered with the utmost Frankness and Sincerity, that he was naturally quick of Resentment; but that he had, by daily Prayer and Meditation, at length attained to this Mastery over himself.

As soon as he rose in the Morning, it was, throughout his whole Life, his daily Practice to retire for an Hour to private Prayer and Meditation: This, he often told his Friends, gave him Spirit and Vigour in the Business of the Day; and this he therefore recommended as the best Rule of Life; for nothing, he knew, could support the Soul in all Distresses, but a Confidence in the Supreme Being; nor can a steady and rational Magnanimity flow from any other Source, than a Consciousness of the Divine Favour.

He asserted on all Occasions the Divine Authority and sacred Efficacy of the Holy Scriptures; and maintained that by them alone was taught the Way of Salvation, and that they only could give Peace of Mind.

The

The Excellency of the Christian Religion was the frequent Subject of his Conversation. A strict Obedience to the Doctrine, and a diligent Imitation of the Example of our Blessed Saviour, he often declared to be the Foundation of true Tranquillity. He recommended to his Friends a careful Observation of the Precept of *Moses* concerning the love of God and Man. He worshipped God as he is in himself, without attempting to inquire into his Nature. He desired only to think of God, what God has revealed of himself. There he stopped; lest, by indulging his own Ideas, he should form a Deity from his own Imagination, and commit Sin by falling down before him. To the Will of God he paid an absolute Submission, without endeavouring to discover the Reason of his Determinations; and this he accounted the first and most inviolable Duty of a Christian. When he heard of a Criminal condemned to die, he used to think, and often to say, ' Who can ' tell whether this Man is not better than I? Or, if ' I am better, it is not to be ascribed to myself, but ' to the Goodness of God.'

So far was this Man from being made impious by Philosophy, or vain by Knowledge, or by Virtue, that he ascribed all his Abilities to the Bounty, and all his Goodness to the Grace of God. May his Example extend its Influence to his Admirers and Followers! May those who study his Writings, imitate his Life; and those who endeavour after his Knowledge, aspire likewise to his Piety!

He married, *September* 17, 1710, *Mary Droleneveaux*, the only Daughter of a Burgomaster of *Leyden*, by whom he had *Joanna Maria*, who survives her Father, and three other Children who died in their Infancy.

The genuine Works of *Boerhaave*, according to his own Catalogue of them, are as follows; and he declares, in 1732, that all others under his Name

are

are fpurious, unlefs fome few Prefaces to new Editions of Books.

*Oratio de commandando Studio Hippocratico, habita
& impreffa Lugd. Bat.* 1701, *apud Abraham Elzevir.*

———— *de ufu Ratiocinij Mechanici in Medicina,*
1703, *apud Joann. Verbeffel.*

———— *qua repurgatæ Medicinæ facilis afferitur fim-
plicitas,* 1703, *apud Joan. Vanderlend.*

———— *de comparando certo in Phyficis,* 1715, *apud
Petr. Vander Aa.*

———— *de Chymia fuos Errores expurgante,* 1718,
apud Petr. Vander Aa.

———— *de Vita & Obitu clariffimi Bernardi Albini,*
1721, *apud eundem.*

——— *quam habui, quum honefta Miffione impetra-
ta, Botanicam & Chymicam Profeffionem publicæ pone-
rem,* 1729, *apud Ifaacum Severinum.*

———— *de Honore Medici, Servitute,* 1731, *apud
eundem.*

*Inftitutiones Medicæ in ufus annuæ Exercitationis do-
mefticos, anno* 1708, *apud J. Vander-Lind. P. & F.
Qui dein auctior aliquoties recufus, in* 8vo.

*Aphorifmi de cognofcendis & curandis Morbis, in
ufum Doctrinæ domefticæ,* 1709, *apud J. Vander-
linden.
Qui dein auctior aliquoties recufue, in* 8vo.

*Index Plantarum quæ in Horto Academico Lugduno
Batavo reperiuntur,* 1710, *apud Cornelium Bontefiein,
in* 8vo.

*Libellus de Materia Medica, & Remediorum Formu-
lis,* 1719, *apud Ifaacum Severinum, in* 8vo.
Qui iterum prodiit, in 8vo.

*Index alter Plantarum, quæ in Horto Academico
Lugduno Batavo aluntur,* 1720, *apud Petrum Vander
Aa, in* 4to.

*Atrocis nec defcripti prius, Morbi Defcriptio, fecun-
dum Medicæ Artis Leges confcripta,* 1724, *apud Bontefiein, in* 8vo.

Atroc-

Atrocis rariſſimique, Morbi Hiſtoria altera 1728, *apud Sam. Luchtmans & Theod. Haak,* 8vo.

Tractatus Medicus de Lue Aphordiſiaca, præfixus Aphrodiſiaco 1728, *apud J. Am. Langerak & Jok. & Herm. Verbrek,* in Folio.

Beſides theſe he communicated to the Royal Society, and to the Royal Academy of Sciences, ſome Obſervations upon Quickſilver, which are publiſhed in the Philoſophical Tranſactions.

Having given this Account of the Life and Writings of *Boerhaave* it remains, that I take ſome Notice of his capital Works, which are his Inſtitutes, his Aphoriſms, and his Chymiſtry.

His Inſtitutes were deſigned as little more than a Syllabus to his Lectures. They are written in a very cloſe and conciſe Style, but abound in Matter containing all the modern Diſcoveries in Anatomy, Phyſiology, and whatever relates to the Laws of the Animal Œconomy, and the Action of Medicines upon the Body, with conſiderable Improvements of his own, which are ſpecified under their proper Articles. This Treatiſe is very methodical and diſtinct; but I apprehend it is utterly unintelligible to any one who is not in ſome Degree previouſly acquainted with the Subjects of which he treats.

His Aphoriſms are, as he tells us himſelf, collected from the *Greek* medicinal Writers, the *Arabians,* and ſome few of the Moderns; and his Reaſonings are founded on the Structure of the Parts and the Laws of Mechanicks. I muſt here obſerve, that *Boerhaave* to his great Honour, ſeems to have gone counter to moſt Writers of Inſtitutes, and Compilers of Syſtems. For they have generally endeavoured to lead Nature captive, and to make her act conformable to their preconceived Notions, however crude and chimerical; impoſing Laws upon the animal Œconomy, which have no Reality, and eſtabliſhing with great Praiſe and Induſtry, Sources of Action, which exiſt no where but in their own Imaginations.

Imaginations. *Boerhaave*, on the contrary, was convinced by daily Experience and a Fund of good Senfe, that the *Greek* Phyficians by diligent Obfervation had determined, with great Accuracy, how Nature acts in producing the Symptoms of Diftempers, and her Methods of relieving herfelf, either with or without the Affiftance of Art, and that their Experience had furnifhed them with very fuccefsful Methods of Cure. The two Points therefore which he feems to have had perpetually in View, were to eftablifh, on mechanical Principles, as much as was poffible, the Doctrine of the Antients with Refpect to the Diagnoftics and Prognoftics of Difeafes, and fhew that they could not be otherwife than they have reprefented them.

But the fecond View is of more Importance than the firft, it being no lefs than to demonftrate, that the Methods of Cure purfued by the antient Phycians were generally the beft that could poffibly have been contrived with the Materials they were acquainted with, though for Reafons to which they were probably Strangers. This appears to me the diftinguifhing Character of *Boerhaave*, and by this he has done almoft as much Service to Phyfic, as his Predeceffors for fome Centuries had done Mifchiefs.

It is greatly to be lamented that our illuftrious Author did not think proper to publifh his Lectures on his Inftitutes and his Aphorifms before his Deceafe. If he had forefeen the fatal Confequences of fuch an Omiffion, I believe his Love to Mankind would have prevailed upon him to have done it, and thereby prevented the Mifchiefs which his great Name, and the Reputation of his Lectures, may poffibly do in the World. That I may explain my Meaning I muft obferve, that it is the Misfortune of the *Englifh* to be very little ufed to converfe in *Latin*, though, perhaps, no People in the World underftand

it

it better. Add to this, that as we pronounce *Latin* in a different Manner from all other Nations, our Ears are not accuftomed to the foreign Accent. Hence Foreigners with Difficulty underftand us, and on the other Hand it is impoffible for us to take their Meaning, efpecially in long Difcourfes, with that Degree of Exactnefs, which Subjects of Importance require; and indeed it is no eafy Matter to take the entire Senfe of long Difcourfes, though delivered in the Languages we are beft acquainted with. This is the Reafon that many of his Pupils who have long attended his Lectures, for two or three Years have frequently miftaken his Meaning, and held their own Errors with an equal Degree of Veneration with the genuine Doctrine of their Profeffor, and have imprudently neglected to fet themfelves right, by examining the Sources from whence *Boerhaave* himfelf drew his Treafures; fometimes perhaps becaufe they imagined the Authority of their Profeffor rendered it fuperfluous, and fometimes becaufe they were Strangers to the Languages in which the beft medicinal Authors wrote thus : either out of Choice or Neceffity, taking a more eafy, though a lefs certain, Way to Knowledge, than *Boerhaave* either advifed or thought proper to purfue himfelf.

That this has been really the Cafe the fpurious Works attributed to *Boerhaave* by his Scholars are glaring Evidences; among which his Method of ftudying Phyfic, as I think it is called deferves fome Notice, being a crude and injudicious Performance, and in a great many Inftances contradictory to the Sentiments of *Boerhaave*, on the Subjects there treated; and as I remember, it recommends fome Authors who never wrote or even exifted. In the fame Rank is the *Praxis Medica* printed in five Volumes in *Holland*, though the Title tells us at *Padua*. In the Preface we are informed, that many of his Au-

ditors

ditors took his Lectures in Writing; that these were carefully compared, and hence this Work was compiled. Yet notwithstanding all this Care, there are not many Pages without some enormous Error, nor even Sentences without false *Latin:* so little did they understand either their Professor or their Subjects.

With respect to his Chymistry, it may be justly said, that his Theory is more philosophical, exact and full, and his Processes more methodical and regular, than those of any preceding Author on the Subject. It is remarkable, that in this Work he has made many chymical Operations subservient to the establishing several important Doctrines of the Antients, and to the Confirmation of their Practice. I shall conclude with remarking, that this Work alone would have been sufficient to raise the Character of any other Man, but is however that in which *Boerhaave* shines mnch less than in his Institutes and Aphorisms, the last of which is, perhaps, more useful than any one Book written upon Physic, and has had the Honour of being translated into *Arabic,* as is said by the *Mufti,* and printed at *Constantinople*

A C H A-

A

CHARACTER

O F

Mr. WILLIAM COLLINS.

MR. *Collins* was a Man of extensive Literature, and of vigorous Faculties. He was acquainted not only with the learned Tongues, but with the *Italian*, *French*, and *Spanish* Languages. He had employed his Mind chiefly upon Works of Fiction, and Subjects of Fancy; and by indulging some peculiar Habits of Thought, was eminently delighted with those Flights of Imagination which pass the Bounds of Nature, and to which the Mind is reconciled only by a passive Acquiescence in popular Traditions. He loved Fairies, Genii, Giants, and Monsters; he delighted to rove through the Meanders of Inchantment, to gaze on the Magnificence of golden Palaces, to repose by the Waterfalls of Elysian Gardens.

This was however the Character rather of his Inclination than his Genius; the Grandeur of Wildness, and the Novelty of Extravagance, were always desired by him, but were not always attained. But Diligence is never wholly lost: if his Efforts sometimes caused Harshness and Obscurity, they likewise produced in happier Moments Sublimity and Splendour. This Idea which he had formed of Excellence, led him to oriental Fictions and allegorical Imagery; and perhaps, while he was intent upon

De-

Defcription, he did not fufficiently cultivate Sentiment. His Poems are the Productions of a Mind
not deficient in Fire, nor unfurnifhed with Knowledge either of Books or Life, but fomewhat ob-
ftructed in its Progrefs, by Deviation in Queft of
miftaken Beauties.

His Morals were pure, and his Opinions pious:
In a long Continuance of Poverty, and long Habits
of Diffipation, it cannot be expected that any Character fhould be exactly uniform. There is a Degree of Want by which the Freedom of Agency is
almoft deftroyed; and long affociation with fortuitous Companions will at laft relax the Strictnefs of
Truth, and abate the Fervour of Sincerity. That
this Man, wife and virtuous as he was, paffed always unentangled through the Snares of Life, it
would be Prejudice and Temerity to affirm; but it
may be faid that at leaft he preferved the Source of
Action unpolluted, that his Principles were never
fhaken, that his Diftinctions of Right and Wrong
were never confounded, and that his Faults had nothing of malignity or Defign, but proceeded from
fome unexpected Preffure, or cafual Temptation.

The latter Part of his Life cannot be remembered, but with Pity and Sadnefs. He languifhed
fome Years under that Depreffion of Mind which
enchains the Faculties without deftroying them, and
leaves Reafon the Knowledge of Right without the
Power of purfuing it. Thefe Clouds which he
found gathering on in his Intellects, he endeavoured to difperfe by Travel, and paffed into *France*; but
found himfelf conftrained to yield to his Malady,
and returned. He was for fome Time confined in
a Houfe of Lunatics, and afterwards retired to the
Care of his Sifter in *Colchefter*, where Death at laft
came to his Relief.

After his Return from *France*, the Writer of this
Character paid him a Vifit at *Iflington*, where he
was

was writing for his Sister, whom he had directed
to meet him: there was then nothing of Disorder
discernible in his Mind by any but himself, but he
had then withdrawn from Study, and travelled with
no other Book than an *English Testament*, such as
Children carry to the School; when his Friend
took it into his Hand, out of Curiosity to see what
Companion a Man of Letters had chosen; ' I have
' but one Book,' says *Collins*, ' but that is the
' best.

A

L E T T E R

T O A

B I S H O P.

C O N C E R N I N G

L E C T U R E S H I P S.

My Lord,

I Would not thus have addrefs'd your Lordfhip in public, but that in thefe our Days the Prefs is the only Method by which I could gain Admif-fion to you, or have the Opportunity, to ufe our old College Phrafe, of a little CONFAB: Bifhops and Curates are, I believe, at prefent feldom feen together, except in the Prayer for the Clergy. For-tune, my Lord, who brought us fo clofe together at the Univerfity, where, you may remember, we were *Chums*, has at Length

Sævo læta negotio,

as the old Bard fings, in one of her ftrange Freaks, thrown us from the moft intimate Connection into Stations of Life at the utmoft Diftance from each other, by making your Lordfhip a Bifhop, and me an ——Affiftant-Curate. I think, my Lord, I have
somewhere

somewhere read, that in the *Roman* Triumphs a Person was always appointed to attend the Conqueror, and as he paſſed along to repeat to him——
' Thou art a Man, The following Pages may be conſidered as a ſalutary Hint of the ſame Nature, and were only meant to lay on your Lordſhip's Table, and as you ſlip on your Lawn, to whiſper to you---' Thou art a Clergyman.'

Though I do not (to uſe the Phraſe of a certain Right Reverend) *baſk in the Sunſhine of the Goſpel,* you will perceive, notwithſtanding, in the Courſe of this Letter, I am not ſo much hurt by Diſappointments, but that I can laugh at a proper Opportunity ; at preſent, however, I am perfectly ſerious, and do from my Heart think and declare, that the leaſt grateful Acknowledgement which our dignified Clergy can make, for the Honours and Rewards conferred on them, is to aſſiſt their diſtreſſed Brethren ; to make uſe of their beſt Endeavours to ſupport the Dignity of the miniſterial Office ; and to gain them ſome Deference and Reſpect, if they *can*, or *will*, procure them nothing elſe : and yet this, my Lord, I will not ſay wherefore, or by whom, is of late Years, moſt ſhamefully neglected.

Your Lordſhip, I am convinced by Experience, is not without Humanity ; I have known ſome Biſhops, (formerly I mean) who had not a Grain of it in their whole Compoſition ; but that is not your Caſe ; I have therefore taken the Liberty to appeal to you, in Behalf of the inferior Clergy of theſe Kingdoms, who, I believe, are the moſt diſtreſſed, deſerted, and deſpiſed Body of Men, at preſent. on the Face of the Earth : into the Cauſes of this, I propoſe cooly and candidly to examine, and to conſult with your Lordſhip concerning the moſt probable Method of removing them.

I have a thousand Things to say to your Lordship, on this copious Head, which I shall reserve
for some future Occasion, and for the Sake of Method, confine myself at present (though I hate Confinement of every Kind) to a particular Branch of
our scanty Revenue, commonly known by the
Name of LECTURESHIPS.

Your Lordship being much better acquainted
with ecclesiastical History than myself, could probably acquaint me with the Origin and Rise of these
PAUPERTATIS SUBSIDIA: as I am not, however,
very ambitious of tracing the Source of this muddy
Spring, I shall defer the Search to another Opportunity, and content myself with observing (a Truth
which I am every Day more and more convinced of)
that the Establishment of *Lectureships*, in and about
London, has been extremely prejudicial to the inferior
Clergy of this Kingdom, and contributed, in a great
Measure, to bring upon the whole Body that Poverty and Contempt into which they are now fallen;
that the Methods by which they are obtained are
highly unbecoming our Character, and the Means
made Use of to support them inadequate to the Duty performed; that they are acquired, in short,
with Difficulty, lost with Ease, and very few of
them worth the keeping: which I will endeavour
to prove to your Lordship in as few Words as possible.

It may not, perhaps, be improper, when I talk
of SERMONISERS, to follow the usual SERMON
Method, and divide my Subject into three or four
general Heads; and though I would not, as Lord
Shaftsbury says, ' Bring my Two's and Three's be-
' fore a fashionable Congregation,' yet, as I am
talking only to your Lordship, and what passes may
never go much further than ourselves, I may as
well adopt the TEXTUAL Manner; (there, my
Lord, is a new Word for *Johnson's* Dictionary).

I shall

I shall proceed therefore,

FIRST,

To confider how LECTURESHIPS are canvaffed for.

SECONDLY,

What is expected from them, And

THIRDLY and LASTLY,

How they are paid, and what Emoluments ufually arife to the Poffeffors of them.

First therefore, my Lord, with Regard to the *canvaffing* for Lectureships, as ufually practifed amongft us, I will venture to affert, it is an Employment utterly inconfiftent with the Character, and unbecoming the Dignity of a Clergyman, an Office greatly beneath the Attention of Genius and Learning, and highly unfuitable to all the Notions of Life imbibed in the Courfe of a genteel and liberal Education.

The Choice of a LECTURER in this Metropolis is generally vefted in the whole Body of the Parifh, confifting, for the moft Part, of ordinary Tradefmen, fometimes very low Mechanics, Perfons not always of the moft refined Manners, or delicate Senfations. Your Lordfhip, I am fure, muft remember, how cavalierly, when we were at *Cambridge,* (for which by the bye, we deferved to be horfe-whipped) we ufed to treat the CANAILLE; if an honeft Tradefman came dunning to our Room of a Morning before Lecture, we tipped the NON DOMI upon him; or if by Chance he gained Admittance, and grew importunate in his Solicitations, without further Ceremony fhewed him the neareft Way down Stairs. Little did fome of us

R 2   think

think what a different Behaviour we fhould one Day be obliged to affume towards fome of their illuftrious Brethren in this Metropolis.

The common People, my Lord, in this Kingdom of Liberty, are of fo combuftible a Nature, that the leaft Point of Difpute blows them up into a Flame: a Conteft about Church-Wardens, the Choice of a felect Veftry-Man, or a paltry Lecturefhip, fhall fet as many fober Citizens together by the Ears as a County Election. To fay the Truth, there is now-a-days almoft as much dirty Work practifed in the canvaffing for one as for the other. The Parfon, as well as the Candidate, muft play over, if he hopes for Succefs, all the little low Tricks of bribing the Indigent, flattering the Proud, cajoling the Rich, abufing and calumniating his Antagonift, buying, making, fplitting, hiding Votes; the whole Catalogue, in fhort, of minifterial Artifices muft be practifed in the Veftry with as little Confcience as on the Huftings; and a Candidate for St. A——'s Church has almoft as much Mire to wade through, as a Candidate for St. S—'s Chapel.

But, as I have heard fay in *Weftminfter-Hall*, there is nothing like a CASE IN POINT; I will therefore treat your Lordfhip with one, to illuftrate the Subject under Confideration, and that Cafe, to prevent any Miftakes, fhall be MY OWN.

Your Lordfhip I believe may remember the Time when my poor Uncle died, which obliged me to quit the Univerfity and feek my Fortune in Town, where I had not been above three Weeks before I ftrolled on *Sunday* Afternoon into a Church in the City, and, after Service, heard the Clerk, by Order of the Veftry, declare the Lecturefhip of the Parifh vacant, and invite the Clergy, however dignified or diftinguifhed, to be Candidates for it, and to give in their Names by the enfuing *Sunday*. No
fooner

fooner did I hear this CHUCH SERJEANT thus
beating up for Recruits, than I immediately refolved to *enlift*; and accordingly, the next Day,
waited on the Worfhipful *Stentor* abovementioned,
who took down my Name and Place of Abode: on
my defiring him at the fame Time to acquaint me
with the beft Method of proceeding, which I was
an utter Stranger to, he advifed me as a Friend, to
apply as fpeedily as poffible, to Mr. ——, a Cheefe-
monger in ——— Lane, who was then firft Church-
warden, a leading Man in the Veftry, and a Perfon, he affured me, on whom the Election would
in a great Meafure depend. I took honeft AMEN's
Advice, and by nine the next Morning, not I muft
own without fome Reluctance, dreffed myfelf as
well as I could, and waited on Mr. Church-warden.
As foon as he faw me enter the Shop in my Canonicals, (for I had hired an excellent new Gown and
Caffock behind St. *Clement*'s on the Occafion) he
made me a very low Bow, gave me the Title of
Doctor, and imagining no Doubt, that I was come
to befpeak Cheefes for the Country, begged to
known my *Honour*'s Commands; to which I replied
in an humble Tone, and looking extremely difcon-
certed, that I came to wait on him on Account of
the Lecturefhip of the Parifh, and begged the Favour of his Vote and Intereft, *&c.* Your Lordfhip I am fure would have fmiled to fee the fudden
Alteration of his Features and Behaviour: he drop-
ped all the Tradefman's Obfequioufnefs, and in a
Moment affumed the magifterial Air and Dignity of
a Church-warden; turned afide to a Woman who
was juft then afking for a Pound of *Chefhire*, and
without addreffing himfelf to me, cried out, ' This
' is the fourth Parfon I have had with me To-day
' on the fame Errand;' then, ftaring me full in
the Face; ' Well, young Man,' fays he, ' you
' intend to be a Candidate for this fame Lecture:

R 3 · ' you

' you are all to mount the *Nostrum*, I suppose, and
' Merit will carry it: For my Part, I promise no-
' body; but remember I tell you before-hand, I
' am for *Voice* and *Action*; so mind your Hits.'
When he had said this, he immediately turned upon
his Heel, and went into the Counting-house. I
took my Leave in an awkward Manner, as you may
suppose, being not a little chagrin'd at his Insolence;
and, as I went out of the Shop, overheard his Lady
observing, from behind the Counter, that I was a
pretty *Sprig of Divinity*, but looked a little *sheepish*,
and had not half the Courage of the Gentleman that
had been recommended to her Husband by Mr.
Squintum.

'The Instant I quitted the Sign of the *Cheshire-
Cheese*, I laid aside all thoughts of further Solicitation, and resolved to return to College, and live on
making Fellow-Commoners Exercises, rather than
subject myself any more to such mortifying Indignities. Good God! thought I to myself, is this the
Fruit of my Studies: this the Reward of all my
Toil and Labour in the University; to have the important Point, whether I shall eat or starve, at last
determined by a Cheesemonger, who declares for
Voice and Action?

In spite notwithstanding of this Resolution (for
Resolutions, your Lordship knows, are much easier
made than kept) I was obliged in less than six
Months, having during that Time taken it into my
Head to fall in Love and marry, to repair once more
to the great City, and put into the ecclesiastical
Lottery; where, by the bye, as in most other Lot-
teries, you buy so dear, meet with so few Prizes,
and run so much Hazard, that none but Desperadoes
ought to venture in them: There, my Lord, I renewed my Solicitations, and experienced all the Miseries and Misfortunes, all the Insults and Indignities, which the Pride and Insolence of the Rich,
both

both Laity and Clergy, inflict on their dependent Brethren : The Difficulties which I met with in Search of
a Lectureship (for that was my *Summum Bonum*) are
inconceivable ; and I can assure your Lordship, that,
trifling as the Emoluments are of this Preferment, all
the Perfections of human Nature united are scarce
sufficient to a Man, without personal Interest, to in-
sure his Success.   The Variety of Distresses which I
encountered from the different Tempers and Dispo-
sitions of the Gentlemen and Ladies (for so I was obliged to call them, who had Votes in the Parish)
the mean and abject Flattery which I was forced to
make Use of, with the many frequent Affronts and
Disappointments I underwent, would swell half a
melancholy Volume.   Without enumerating the necessary Accomplishments generally expected on these
Occasions, of drinking hard with the Husbands, and
saying soft things to their Wives ; in more Parishes
than one, my Lord, where I have been a Candidate, to smoke your Half-dozen of Pipes, and drink
two Bottles at a Sitting, are infinitely more necessary Perfections than any which you could bring
with you from the University ; and it is a Maxim
with many good Citizens, that unless you are what
they call a d----d honest Fellow, you can never be
a good Preacher, or an orthodox Divine ; in short,
my Lord, and to be serious, unless a poor Clergyman is every Thing that he ought *not* to be, he can
never be what is every Man's Wish, independent.

I must not, in this Place, forget to mention one
Rock which young Divines are perpetually splitting
on in this Voyage ; and that is, Party: A Candidate must take great Care how he repeats his political Creed ; as, if he declares himself on *one* Side, he
will inevitably be opposed, slandered and insulted by
the *other* ; it behoves him, therefore, always to join
with the strongest: But, what is worst of all, if he
is of *no* Side (which your Lordship knows is the

moſt prudent Way) it is a million to one if he is ſuffered to continue ſo.

I remember, my Lord, when I ſet up for the
Lectureſhip of Saint ————, the political Thermo-
meter of the Pariſh was very high: I had at that
Time, and retain to this Moment, the utmoſt Contempt for all Parties; being ſatisfied, as every Man
of common Underſtanding muſt be, that there is
nothing but Self intereſt at the Bottom of them: It
was very difficult, however, I found, to perſuade
other Men that I was not as fooliſh as themſelves.

Mr. Alderman *Grub* and Mr. Deputy *Clove*, the
two leading Men in the Pariſh, were at that Time,
or at leaſt profeſſed to be, of oppoſite Principles; the
Alderman a ſtaunch Whig, the Deputy a reputed
Tory: I waited on them both for their Votes and
Intereſt, the Conſequence of which was, that I ſucceeded with neither, both reproaching me with being
of a different Way of thinking from themſelves.
The Alderman was extremely ſorry he could not
ſerve me: He had a Regard, he had heard, he admired, &c. but, to be plain with me, he was aſſur-
ed I had drank Tea at the Deputy's. And when I
went to the Deputy: ' For my Part' (I ſhall never
forget it, my Lord, to my dying Day) ' For my
' Part' (ſaid he) ' I am of no Side; I deſpiſe all
' Parties whatſomdever; but there are People whom
' ſome People can't like like other People: In ſhort,
' I ſhall always be glad to ſee you whilſt you are
' what you are; but remember, Mr. Parſon, if
' ever you dine with Alderman *Grub* again —— you
' underſtand me —— Your humble Servant.'

Theſe, my Lord, are but an inconſiderable Part
of the Miſeries and Indignities which a poor Parſon
is ſure to encounter with on this Occaſion, but half

> the Spurns
> Which patient Merit from th'Unworthy takes.

For

For my own Part, I cannot but think the very single Circumstance of trapesing about from Door to Door in one's Canonicals, perhaps for a Week, is sufficient to deter any Man, who has the least Regard for Cleanliness and Decorum, from canvassing for a City Lectureship. There is not in Nature a more ridiculous Sight than a draggletail Divine, holding up his spattered Sacerdotals, and dabbling through dirty Streets and blind Alleys, in Search of Civic Preferment.

And now I am upon this Head, my Lord, you must pardon me

A

SHORT DIGRESSION

CONCERNING

GOWNS and CASSOCKS.

A certain right reverend Prelate, now with God, (that I think, my Lord, is the Phrase when we speak of departed Episcopacy) had, amongst other reforming Schemes, entertained a Design of obliging all the Clergy, and especially those of the Metropolis, to appear constantly in their proper Uniform, and on no Account permitting them to be seen in publick without a Gown and Cassock. Of what Service this Reformation could possibly be to Religion and Virtue, I must own I could never discover, whilst the Inconveniencies attending it to the poor Clergy are sufficiently obvious. It has been said, I know, by the Advocates for this Plan, that whenever a Clergyman appears as such, he will always meet with the Respect due to his Function; and that if he is not treated with Civility, he may thank himself for it. But let us examine a little, and see if these Things are so.

You, my Lord, I make no doubt, meet with all the Deference and Respect which are due to your
exalted

exalted Station and Character: But I muſt beg your
Lordſhip not to attribute it to wrong Motives, or
imagine that the Bows made to you in the Street are
a Tribute to your Roſe and Beaver: The Incenſe,
I aſſure your Lordſhip, is offered to the Mitre only.
The Reverence is not paid to you as a Paſtor of the
Flock of Chriſt; it is your temporal, and not your
ſpiritual Dignity, that attracts the Attention, and
commands the Homage of the Multitude: It is not
becauſe you have Three thouſand Souls under your
Care, but that you have Three thouſand Pounds
per Annum. I have read, my Lord, and do verily
believe, that there was a Time, though not within
our Memory, when the Clergy of all Ranks, dignified or undignified, met with ſome Degree of Reſpect, as ſuch, even in this Kingdom; but thoſe
Days are gone and paſt, and ſo very different are
the Manners of this Age, that I would venture one
of my beſt Sermons againſt your Lordſhip's laſt
new Gown and Caſſock, (we Philoſophers, my
Lord, conſider one another's Wants) that if your
Lordſhip, when you go next to the Houſe of Peers,
will ſtep out of your Chariot at _Charing-Croſs_, without your purple-fringed Gloves, your Footman behind, or any other external Mark that might betray
your Quality, you ſhall walk from thence to _Palace-
yard_, without once being obliged to pull off your
Hat, in Return for any Compliments paid to your
Cloth. Nobody, my Lord, in theſe our Days,
takes any Notice of a Gown and Caſſock, except
perhaps a Pariſh Girl, a Chimney-ſweeper's Boy,
who ſalutes you as a Brother Black, or now and
then a common Soldier, who does not know, (as
Chaplains ſeldom attend) but you may belong to
his Regiment. On the other Hand, it is at leaſt
forty to one that you meet with ſome groſs Affront
before you get half way: It is odds but a Hackney
Coachman gives his Horſes a Lick as ſoon as he ſees
you,

you, splashes you all over, and then winks to his Brother, with — ' Smoke the Doctor's new Caf- ' sock.' Add to this, that if you do not give the Wall to every Tinker and Taylor you meet, you will be called a proud Priest: If you happen to be fat, they will be sure to say you have got the Church in your Belly; if you walk fast, you are in a d——d Hurry for your Dinner; if you go slow, and pick your Way, it is,—' Mind Parson *Prim*, how gin- ' gerly he steps.' If your Gown is draggled, a Car- man will call out to you to hold up your Petticoats; and if you chance to turn up an Alley on any ne- ceffary Occafion, the Witticifms upon you are in- numerable: For after all, my Lord, it is a ftrange Thing, and what all the World wonders at, that Parfons fhould eat and drink, and fleep, and do a hundred vulgar Things, juft like other Men.

And now, my Lord, do you ferioufly think it would be any Advantage, or contribute to the Honour and Dignity of the Cloth, to be for ever fcarfed and caffocked in the Streets of *London?* For my own Part, till I am forced to do otherwife, I fhall con- tent myfelf with fkulking unnoticed in my Iron Grey; as, whilft I am miftaken for a Parifh Clerk, a Grazier, or an Undertaker, I may at leaft efcape without Ridicule and Abufe, which, if I appear in my Regimentals, as Things are now circumftanced, I can never expect.

But to return to my Subject, or, as we fay every *Sunday*, to proceed to my fecond Head, and con- fider

What is expected from Lecturers, and how they are generally treated when they become fo. Let us now then fuppofe that the poor Candidate, after going through all thefe fiery Trials, fhould at length be fo fortunate as to make his Calling and Election fure; behold him chofen, licenfed, and in-pulpited, (there, my Lord, is another new Word for you,

3   and

and I fee no Reafon why it is not as good as in-
ftalled) he will find that Seat, or rather Standing of
Honour, a painful Pre-eminence; for, as high as
he may there imagine himfelf, not a Creature who
fits below, but thinks himfelf far above him. Every
Man that gave you his Vote will confider you, from
that Day forth, and as long as you continue in that
Situation, as his Inferior: He looks upon himfelf as
one of your Feeders, to whom you are indebted for
your daily Bread, and therefore expects you will
honour him accordingly; and for this fpecial Reafon,
becaufe if you withdraw your *Complaifance*, he may
withdraw his *Subfcription*. But let us attend a little to the precarious Tenure on which he holds his
new Preferment. When a Man is in peaceable Poffeffion of a good Living, fcarce any Body takes Notice of his Preaching; it matters very little whether
he is as elegant as * —————, or as contemptible as
Dr. —————. But with a *Lecturer* the Cafe is
extremely different: He is confidered by his Hearers
as a Kind of Divinity-cook, and is expected, like
other Cooks, to adapt every Thing to every Body's
Palate: And let him have ever fo much Merit, it is
a Hundred to one he does not pleafe one in a Hundred, for it is all Whim and Caprice. If he has a
loud Voice, perhaps he may be called a Brawler, he
takes too much Pains, labours, and fo forth; if he
is weak and low, he is cenfured as fpiritlefs and inanimate; if his Action is flow and folemn, he fhall
be termed liftlefs and indolent; if it be ftrong, and
varied, it fhall be called vehement and theatrical:
For the poor Judges he is talking to never confider
the different Subjects to be treated; that one may
require fober and compofed Behaviour in the Utterance, another lively, fpirited, and diffufed Gefture.

* The Reader is defired to fill up thefe blank Spaces with the
Names of the beft and worft Preacher he is acquainted with.

In moſt other Profeſſions, thoſe who apply for your Aid and Inſtruction will at leaſt allow you ſome Knowledge in your *own* Buſineſs, and have Complaiſance enough to ſuppoſe you have a tolerable Idea of and Acquaintance with the Matter of it; but in *Divinity* it is quite otherwiſe : Every Auditor in a Church is as good a Judge (or at leaſt thinks himſelf ſo) both of the Subject and the Manner of treating it as yourſelf, and will not fail to ſhew his Judgment with regard to Stile, Sentiment, and Delivery, tho' he knows no more of either than the Deſk you write upon.

They will tell you the Sermon you preached was borrowed from another, when it is really your own; and, *vice verſa*, Compliment you upon it as your own, when it is every Word of it ſtolen from another.

The following, my Lord, is a Fact which happened to myſelf.

Being engaged one whole Week in Writing an Anſwer to a political Pamplet againſt the D——— of N———, for which I had twenty Pieces (more, by the bye, than I got by Preaching in a Twelvemonth) I ventured on the *Saturday* Night to tranſcribe a Diſcourſe of *Tillotſon*'s, and preached it on the *Sunday* Morning to a very polite Audience. On my coming out of Church, I was ſaluted by one of the Overſeers with ' Thank you, Doctor, for your ' excellent Sermon; but let me tell you, it was a ' dangerous Topic for a young Man ; to be ſure you ' might have treated it a little more fully *(obſerve his* ' *Complaiſance)* but upon the Whole it was really a ' good Diſcourſe, and I am ſure all your own; but ' I remember a glorious one of *Tillotſon*'s on that ' very Subject. I remember'---' That you do not ' indeed, my Friend,' replied I (I could not help it, my Lord, for the Life of me) ' for the Sermon ' you juſt now heard is the very ſame, Word for
' Word,

' Word, I aſſure you, and you will find it when you
' go home, Vol. and Page---ſo and ſo.'

But let a Man preach his own Sermons, or any
Body's elſe, he can never expect to pleaſe for any
Length of Time; I have ſcarce ever known a Lecturer continue a Favourite above two or three Years:
If he always preaches himſelf he grows tireſome, and
if he puts in another he is cenſured as Idle and
Negligent: If his Deputy preaches better, or which
is the ſame Thing, appears to preach better than
himſelf, it ſinks the Principal into Contempt; and
if the Deputy does not preach ſo well, Hints are
given him that it would be better if ſome Folks
would do their own Duty; add to this, that your
conſtant Church-trotters and Text-markers, who
take down the Heads in their Pocket-Books, are
always ſmoaking your ſtale Divinity, and expect a
new Diſcourſe to tickle their Ears every *Sunday*. We
can ſee the ſame Play at the Theatre, hear the ſame
Story abroad, or read the ſame Book at home, perhaps once in a Month at leaſt, with Pleaſure; but to
liſten to the ſame Diſcourſe from a Pulpit once in
three Years, though perhaps we do not actually remember a Line more than the Text, is, for what
Reaſon I know not, moſt intolerable.

I am as thoroughly convinced, as I am of my
own Exiſtence, that Lectureſhips greatly promote
and increaſe Methodiſm. A Deſire of ſtriking out
ſomething new and uncommon to tickle the Ears of
the Groundlings, has led many a plain well-mean-
ing Preacher into romantic Sallies, and theatrical
Geſtures, and inſenſibly drawn them into metho-
diſtical Rant and Enthuſiaſm.

There never was a duller Hound than that * Hound
of *King's*, whom your Lordſhip muſt remember as

* The Servitors, as they are termed at *Oxford*, or what we call in
Cambridge Sizers, go, at *King's College*, and there only, by the Name
of Hounds. Mr. *Jones* was a Hound of *King's*.

well

well as myfelf, the famous Mr. *Jones* of *St. Saviour's:* He had preached for fome Time in the old dog-trot Stile of Firft to the Firft, Secondly to the Second, and adminiftered his gentle Soporifics to no Purpofe for a Year or two, when, finding it would not do, all on a fudden he fhook his Ears, fet up a loud Bark, and by mere Dint of Noife, Vociferation and Grimace, mouthed and bellowed himfelf into Reputation amongft the Gentlemen of the *Clink,* out heroded *Herod,* and almoft eclipfed the Fame of *Wefley, Whitefield,* and *Madan.*

I fhall now proceed, my Lord (to fpeak in the Parfonick Stile) to my third general Head, *viz.* the Manner in which Lecturefhips are ufually paid, which is equally injurious to our Character and Function.

I know a little too much of the World, my Lord, to expect that a Parfon fhould be paid like a firft-rate Player, a Pimp, or a Lord of the Treafury, whofe Incomes I believe are pretty near equal ; but at the fame Time cannot help thinking, that a La-bourer in the Vineyard is as well worthy of his Hire, as a Journeyman Carpenter, Mafon, *&c.* and has as good a Right to two Pound two on a *Sunday* as he has on a *Saturday* Night; and yet not one in a Hundred of us is paid in that Proportion.

The Lecturer's Box generally goes about with the reft of the Parifh Beggars a little after *Chriftmas*; and every Body throws in their Charity (for it is always confidered in that Light) as they think proper. Were I to tell your Lordfhip how many paltry Excufes are made to evade this little annual Tribute by the Mean and Sordid, how very little is given even by the moft Generous, and what an inconfiderable Sum the Whole generally amounts to, the Recital would not afford you much Entertainment, and, for aught I know, might even give you fome fmall Concern.

You

You cannot imagine, my Lord, with what an envious Eye we poor Lecturers have often looked over a Waiter's Book at a Coffee-houfe, where I have feen fuch a Collection of Guineas and half Guineas as made my Mouth water: To give lefs than a Crown at leaft, would be to the laft Degree ungenteel, for the immenfe Trouble of handing a Difh of Coffee, or a News-paper; whilft the poor Divine, who has toiled in the Miniftry for a Twelve-month, and half worn out a Pair of excellent Lungs in the unprofitable Service, fhall think himfelf well rewarded with the noble Donation of *Half a Crown*.

But to illuftrate my Subject, I will give your Lordfhip another Story: There is nothing like a little Painting from the Life on thefe Occafions: Suppofe yourfelf then, my Lord, an Eye-witnefs of the following Scene, which paffed not long fince in a certain Part of this Metropolis.

Enter the Church-warden and Overfeer into the Shop of Mr. *Prim* the Mercer---Well, Mr. *Twift*, what are your Commands with me?---We are come to wait on your Honour, with the Lecturer's Book, Sir,---a voluntary Subfcription of the Inhabitants of the Parifh of St. —— for the Support of —— Well, well, you need not read any further; what is it?—— Whatever you pleafe, Sir,—Aye, here's another Load, another Burthen: D'ye think I am made of Gold? There's the Poor's Rate, the Doctor's Rate, the Window Rates; the Devil's in the Rates, I think— however, I can't refufe *you*; but I'll not give an-other Year—here, *Buckram*, reach me Half a Crown out of the Till—your Servant, Madam—

[*A Lady comes out of a back Parlour, walks through the Shop, and gets into a Chair.*]

Aye, there's another Tax—a Guinea for two Box Tickets, as fure as the Benefit comes round, for my Wife and Daughter, befides Chair-hire.

[*Twift fhakes his Head.*]

O Mafter

O Mafter *Prim*, Mafter *Prim!* had not you better now have given us a Guinea for the Doctor and
his four Children, and referved your Half Crown
for the Lady, who, if I may judge from her Garb
and Equipage, does not want it half fo much as the
poor *Parfon*; but you will be in the Fafhion, fo
give us your Mite ; fet down Mr. *Prim* Two and
Sixpence.—Sir, Good Morrow to you—Gentlemen,
your Servant—

Such, my Lord, you fee, is the Force of Fafhion, and fuch the Influence of Example, that a
conftant Church-goer, and one perhaps who fancies
himfelf a very good Chriftian, fhall throw away *one
Pound one* with all the Pleafure imaginable for an
Evening's Entertainment at the Theatre, and at the
fame Time grudge *Half a Crown* for two and fifty
Difcourfes from the Pulpit, which, if he turns to
his Arithmetic Book, he will fee amounts to about
---three Farthings a Sermon---and a fober Citizen
too, as Lady *Townly* fays, ' Fye ! fye !'

Thefe, my Lord, are melancholy Truths, and,
though you and I who are Philofophers may laugh
at them, have made many an honeft Man's Heart
ake.

I will leave your Lordfhip to imagine, without
entering any further into this Subject, what the
great and defirable Emoluments muft be arifing from
a *Town Lectureship* ; hardly equal at the beft to the
Wages of a Journeyman Staymaker, and by no
Means upon a Level with the Profits of Drawers,
Coffee-houfe Waiters, or the Footmen of our Nobility.   This very lucrative Employment, notwithftanding, as being too confiderable for one Man, is
frequently fplit in two and divided, like the Places
of Poft Mafter General, Secretary, &c. amongft
the Great.   I have myfelf the Honour, my Lord,
of being what is called a *Joint-Lecturer*, not having
Intereft enough in the Parifh, where I had been *Cu-*

rate for twenty Years, to fecure the Whole. I cannot indeed fo far agree with our old Friend *Hefiod* as to think * the Half better than the Whole, but, embracing the † *Englifh* inftead of the *Greek* Proverb, fit myfelf down contentedly, and eat my *half Loaf* in Quiet. But, to confefs the Truth, I find the Profits of both Preferments (for your Lordfhip fees I am a *Pluralift*) rather too fmall, to provide, in thefe hard Times, for the Neceffities of a growing Family, and have lately been obliged to *eke out* Matters by entering myfelf on my Friend *H---w's* Lift. As there is fomething curious in this Mr. *H——*, both with Regard to himfelf, and the Bufinefs he is engaged in, I fhall beg Leave to introduce him to your Lordfhip's Acquaintance, as I believe, during what I may call your *Minority* in the *Church*, no fuch Character or Occupation was in being.

You muft know then, my Lord, that the ingenious Mr. H—— has found out a new Method of being ferviceable to the *Clergy* and himfelf, by keeping a Kind of *Ecclefiaftical Regifter Office*, or, more properly fpeaking, *Divinity-Shop*, in the City, where *Parfons* are *hired* by the Day, Week, Month, &c. as Occafion requires. For this Purpofe he keeps a regular alphabetical Lift of unemployed *Divines*, from the Age of threefcore and ten, to two and twenty, ready to be *let out* for certain ftipulated Sums, deducting a proper *Premium* for the *Agent* from every one of them. If any labouring *Curate*, *Lecturer*, *Morning Preacher*, &c. is too bufy or too idle to perform his own Duty, he may immediately repair to the faid Office, and be fupplied with as much found and orthodox Divinity as he is able or willing to pay for. To this very ufeful Gentleman, I had myfelf, not long fince, Occafion to apply,

---

* πλεον ημισυ παντ☉.

† Half a Loaf is better than no Bread.

being obliged to leave my *Church* for a Fortnight ;
when the following Converfation, as near as I can
remember, paffed between us : if it does not make
you fmile, I can only fay, your Lordfhip's rifible
Mufcles are not fo pliant as they ufed to be.

Curate.

Mr. *H——* your Servant.

Mr. *H——*

Doctor, your's.

Curate.

I fuppofe, Mr. *H——*, you can guefs my Errand ; I am going out of Town To-morrow, and
fhall want a Supply, and withal, Mafter *H——*,
I come to inform you, I fhall commence from this
Day both *Agent* and *Patient*, and intend to hire and
to be hired : fo, as I am likely to be a pretty conftant Dealer, and am befides an old Acquaintance,
hope you will give me the Turn of the Scale : fo
put me down in your Lift immediately.

Mr. *H——* [*pulling out the Lift.*

It fhall be done, Sir : and a moft refpectable
Lift it is, I affure you ; I have juft got a frefh Cargo of *Scotch Divines*, piping hot from *Edinburgh* ;
befides the old Corps—my Collection ends with---
let me fee---fourteen School-Mafters, five Doctors
of Divinity, (pray, my Lord mind the *Climax*) two
Reviewers, three political Writers, two Bible-ma-
kers, and a K——'s C——n.

Curate.

All Men of Erudition, I fuppofe.

Mr. *H——*

Excellent Scholars, charming Preachers, I affure
you : but, *entre nous*, not one of them worth Sixpence in the World---but to your Bufinefs.

Curate.

Aye, Mr. *H——*, I muft have good Voice for
Wednefdays and *Fridays*, and one of your beft Ora-

tors

tors for *Sunday next:* you know, *my* Congregation
is a little delicate.

Mr. *H——*

Aye; more nice than wife perhaps---but let us
look fharp---here's *Parfon Rawbones,* one of my
Athletic, able-bodied Divines, it is not long fince
he knock'd down a Clerk in the Defk for interrupt-
ing him in the Middle of a Prayer; this, you know,
fhew'd a good Spirit, and keeps up the *Dignity* of
the *Cloth:* but I doubt whether he'll do for *you;*
for he's a *North country Man,* and has got the *Burr*
in his Throat; he'll never pafs at *your* End of the
Town: I fhall fport him, however, at a *Day-lec-
ture,* or an early *Sacrament.*

Curate.

You are fo facetious Mr. *H——*, but pray find
me out fomebody, for I am in Hafte.

Mr. *H——*

If you had wanted a Brawler for a Charity Ser-
mon, I could have help'd you to the beft *Beggar*
in *England,* an Errant Pick-pocket for the *Middle
Ifle;* beats your D——'s and W——'s out of the
Pit, a Doctor of Divinity too, and a Juftice of
Peace; but he won't do for *you,* for the Dog's over
Head and Ears in Debt, and durft not ftir out on
a Week-day for Fear of the Bum-bailiffs; but---
here I have him for you---the quickeft Reader in
England: I'll bet my *Stackhoufe's* Bible to a *Common-
Prayer* Book, he gives Dr. *Drawl* to the Te-Deum,
and overtakes him before he comes to the Thankfgiving! O, he's a *rare Hand* at a Collect; but,
remember, if he preaches, you muft furnifh him
with the *Paraphernalia;* for he's but juft got upon
the Lift, and has not Money enough yet to purchafe *Canonicals.*

Curate.

O, we can equip him with *them,* but what's his
Price?

Mr.

Mr. *H——*   [*whispers.*

Why, you would not offer him lefs than——
for the Sake of your Brethren, for your own Sake.
Let me tell you, Sir, I am one of the beft Friends
to the inferior *Clergy*, and have done more for them,
(and that's a bold Word) than the whole Bench of
B——p's.   I believe I may fafely fay, I have raifed
the Price of *Lungs* at leaft *Cent. per Cent :* I knew
the Time, and fo did·you, when a well caffock'd
Divine was glad to read Prayers, and on a Holiday
too, for Twelve-pence ; Old *C——* never had
more in his Life ; now, Sir, I never let a *Tit* go out
of *my* Stable, (you'll pardon my Jocularity) under
five Shillings.---

My Friend *H——* was running on in this un-
merciful Manner, and would, for aught I know,
have talked to this Time, if I had not ftopp'd him
fhort, pretended immediate Bufinefs, paid my Ear-
neft, and took my Leave: not a little chagrin'd,
you may imagine, at the contemptuous Kindnefs
he expreffed for the *Cloth*, and the degrading Familiarity with which he treated that *Function* to which
your Lordfhip, equally with myfelf, has the Honour
to belong.

To fay the Truth ——But this muft be deferred,
with many other Confiderations, to *another Letter* ;
my Wife having juft now broke into my Study to
remind me, that I have a Sermon to finifh before
Ten, To-morrow, which will fcarce give me Time
to fubfcribe myfelf,

My Lord,

Your Lordship's

Moft obedient, &c.

F. T.

CRITICAL REFLECTIONS

ON THE OLD

ENGLISH DRAMATICK WRITERS.

To DAVID GARRICK, Efq.

SIR,

IT is not unnatural to imagine that, on the firſt Glance of your Eye over the Advertiſement of a new Pamphlet, addreſſed to yourſelf, you are apt to feel ſome little Emotion ; that you beſtow more than ordinary Attention on the Title, as it ſtands in the News-Paper, and take Notice of the Name of the Publiſher.----Is it Compliment or Abuſe?---One of theſe being determined, you are perhaps eager to be ſatisfied, whether ſome coarſe Hand has laid on Encomiums with a Trowel, or ſome more elegant Writer (ſuch as the Author of *The Actor* for Inſtance) has done Credit to himſelf and you by his Panegyrick ; or, on the other Hand, whether any offended Genius has employed thoſe Talents againſt you, which he is ambitious of exerciſing in the Service of your Theatre ; or ſome common Scribe has taken your Character, as he would that of any other Man or Woman, or Miniſter, or the King, if he durſt, as a popular Topick of Scandal.

Be not alarmed on the preſent Occaſion ; nor, with that Conſciouſneſs of your own Merit, ſo natural to the Celebrated and Eminent, indulge yourſelf in an Acquieſcence with the Juſtice of ten thouſand fine Things, which you may ſuppoſe ready to be

3 be

be said to you. No private Satire or Panegyrick, but the general Good of the Republick of Letters, and of the Drama in particular, is intended. Though Praise and Dispraise stand ready on each Side, like the Vessels of Good and Evil on the Right and Left Hand of *Jupiter*, I do not mean to dip into either: Or, if I do, it shall be, like the Pagan Godhead himself, to mingle a due Proportion of each. Sometimes, perhaps, I may find Fault, and sometimes bestow Commendation: But you must not expect to hear of the Quickness of your Conception, the Justice of your Execution, the Expression of your Eye, the Harmony of your Voice, or the Variety and Excellency of your Deportment; nor shall you be maliciously informed, that you are shorter than *Barry*, leaner than *Quin*, and less a Favourite of the Upper Gallery than *Woodward* or *Shuter*.

The following Pages are destined to contain a Vindication of the Works of *Massinger*, one of our old Dramatick Writers, who very seldom falls much beneath *Shakespeare* himself, and sometimes almost rises to a proud Rivalship of his chiefest Excellencies. They are meant too as a laudable, though faint, Attempt to rescue these admirable Pieces from the too general Neglect which they now labour under, and to recommend them to the Notice of the Publick. To whom then can such an Essay be more properly inscribed than to you, whom that Publick seems to have appointed, as its chief *Arbiter Deliciarum*, to preside over the Amusements of the Theatre?—But there is also, by the bye, a private Reason for addressing you. Your honest Friend *Davies*, who, as is said of the provident Comedian in *Holland*, spends his Hours of Vacation from the Theatre in his Shop, is too well acquainted with the Efficacy of your Name at the Top of a Play-Bill, to omit an Opportunity of prefixing it to a new Publication, hoping it may prove a Charm

to

to draw in Purchasers, like the Head of *Shakespeare* on his Sign. My Letter too being anonymous, your Name at the Head, will more than compensate for the Want of mine at the End of it: And our above-mentioned Friend is, no Doubt, too well versed in both his Occupations, not to know the Consequence of Secrecy in a Bookseller, as well as the Necessity of concealing from the Publick many Things that pass *behind the Curtain*.

There is perhaps no Country in the World more subordinate to the Power of Fashion than our own. Every Whim, every Word, every Vice, every Virtue, in its Turn becomes the Mode, and is followed with a certain Rage of Approbation for a Time. The favourite Stile in all the polite Arts, and the reigning Taste in Letters, are as notoriously Objects of Caprice as Architecture and Dress. A new Poem, or Novel, or Farce, are as inconsiderately extolled or decried as a Ruff or a *Chinese* Rail, a Hoop or a Bow Window. Hence it happens, that the publick Taste is often vitiated: Or if, by Chance, it has made a proper Choice, becomes partially attached to one Species of Excellence, and remains dead to the Sense of all other Merit, however equal, or superior.

I think I may venture to assert, with a Confidence, that on Reflection it will appear to be true, that the eminent Class of Writers, who flourished at the Beginning of this Century, have almost entirely superseded their illustrious Predecessors. The Works of *Congreve*, *Vanbrugh*, *Steele*, *Addison*, *Pope*, *Swift*, *Gay*, &c. &c. are the chief Study of the Million: I say, of the Million; for as to those few, who are not only familiar with all our own Authors, but are also conversant with the Ancients, they are not to be circumscribed by the narrow Limits of the Fashion. *Shakespeare* and *Milton* seem to stand alone, like first-rate Authors, amid the general Wreck of old *English*

z   Litera-

Literature. *Milton* perhaps owes much of his prefent Fame to the generous Labours and good Tafte
of *Addifon*. *Shakefpeare* has been tranfmitted down
to us with fucceffive Glories; and you, Sir, have
continued, or rather increafed, his Reputation.
You have, in no fulfome Strain of Compliment,
been ftiled the Beft Commentator on his Works:
But have you not, like other Commentators, contracted a narrow, exclufive, Veneration of your
Author? Has not the Contemplation of *Shakefpeare's*
Excellencies almoft dazzled and extinguifhed your
Judgement, when directed to other Objects, and
made you blind to the Merit of his Cotemporaries?
Under your Dominion, have not *Beaumont* and *Fletcher*, nay even *Johnfon*, fuffered a Kind of theatrical Difgrace? And has not poor *Maffinger*, whofe
Caufe I have now undertaken, been permitted to
languifh in Obfcurity, and remained almoft entirely
unknown?

To this perhaps it may be plaufibly anfwered, nor
indeed without fome Foundation, that many of our
old Plays, though they abound with Beauties, and
are raifed much above the humble Level of later
Writers, are yet, on feveral Accounts, unfit to be
exhibited on the modern Stage; that the Fable, inftead of being raifed on probable Incidents in real
Life, is generally built on fome foreign Novel, and
attended with romantick Circumftances; that the
Conduct of thefe extravagant Stories is frequently
uncouth, and infinitely offenfive to that dramatick
Correctnefs prefcribed by late Criticks, and practifed, as they pretend, by the *French* Writers; and
that the Characters, exhibited in our old Plays, can
have no pleafing Effect on a modern Audience, as
they are fo totally different from the Manners of the
prefent Age.

Thefe, and fuch as thefe, might once have appeared reafonable Objections: But you, Sir, of all
Perfons,

Persons, can urge them with the least Grace, since your Practice has so fully proved their Insufficiency. Your Experience must have taught you, that when a Piece has any striking Beauties, they will cover a Multitude of Inaccuracies: and that a Play need not be written on the severest Plan, to please in the Representation. The Mind is soon familiarized to Irregularities, which do not sin against the Truth of Nature, but are merely Violations of that strict Decorum of late so earnestly insisted on What patient Spectators are we of the Inconsistencies that confessedly prevail in our darling *Shakespeare!* What critical Catcall ever proclaimed the Indecency of introducing the Stocks in the Tragedy of *Lear?* How quietly do we see *Gloster* take his imaginary Leap from *Dover* Cliff! Or to give a stronger Instance of Patience, with what a philosophical Calmness do the Audience dose over the tedious, and uninteresting, Love-Scenes, with which the bungling Hand of *Tate* has coarsely pieced and patched that rich Work of *Shakespeare!*— To instance further from *Shakespeare* himself, the Grave-diggers in *Hamlet* (not to mention *Polonius*) are not only endured, but applauded; the very Nurse in *Romeo* and *Juliet* is allowed to be Nature; the Transactions of a whole History are, without Offence, begun and compleated in less than three Hours; and we are agreeably wafted by the *Chorus,* or oftener without so much Ceremony, from one End of the World to another.

It is very true, that it was the general Practice of our old Writers, to found their Pieces on some foreign Novel; and it seemed to be their chief Aim to take the Story, as it stood, with all its appendant Incidents of every Complexion, and throw it into Scenes. This Method was, to be sure, rather inartificial, as it at once overloaded and embarrassed the Fable, leaving it destitute of that beautiful dramatick Connection, which enables the Mind to take in all

its

its Circumſtances with Facility and Delight. But I
am ſtill in Doubt, whether many Writers, who come
nearer to our own Times, have much mended the
Matter. What with their Plots, and Double-Plots,
and Counter-Plots, and Under-Plots, the Mind is as
much perplexed to piece out the Story, as to put together the disjointed Parts of our ancient Drama.
The Comedies of *Congreve* have, in my Mind, as
little to boaſt of Accuracy in their Conſtruction, as
the Plays of *Shakeſpeare*; nay, perhaps, it might be
proved that, amidſt the moſt open Violation of the
leſſer critical Unities, one Point is more ſteadily per-
ſued, one Character more uniformly ſhewn, and one
grand Purpoſe of the Fable more evidently accom-
pliſhed in the Production of *Shakeſpeare* than of
Congreve.

These Fables (it may be further objected) founded
on romantick Novels, are unpardonably wild and extravagant in their Circumſtances, and exhibit too
little even of the Manners of the Age in which they
were written. The Plays too are in themſelves a
Kind of heterogeneous Compoſition; ſcarce any of
them being, ſtrictly ſpeaking, a Tragedy, Comedy,
or even Tragi-Comedy, but rather an indigeſted
Jumble of every Species thrown together.

This Charge muſt be confeſſed to be true: But
upon Examination it will, perhaps, be found of leſs
Conſequence than is generally imagined. Theſe
Dramatick Tales, for ſo we may beſt ſtile ſuch Plays,
have often occaſioned much Pleaſure to the Reader
and Spectator, which could not poſſibly have been
conveyed to them by any other Vehicle. Many an
intereſting Story, which, from the Diverſity of its
Circumſtances, cannot be regularly reduced either
to Tragedy or Comedy, yet abounds with Character, and contains ſeveral affecting Situations: And
why ſuch a Story ſhould loſe its Force, dramatically
related and aſſiſted by Repreſentation, when it
pleaſes,

pleafes, under the colder Form of a Novel, is difficult to conceive. Experience has proved the Effect of fuch Fictions on our Minds; and convinced us, that the Theatre is not that barren Ground, wherein the Plants of Imagination will not flourifh. *The Tempeſt, the Midſummer Night's Dream, the Merchant of Venice, As you like it, Twelfth Night, the Faithful Shepherdeſs of Fletcher,* (with a much longer Liſt that might be added from *Shakeſpeare, Beaumont and Fletcher,* and their Cotemporaries, or immediate Succeſſors) have moſt of them, within all our Memories, been ranked among the moſt popular Entertainments of the Stage. Yet none of theſe can be denominated Tragedy, Comedy, or Tragi-Comedy. The Play Bills, I have obſerved, cautioufly ſtile them Plays: And Plays indeed they are, truly ſuch, if it be the End of Plays to delight and inſtruct, to captivate at once the Ear, the Eye, and the Mind, by Situations forcibly conceived, and Characters truly delineated.

There is one Circumſtance in Dramatick Poetry, which, I think, the chaſtiſed Notions of our modern Criticks do not permit them ſufficiently to conſider. Dramatic Nature is of a more large and liberal Quality than they are willing to allow. It does not conſiſt merely in the Repreſentation of real Characters, Characters acknowledged to abound in common Life; but may be extended alſo to the Exhibition of imaginary Beings. To create, is to be a Poet indeed; to draw down Beings from another Sphere, and endue them with ſuitable Paſſions, Affections, Diſpoſitions, allotting them at the ſame Time proper Employment; to body forth, by the Powers of Imagination, the Forms of Things unknown, and to give to airy Nothing a local Habitation and a Name, ſurely requires a Genius for the Drama equal, if not ſuperior, to the Delineation of Perſonages, in the ordinary Courſe of Nature.

Shake-

Shakespeare, in particular, is univerfally acknowledged
never to have foared fo far above the Reach of all
other Writers, as in thofe Inftances, where he feems
purpofely to have tranfgreffed the Laws of Criticifm.
He appears to have difdained to put his free Soul
into Circumfcription and Confine, which denied his
extraordinary Talents their full Play, nor gave Scope
to the Boundlefnefs of his Imagination. His Witches,
Ghofts, Fairies, and other imaginary Beings, fcattered through his Plays, are fo many glaring Violations of the common Table of Dramatick Laws.
What then fhall we fay? Shall we confefs their
Force and Power over the Soul, fhall we allow them
to be Beauties of the moft exquifite Kind, and yet
infift on their being expunged? And why? except
it be to reduce the Flights of an exalted Genius, by
fixing the Standard of Excellence on the Practice of
inferior Writers, who wanted Parts to execute fuch
great Defigns; or to accommodate them to the narrow Ideas of fmall Cricks, who want Souls large
enough to comprehend them?

Our old Writers thought no Perfonage whatever,
unworthy a Place in the Drama, to which they could
annex what may be called a *Seity*; that is, to which
they could allot Manners and Employment peculiar
to itfelf. The fevereft of the Antients cannot be
more eminent for the conftant Prefervation of Uniformity of Character, than *Shakefpeare*; and *Shake-*
fpeare, in no Inftance, fupports his Characters with
more Exactnefs, than in the Conduct of his ideal
Beings. The Ghoft in *Hamlet* is a fhining Proof
of this Excellence.

But, in Confequence of the Cuftom of tracing the
Events of a Play minutely from a Novel, the Au-
thors were fometimes led to reprefent a mere human
Creature in Circumftances not quite confonant to
Nature, of a Difpofition rather wild and extravagant,
and in both Cafes more efpecially repugnant to mo-
                                                    dern

dern Ideas. This indeed required particular Indulgence from the Spectator, but it was an Indulgence, which seldom missed of being amply repaid. Let the Writer but once be allowed, as a necessary *Datum*, the Possibility of any Character's being placed in such a Situation, or possest of so peculiar a Turn of Mind, the Behaviour of the Character is perfectly natural. *Shakespeare*, though the Child of Fancy, seldom or never dreft up a common Mortal in any other than the modest Dress of Nature: But many shining Characters in the Plays of *Beaumont* and *Fletcher* are not so well grounded on the Principles of the human Heart; and yet, as they were supported with Spirit, they were received with Applause. *Shylock*'s Contract, with the Penalty of the Pound of Flesh, though not *Shakespeare*'s own Fiction, is perhaps rather improbable; at least it would not be regarded as a happy Dramatick Incident in a modern Play; and yet, having once taken it for granted, how beautifully, nay, how naturally, is the Character sustained!—Even this Objection therefore, of a Deviation from Nature, great as it may seem, will be found to be a Plea insufficient to excuse the total Exclusion of our antient Dramatists from the Theatre. *Shakespeare*, you will readily allow, possest Beauties more than necessary to redeem his Faults; Beauties, that excite our Admiration, and obliterate his Errors. True. But did no Portion of that divine Spirit fall to the Share of our other old Writers? And can their Works be suppressed, or concealed, without Injustice to their Merit?

One of the best and most pleasing Plays in *Massinger*, and which, we are told, was originally received with general Approbation, is called, *The Picture*. The Fiction, whence it takes its Title, and on which the Story of the Play is grounded, may be collected from the following short Scene. *Mathias*, a Gentleman of *Bohemia*, having taken an affecting Leave

of

of his Wife *Sophia*, with a Refolution of ferving in
the King of *Hungary's* Army againft the *Turks*, is
left alone on the Stage, and the Play goes on, as
follows :

Math. I am ftrangely troubled : Yet why fhould I
A Fury here, and with imagin'd Food? [nourifh
Having no real Grounds on which to raife
A Building of Sufpicion fhe ever was,
Or can be falfe hereafter? I in this
But foolifhly inquire the Knowledge of
A future Sorrow, which, if I find out,
My prefent Ignorance were a cheap Purchafe,
Though with my Lofs of Being. I have already
Dealt with a Friend of mine, a general Scholar,
One deeply read in Nature's hidden Secrets,
And (though with much Unwillingnefs) have won
To do as much as Art can to refolve me   [him
My Fate that follows—To my Wifh he's come.
                Enter Baptifta.
Julio Baptifta, now I may affirm
Your Promife and Performance walk together ;
And therefore, without Circumftance, to the Point,
Inftruct me what I am.
    Bapt. I could wifh you had
Made Trial of my Love fome other Way.
    Math. Nay, this is from the Purpofe.
    Bapt. If you can,
Proportion your Defire to any Mean,
I do pronounce you happy : I have found,
By certain Rules of Art, your matchlefs Wife
Is to this prefent Hour from all Pollution
Free and untainted.
    Math. Good.
    Bapt. In Reafon therefore
You fhould fix here, and make no farther Search
Of what may fall hereafter.
    Math. O *Baptifta!*

'Tis

'Tis not in me to master so my Passions;
I must know farther, or you have made good
But half your Promise.—While my Love stood by,
Holding her upright, and my Presence was
A Watch upon her, her Desires being met too
With equal Ardour from me, what one Proof
Could she give of her Constancy, being untempted?
But when I am absent, and my coming back
Uncertain, and those wanton Heats in Women
Not to be quench'd by lawful Means, and she
The absolute Disposer of herself,
Without Controul or Curb; nay more, invited
By Opportunity and all strong Temptations,
If then she hold out——

   Bapt. As no Doubt she will.

   Math. Those Doubts must be made Certainties,
By your Assurance, or your boasted Art   [*Baptista,*
Deserves no Admiration. How you trifle——
And play with my Affliction! I'm on
The Rack, till you confirm me.

   Bapt. Sure, *Mathias,*
I am no God, nor can I dive into
Her hidden Thoughts, or know what her Intents are;
That is deny'd to Art, and kept conceal'd
E'en from the Devils themselves: They can but guess,
Out of long Observation, what is likely;
But positively to foretell that this shall be,
You may conclude impossible; all I can,
I will do for you. When you are distant from her
A thousand Leagues, as if you then were with her,
You shall know truly when she is solicited,
And how far wrought on.

   Math. I desire no more.

   Bapt. Take then this little Model of *Sophia,*
With more than human Skill limn'd to the Life;
Each Line and Lineament of it in the Drawing
So punctually observ'd, that, had it Motion,
In so much 'twere herself.

                         Math.

Math. It is, indeed,
An admirable Piece ; but if it have not
Some hidden Virtue that I cannot guefs at,
In what can it advantage me ?
　Bapt. I'll inftruct you.
Carry it ftill about you, and as oft
As you defire to know how fhe's affected,
With curious Eyes perufe it : While it keeps
The Figure it now has, entire and perfect,
She is not only innocent in Fact,
But unattempted ; but if once it vary
From the true Form, and what's now White and Red
Incline to Yellow, reft moft confident
She's with all Violence courted, but unconquer'd.
But if it turn all Black, 'tis an Affurance
The Fort, by Compofition or Surprize,
Is forc'd, or with her free Confent, furrender'd.

Nothing can be more fantaftick, or more in the
extravagant Strain of the *Italian* Novels, than this
Fiction : And yet the Play raifed on it is extremely
beautiful, abounds with affecting Situations, true
Character, and a faithful Reprefentation of Nature.
The Story, thus opened, proceeds as follows : *Mathias* departs, accompanied by his Friend, and ferves
as a Volunteer in the *Hungarian* Army againft the
Turks. A complete Victory being obtained, chiefly
by Means of his Valour, he is brought by the General to the *Hungarian* Court, where he not only receives many Honours from the King, but captivates
the Heart of the Queen ; whofe Paffion is not fo
much excited by his known Valour, or perfonal At-
tractions, as by his avowed Conftancy to his Wife,
and his firm Affurance of her reciprocal Affection and
Fidelity to him. Thefe Circumftances touch the
Pride, and raife the Envy of the Queen. She refolves therefore to deftroy his conjugal Faith by
giving up her own, and determines to make him a

desperate Offer of her Person; and, at the same Time, under Pretence of Notice of *Mathias*'s being detained for a Month at Court, she dispatches two young Noblemen to tempt the Virtue of *Sophia*. These Incidents occasion several affecting Scenes both on the Part of the Husband and Wife. *Mathias* (not with an unnatural and untheatrical Stoicism, but with the liveliest Sensibility) nobly withstands the Temptations of the Queen. *Sophia*, though most virtuously attached to her Husband, becomes uneasy at the feigned Stories which the young Lords recount to her of his various Gallantries at Court, and in a Fit of Jealousy, Rage, and Resentment, makes a momentary Resolution to give up her Honour. While she is supposed to be yet under the Dominion of this Resolution, occurs the following Scene between the Husband and his Friend.

MATHIAS and BAPTISTA.

Bapt. We are in a desperate Straight; there's no
       Evasion,
Nor Hope left to come off, but by your yielding
To the Necessity; you must feign a Grant
To her violent Passion, or——
   Math. What, my *Baptista?*
Bapt. We are but dead else.
   Math. Were the Sword now heav'd up,
And my Neck upon the Block, I would not buy
An Hour's Reprieve with the Loss of Faith and Virtue,
To be made immortal here. Art thou a Scholar,
Nay, almost without a Parallel, and yet fear
To die, which is inevitable? You may urge
The many Years that by the Course of Nature
We may travel in this tedious Pilgrimage,
And hold it as a Blessing, as it is,
When Innocence is our Guide; yet know, *Baptista*,
Our Virtues are preferr'd before our Years,
By the Great Judge. To die untainted in

Our

Our Fame and Reputation is the greateſt ;
And to loſe that, can we deſire to live?
Or ſhall I, for a momentary Pleaſure,
Which ſoon comes to a Period, to all Times
Have Breach of Faith and Perjury remembred
In a ſtill living Epitaph? No, *Baptiſta*,
Since my *Sophia* will go to her Grave
Unſpotted in her Faith, I'll follow her
With equal Loyalty : But look on this,
Your own great Work, your Maſter-piece, and then
She being ſtill the ſame, teach me to alter.
Ha ! ſure I do not ſleep ! Or, if I dream,
                              [*The Picture altered.*
This is a terrible Viſion ! I will clear
My Eyeſight, perhaps Melancholy makes me
See that which is not.

   Bapt. It is too apparent.
I grieve to look upon't ; beſides the Yellow,
That does aſſure ſhe's tempted, there are Lines
Of a dark Colour, that diſperſe themſelves
O'er every Miniature of her Face, and thoſe
Confirm——

   Math. She is turn'd Whore.

   Bapt. I muſt not ſay ſo,
Yet as a Friend to Truth, if you will have me
Interpret it, in her Conſent, and Wiſhes
She's falſe, but not in Fact yet.

   Math. Fact ! *Baptiſta ?*
Make not yourſelf a Pandar to her Looſeneſs,
In labouring to palliate what a Vizard
Of Impudence cannot cover.   Did e'er Woman
In her Will decline from Chaſtity, but found Means
To give her hot Luſt full Scope? It is more
Poſſible in Nature for groſs Bodies
Deſcending of themſelves, to hang in the Air,
Or with my ſingle Arm to underprop
A falling Tower ; nay, in its violent Courſe
To ſtop the Light'ning, than to ſtay a Woman

Hurried by two Furies, Luſt and Falſhood,
In her full Career to Wickedneſs.

    Bapt Pray you temper
The Violence of your Paſſion.

    Math. In Extremes
Of this Condition, can it be in Man
To uſe a Moderation? I am thrown
From a ſteep Rock headlong into a Gulph
Of Miſery, and find myſelf paſt Hope,
In the ſame Moment that I apprehend
That I am falling.   And this, the Figure of
My Idol, few Hours ſince, while ſhe continued
In her Perfection, that was late a Mirror,
In which I ſaw miraculous Shapes of Duty,
Staid Manners, with all Excellency a Huſband
Could wiſh in a chaſte Wife, is on the ſudden
Turn'd to a magical Glaſs, and does preſent
Nothing but Horns and Horror.

    Bapt   You may yet
(And 'tis the beſt Foundation) build up Comfort
On your own Goodneſs.

    Math. No, that hath undone me,
For now I hold my Temperance a Sin
Worſe than Exceſs, and what was Vice a Virtue.
Have I refus'd a Queen, and ſuch a Queen   [ed
(Whoſe raviſhing Beauties at the firſt Sight had tempt-
A Hermit from his Beads, and chang'd his Prayers
To amorous Sonnets) to preſerve my Faith
Inviolate to Thee, with the Hazard of
My Death with Torture, ſince ſhe could inflict .
No leſs for my Contempt, and have I met
Such a Return from Thee? I will not curſe Thee,
Nor for thy Falſhood rail againſt the Sex ;
"Tis poor, and common ; I'll only with wiſe Men
Whiſper unto myſelf, howe'er they ſeem,
Nor preſent, nor paſt Times, nor the Age to come
Hath heretofore, can now, or ever ſhall ʼ
Produce one conſtant Woman.

              I   *Bapt.*

Bapt. This is more
Than the Satyrifts wrote againft 'em.
    Math. There's no Language
That can exprefs the Poifon of thefe Afpicks,
Thefe weeping Crocodiles, and all too little
That hath been faid againft 'em.   But I'll mould
My Thoughts into another Form, and if
She can outlive the Report of what I have done,
This Hand, when next fhe comes within my Reach,
Shall be her Executioner.

The Fiction of *the* PICTURE being firft allowed,
the moft rigid Critick will, I doubt not, confefs,
that the Workings of the human Heart are accurately fet down in the above Scene.   The Play is
not without many others, equally excellent, both
before and after it ; nor in thofe Days, when the
Tower of Magick was fo generally believed, that
the fevereft Laws were folemnly enacted againft
Witches and Witchcraft, was the Fiction fo bold
and extravagant, as it may feem at prefent   Hoping
that the Reader may, by this Time, be fomewhat reconciled to the Story, or even interefted in
it, I will venture to fubjoin to the long Extracts
I have already made from this Play one more
Speech, where *the* PICTURE is mentioned very
beautifully.   *Mathias* addreffes himfelf to the Queen
in thefe Words.

    Math. To flip once
Is incident, and excus'd by human Frailty ;
But to fall ever, damnable.   We were both
Guilty, I grant, in tendering our Affection,
But, as I hope you will do, I repented.
When we are grown up to Ripenefs, our Life is
Like to this Picture.   While we run
A conftant Race in Goodnefs, it retains
The juft Proportion.   But the Journey being

Tedious,

Tedious, and fweet Temptations in the Way,
That may in fome Degree divert us from
The Road that we put forth in, e'er we end
Our Pilgrimage, it may, like this, turn Yellow,
Or be with Blacknefs clouded. But when we
Find we have gone aftray, and labour to
Return unto our never-failing Guide
Virtue, Contrition (with unfeigned Tears,
The fpots of Vice wafh'd off) will foon reftore it
To the firft Purenefs.

Thefe feveral Paffages will, I hope, be thought
by the judicious Reader to be written in the free
Vein of a true Poet, as well as by the exact Hand
of a faithful Difciple of Nature. If any of the
above Arguments, or, rather, the uncommon Excellence of the great Writers themfelves, can in-
duce the Critic to allow the Excurfions of Fancy
on the Theatre, let him not fuppofe that he is here
advifed to fubmit to the Perverfion of Nature, or
to admire thofe who over-leap the modeft Bounds,
which fhe has prefcribed to the Drama. I will
agree with him, that Plays, wherein the Truth of
Dramatick Character is violated, can convey neither
Inftruction nor Delight, *Shakefpeare*, *Jonfon*, *Beaumont* and *Fletcher*, *Maffinger*, &c. are guilty of no
fuch Violation. Indeed the Heroick Nonfenfe, which
overruns the Theatrical Productions of *Dryden* *,
Howard,

---

* Nobody can have a truer Veneration for the Poetical Genius of
Dryden, than the Writer of thefe Reflections; but furely that Genius is no where fo much obfcured, notwithftanding fome tranfient
Gleams, as in his Plays; of which He had Himfelf no great Opinion, fince the only Plea He ever urged in their Favour, was, that
the Town had received with Applaufe Plays *equally bad*. Nothing,
perhaps, but the abfurd Notion of Heroick Plays, cou'd have carried
the immediate Succeffors to the Old Clafs of Writers into fuch ridiculous Contradictions to Nature. That I may not appear fingular in
my Opinion of *Dryden's* Dramatick Pieces. I muft beg Leave to refer
the Reader to *the Rambler*, No. 125, where that judicious Writer
has

Howard, and the other illuftrious Prototypes of *Bayes* in the *Rehearfal*, muft naufeate the moft indulgent Spectator. The temporary Rage of falfe Tafte may perhaps betray the Injudicious into a foolifh Admiration of fuch Extravagance for a fhort Period: But how will thefe Plays ftand the Brunt of critical Indignation, when the Perfonages of the Drama are found to refemble no Characters in Nature, except, perhaps, the difordered Inhabitants of *Bedlam?*

If then it muft be confeffed, both from Reafon and Experience, that we cannot only endure, but attend with Pleafure to Plays, which are almoft merely Dramatick Reprefentations of romantick Novels; it will furely be a further Inducement to recur to the Works of our old Writers, when we find among them many Pieces written on a feverer Plan; a Plan more accommodated to real Life, and approaching more nearly to the modern Ufage. *The Merry Wives of Windfor*, of *Shakefpeare*; the *Fox*, the *Alchymift*, the *Silent Woman*, *Every Man in his Humour* of *Jonfon*; the *New Way to pay Old Debts*, the *City Madam*, of *Maffinger*, *&c. &c.* all urge their Claim for a Rank in the ordinary Courfe of our Winter-Evening Entertainments, not only clear of every Objection made to the above-mentioned Species of Dramatick Compofition, but adhering more ftrictly to ancient Rules, than moft of our later Comedies.

In Point of Character (perhaps the moft effential Part of the Drama) our Old Writers far tranfcend the Moderns. It is furely needlefs, in Support of this Opinion, to recite a long Lift of Names, when the Memory of every Reader muft fuggeft them to himfelf. The Manners of many of them, it is true, do not prevail at prefent. What then? Is it dif-

---

has produced divers Inftances from *Dryden*'s Plays, *fufficient* (to ufe the *Rambler*'s own Language) *to awaken the moft torpid Rifibility.*

pleafing

pleasing or uninstructive to see the Manners of a former Age pass in Review before us? Or is the Mind undelighted at recalling the Characters of our Ancestors, while the Eye is confessedly gratified at the Sight of the Actors drest in their Antique Habits? Moreover, Fashion and Custom are so perpetually fluctuating, that it must be a very accurate Piece indeed, and one quite new and warm from the Anvil, that catches the *Damon* or *Cynthia* of this Minute. Some Plays of our latest and most fashionable Authors are grown as obsolete in this Particular, as those of the first Writers; and it may with Safety be affirmed, that *Bobadil* is not more remote from modern Character, than the ever-admired and every-where-to-be-met-with Lord *Foppington*. It may, also, be further considered, that most of the best Characters in our old Plays are not merely fugitive and temporary. They are not the sudden Growth of Yesterday or To-day, sure of fading or withering To-morrow; but they were the Delight of past Ages, still continue the Admiration of the present, and (to use the Language of true Poetry)

———— To Ages yet unborn appeal,
And latest Times th' ETERNAL NATURE feel.

The ACTOR.

There is one Circumstance peculiar to the Dramatick Tales, and to many of the more regular Comedies of our old Writers, of which it is too little to say, that it demands no Apology. It deserves the highest Commendation; since it hath been the Means of introducing the most capital Beauties into their Compositions, while the same Species of Excellence could not possibly enter into those of a later Period. I mean the Poetical Stile of their Dialogue. Most Nations, except our own, have imagined mere Prose, which, with *Meliere's Bourgeois Gentilhomme*, the meanest of us have talked from our Cradle, too little

elevated

elevated for the Language of the Theatre. Our
Neighbours, the *French*, at this Day write moſt of
their Plays, Comedies as well as Tragedies, in
Rhime; a *Gothick* Practice, which our own Stage
once admitted, but long ago wiſely rejected. The
Grecian Iambick was more happily conceived in the
true Spirit of that elegant and magnificent Simplicity, which characterized the Taſte of that Nation.
Such a Meaſure was well accommodated to the Expreſſions of the Mind; and though it refined indeed
on Nature, it did not contradict it. In this, as
well as in all other Matters of Literature, the Uſage
of *Greece* was religiouſly obſerved at *Rome*. *Plautus*,
in his richeſt Vein of Humour, is numerous and poetical. The Comedies of *Terence*, though we cannot agree to read them after Biſhop *Hare*, were evidently not written without Regard to Meaſure;
which is the invincible Reaſon, why all Attempts to
render them into downright Proſe have always proved,
and ever muſt prove, unſuccefsful; and if a faint
Effort, now under Contemplation, to give a Verſion
of them in familiar Blank Verſe (after the Manner of
our old Writers, but without a ſervile Imitation of
them) ſhould fail, it muſt, I am confident, be owing to the Lameneſs of the Execution. The *Engliſh*
Heroick Meaſure, or, as it is commonly called, Blank
Verſe, is perhaps of a more happy Conſtruction even
than the *Grecian* Iambick; elevated equally, but approaching nearer to the Language of Nature, and as
well adapted to the Expreſſion of Comick Humour,
as to the *Pathos* of Tragedy.

The mere modern Critick, whoſe Idea of Blank
Verſe is perhaps attached to that empty Swell of
Phraſeology, ſo frequent in our late Tragedies, may
conſider theſe Notions as the Effect of Bigotry to our
old Authors, rather than the Reſult of impartial
Criticiſm. Let ſuch an one carefully read over the
Works of thoſe Writers, for whom I am an Advo-
cate.

cate. There he will feldom or ever find that Tumour of Blank Verfe, to which he has been fo much accuftomed. He will be furprized with a familiar Dignity, which, though it rifes fomewhat above ordinary Converfation, is rather an Improvement than Perverfion of it. He will foon be convinced that Blank Verfe is by no Means appropriated folely to the Bufkin, but that the Hand of a Mafter may mould it to whatever Purpofes he pleafes ; and that in Comedy it will not only admit Humour, but heighten and embellifh it. Inftances might be produced without Number. It muft however be lamented, that the modern Tragick Stile, free, indeed, from the mad Flights of *Dryden*, and his Cotemporaries, yet departs equally from Nature. I am apt to think it is in great Meafure owing to the almoft total Exclufion of Blank Verfe from all modern Compofitions, Tragedy excepted. The common Ufe of an elevated Diction in Comedy, where the Writer was often, of Neceffity, put upon expreffing the moft ordinary Matters, and where the Subject demanded him to paint the moft ridiculous Emotions of the Mind, was perhaps one of the chief Caufes of that *eafy Vigour*, fo confpicuous in the Stile of the old Tragedies. Habituated to poetical Dialogue in thofe Compofitions, wherein they were obliged to adhere more ftrictly to the Simplicity of the Language of Nature, the Poets learnt, in thofe of a more raifed Species, not to depart from it too wantonly. They were well acquainted alfo with the Force as well as Elegance of their Mother-Tongue, and chofe to ufe fuch Words as may be called Natives of the Language, rather than to *harmonize* their Verfes, and *agonize* the Audience with *Latin* Terminations. Whether the refined Stile of *Addifon's Cato*, and the flowing Verfification of *Rowe*, firft occafioned this Departure from ancient Simplicity, it is difficult to determine : But it is too true, that *Southern* was the

laſt of our Dramatic Writers, who was, in any Degree, poſſeſt of that magnificent Plainneſs, which is
the genuine Dreſs of Nature; though indeed the
Plays even of *Rowe* are more ſimple in their Stile,
than thoſe which have been produced by his Succeſſors. It muſt not, however, be diſſembled in this
Place, that the Stile of our old Writers is not without Faults; that they were apt to give too much
into Conceits; that they often purſued an allegorical
Train of Thought too far; and were ſometimes be-
trayed into forced, unnatural, quaint, or gigantick
Expreſſions. In the Works of *Shakeſpeare* himſelf,
every one of theſe Errors may be found; yet it may
be ſafely aſſerted, that no other Author, antient or
modern, has expreſſed himſelf on ſuch a Variety of
Subjects with more Eaſe, and in a Vein more truly
poetical, unleſs, perhaps, we ſhould except *Homer*:
Of which, by the bye, the deepeſt Critick, moſt
converſant with Idioms and Dialects, is not quite a
competent Judge.

I would not be underſtood, by what I have here
ſaid of Poetical Dialogue, to object to the Uſe of
Proſe, or to inſinuate that our modern Comedies are
the worſe for being written in that Stile. It is
enough for me, to have vindicated the Uſe of a
more elevated Manner among our old Writers. I
am well aware that moſt Parts of *Falſtaff*, *Ford*,
Benedick, *Malvolio*, &c. are written in Proſe; nor
indeed would I counſel a modern Writer to attempt
the Uſe of Poetical Dialogue in a mere Comedy: A
Dramatick Tale, indeed, chequered, like Life itſelf, with various Incidents, ludicrous and affecting,
if written by a maſterly Hand, and ſomewhat more
ſeverely than thoſe abovementioned, would, I doubt
not, ſtill be received with Candour and Applauſe.
The Publick would be agreeably ſurpriſed with the
Revival of Poetry on the Theatre, and the Opportunity of employing all the beſt Performers, ſerious

as well as comick, in one Piece, would render it still more likely to make a favourable Impreſſion on the Audience. There is a Gentleman, not unequal to ſuch a Taſk, who was once tempted to begin a Piece of this Sort; but, I fear, he has too much Love of Eaſe and Indolence, and too little Ambition of literary Fame, ever to complete it.

But to conclude:

Have I, Sir, been waſting all this Ink and Time in vain? Or may it be hoped that you will extend ſome of that Care to the reſt of our old Authors, which you have ſo long beſtowed on *Shakeſpeare*, and which you have ſo often laviſhed on many a worſe Writer, than the moſt inferior of thoſe here recommended to you? It is certainly your Intereſt to give Variety to the Publick Taſte, and to diverſify the Colour of our Dramatick Entertainments. Encourage new Attempts; but do Juſtice to the Old! The Theatre is a wide Field. Let not one or two Walks of it alone be beaten, but lay open the Whole to the Excurſions of Genius! This, perhaps, might kindle a Spirit of Originality in our modern Writers for the Stage; who might be tempted to aim at more Novelty in their Compoſitions, when the Liberality of the popular Taſte rendered it leſs hazardous. That the Narrowneſs of Theatrical Criticiſm might be enlarged, I have no Doubt. Reflect, for a Moment, on the uncommon Succeſs of *Romeo* and *Juliet*, and *Every Man in his Humour!* and then tell me, whether there are not many other Pieces of as antient a Date, which, with the like proper Curtailments and Alterations, would produce the ſame Effect? Has an induſtrious Hand been at the Pains to ſcratch up the Dunghill of *Dryden's Amphitryon* for the few Pearls that are buried in it, and ſhall the rich Treaſures of *Beaumont* and *Fletcher*, *Jonſon* and *Maſſinger*, lie (as it were) in the Ore, untouched and diſregarded? Reform your Liſt of

Plays!

Plays! In the Name of *Burbage*, *Taylor*, and *Betterton*, I conjure you to it! Let the veteran Criticks once more have the Satisfaction of feeing *The Maid's Tragedy*, *Philafter*, *King and no King*, &c. on the Stage!—Reftore *Fletcher*'s *Elder Brother* to the Rank unjuftly ufurped by *Cibber*'s *Love Makes a Man!* and fince you have wifely defifted from giving an annual Affront to the City by acting *The London Cuckolds* on Lord-Mayor's Day, why will you not pay them a Compliment, by exhibiting *The City Madam* of *Maffinger* on the fame Occafion?

If after all, Sir, thefe Remonftrances fhould prove without Effect, and the Merit of thefe great Authors fhould plead with you in vain, I will here fairly turn my Back upon you, and addrefs myfelf to the Lovers of Dramatick Compofitions in general. They, I am fure, will perufe thofe Works with Pleafure in the Clofet, though they lofe the Satisfaction of feeing them reprefented on the Stage: Nay, fhould they, together with you, concur in determining that fuch Pieces are unfit to be acted, you, as well as they, will, I am confident, agree, that fuch Pieces are, at leaft, very worthy to be read. There are many modern Compofitions, feen with Delight at the Theatre, which ficken on the Tafte in the Perufal; and the honeft Country Gentleman, who has not been prefent at the Reprefentation, wonders with what his *London* Friends have been fo highly entertained, and is as much perplexed at the *Town-manner* of Writing as Mr. *Smith* in *The Rehearfal*. The Excellencies of our old Writers are, on the contrary, not confined to Time and Place, but always bear about them the Evidences of true Genius.

Maffinger is perhaps the leaft known, but not the leaft meritorious of any of the old Clafs of Writers. His Works declare him to be no mean Proficient in the fame School. He poffeffes all the Beauties and

Blemifhes

Blemishes common to the Writers of that Age. He has, like the rest of them, in Compliance with the Custom of the Times, admitted Scenes of a low and gross Nature, which might be admitted with no more Prejudice to the Fable, than the Buffoonry in *Venice Preserved.* For his few Faults he makes ample Atonement. His Fables are, most of them, affecting; his Characters well conceived, and strongly supported; and his Diction, flowing, various, elegant, and manly. His two Plays, revived by *Betterton*, *The Bondman*, and *The Roman Actor*, are not, I think, among the Number of his best. *The Duke of Milan*, *The Renegado*, *The Picture*, *The Fatal Dowry*, *The Maid of Honour*, *A New Way to pay Old Debts*, *The Unnatural Combat*, *The Guardian*, *The City Madam*, are each of them, in my Mind, more excellent. He was a very popular Writer in his own Times, but so unaccountably, as well as unjustly, neglected at present, that the accurate Compilers of a Work, called, *The Lives of the Poets*, published under the learned Name of the late Mr. *Theophilus Cibber*, have not so much as mentioned him. He is, however, take him for all in all, an Author, whose Works the intelligent Reader will peruse with Admiration: And that I may not be supposed to withdraw my Plea for his Admission to the modern Stage, I shall conclude these Reflections with one more Specimen of his Abilities; submitting it to all Judges of Theatrical Exhibitions, whether the most masterly Actor would not here have an Opportunity of displaying his Powers to Advantage.

The Extract I mean to subjoin is from the last Scene of the first Act of *The Duke of Milan.*—*Sforza*, having espoused the Cause of the King of *France* against the Emperor, on the King's Defeat, is advised by a Friend, to yield himself up to the Emperor's Discretion. He consents to this Measure,

fure, but provides for his Departure in the following
Manner:

    Sfor. ——Stay you, *Francifco.*
—You fee how Things ftand with me?
    Fran. To my Grief:
And if the Lofs of my poor Life could be
A Sacrifice, to reftore them as they were,
I willingly would lay it down.
    Sfor. I think fo;
For I have ever found you true and thankful,
Which makes me love the Building I have rais'd,
In your Advancement; and repent no Grace
I have confer'd upon you: And, believe me,
Though now I fhould repeat my Favours to you,
The Titles I have given you, and the Means
Suitable to your Honours; that I thought you
Worthy my Sifter, and my Family,
And in my Dukedom made you next myfelf;
It is not to upbraid you; but to tell you
I find you're worthy of them,, in your Love
 And Service to me.
    Fran. Sir, I am your Creature;
And any Shape that you would have me wear,
I gladly will put on.
    Sfor. Thus, then, *Francifco;*
I now am to deliver to your Truft
A weighty Secret, of fo ftrange a Nature,
And 'twill, I know, appear fo monftrous to you,
That you will tremble in the Execution,
As much as I am tortur'd to command it:
For 'tis a Deed fo horrid, that, but to hear it,
Would ftrike into a Ruffian flefh'd in Murthers,
Or an obdurate Hangman, foft Compaffion;
And yet, *Francifco* (of all Men the deareft,
And from me moft deferving) fuch my State
And ftrange Condition is, that Thou alone
Muft know the fatal Service, and perform it.

                                    Fran.

Fran. These Preparations, Sir, to work a Stranger,
Or to one unacquainted with your Bounties,
Might appear useful ; but, to Me, they are
Needless Impertinencies : For I dare do
Whate'er you dare command.

Sfor. But thou must swear it,
And put into thy Oath, all Joys, or Torments
That fright the Wicked, or confirm the Good :
Not to conceal it only (that is nothing)
But, whensoe'er my Will shall speak, strike now !
To fall upon't like Thunder.

Fran. Minister
The Oath in any Way, or Form you please,
I stand resolv'd to take it.

Sfor. Thou must do, then,
What no malevolent Star will dare to look on;
It is so wicked : For which, Men will curse thee
For being the Instrument ; and the Angels
Forsake me at my Need, for being the Author :
For 'tis a Deed of Night, of Night, *Francisco*,
In which the Memory of all good Actions,
We can pretend to, shall be buried quick :
Or, if we be remember'd, it shall be
To fright Posterity by our Example,
That have outgone all Precedents of Villains
That were before us ; and such as succeed,
Though taught in Hell's black School, shall ne'er
——Art thou not shaken yet !   [come near us.

Fran. I grant you move me :
But to a Man confirm'd—

Sfor. I'll try your Temper :
What think you of my Wife?

Fran. As a Thing sacred ;
To whose fair Name and Memory I pay gladly
These Signs of Duty.   [*Kneels.*

Sfor. Is she not the Abstract
Of all that's rare, or to be wish'd in Woman?

Fran. It were a Kind of Blasphemy to dispute it :
——But to the Purpose, Sir.

Sfor. Add to her Goodnefs,
Her Tendernefs of me, her Care to pleafe me,
Her unfufpected Chaftity, ne'er equall'd,
Her Innocence, her Honour—O I am loft
In the Ocean of her Virtues, and her Graces,
When I think of them.

Fran. Now I find the End
Of all your Conjurations: There's fome Service
To be done for this fweet Lady. If fhe have Enemies
That fhe would have remov'd——

Sfor. Alas! *Francifco,*
Her greateft Enemy is her greateft Lover;
Yet, in that Hatred, her Idolater.
One Smile of her's would make a Savage tame:
One Accent of that Tongue would calm the Seas,
Though all the Winds at once ftrove there for Empire.
Yet I, for whom fhe thinks all this too little,
Should I mifcarry in this prefent Journey,
(From whence it is all Number to a Cypher,
I ne'er return with Honour) by thy Hand
Muft have her murther'd.

Fran. Murther'd!—She that loves fo,
And fo deferves to be belov'd again?
And I, who fometimes you were pleas'd to favour,
Pick'd out the Inftrument?

Sfor. Do not fly off:
What is decreed, can never be recall'd.
'Tis more than Love to her, that marks her out
A wifh'd Companion to me, in both Fortunes:
And ftrong Affurance of thy zealous Faith,
That gives up to thy Truft a Secret, that
Racks fhould not have forc'd from me.—O *Francifco,*
There is no Heav'n without her; nor a Hell,
Where fhe refides. I afk from her but Juftice,
And what I would have paid to her, had Sicknefs,
Or any other Accident, divorc'd
Her purer Soul from her unfpotted Body.
The flavifh *Indian* Princes, when they die,

VOL. II.   U   Are

Are chearfully attended to the Fire
By the Wife and Slave, that living they lov'd beft,
To do them Service in another World:
Nor will I be lefs honour'd, that love more.
And therefore trifle not, but in thy Looks
Exprefs a ready Purpofe to perform
What I command; or, by *Marcelia*'s Soul,
This is thy lateft Minute.

 Fran. 'Tis not Fear
Of Death, but Love to you, makes me embrace it.
But, for mine own Security, when 'tis done,
What Warrant have I? If you pleafe to fign one,
I fhall, though with Unwillingnefs and Horror,
Perform your dreadful Charge.

 Sfor. I will, *Francifco:*
But ftill remember, that a Prince's Secrets
Are Balm, conceal'd; but Poifon, if difcover'd.
I may come back; then this is but a Trial,
To purchafe thee, if it were poffible,
A nearer Place in my Affection—but
I know thee honeft.

 Fran. 'Tis a Character
I will not part with.

 Sfor. I may live to reward it.   [*Exeunt.*

PRO.

P R O L O G U E

S P O K E N

By Mr. G A R R I C K

At the Opening of the THEATRE in DRURY-
LANE, 1747.

WHEN Learning's Triumph o'er her bar-
barous Foes,
Firſt rear'd the Stage, immortal *Shakeſpeare* roſe,
Each Change of many-colour'd Life he drew,
Exhauſted Worlds, and then imagin'd new:
Exiſtence ſaw him ſpurn her bounded Reign,
And panting Time toil'd after him in vain.
His powerful Strokes preſiding Truth impreſs'd,
And unreſiſting Paſſion ſtorm'd the Breaſt.
　　Then *Jonſon* came, inſtructed from the School,
To pleaſe in Method. and invent by Rule;
His ſtudious Patience, and laborious Art,
By regular Approach aſſail'd the Heart:
Cold Approbation gave the ling'ring Bays
For thoſe who durſt not cenſure, ſcarce could praiſe.
A Mortal born, he met the general Doom,
But left, like *Egypt's* Kings, a laſting Tomb.
The Wits of *Charles* found eaſier Ways to Fame,
Nor wiſh'd for *Jonſon's* Art, or *Shakeſpeare's* Flame;

Them-

Themselves they studied, as they felt they writ;
Intrigue was Plot, Obscenity was Wit.
Vice always found a sympathetic Friend,
They pleas'd their Age, and did not aim to mend.
Yet Bards like these aspir'd to lasting Praise,
And proudly hop'd to pimp in future Days.
Their Cause was gen'ral, their Supports were strong,
Their Slaves were willing, and their Reign was
      long;
Till Shame regain'd the Post that Sense betray'd,
And Virtue call'd Oblivion to her Aid.
    Then crush'd by Rules, and weaken'd as refin'd,
For Years the Power of Tragedy declin'd:
From Bard to Bard the frigid Caution crept
Till Declamation soar'd, while Passion slept.
Yet still did Virtue deign the Stage to tread,
Philosophy remain'd, though Nature fled.
But forc'd at length her ancient Reign to quit,
She saw great *Faustus* lay the Ghost of Wit;
Exulting Folly hail'd the joyful Day,
And Pantomime and Song confirm'd her Sway.
    But who the coming Changes can presage,
And mark the future Periods of the Stage?
Perhaps if Skill could distant Times explore,
New *Bhens*, new *Durfeys*, yet remain in Store.
Perhaps, where *Lear* has rav'd, and *Hamlet* dy'd,
On flying Cars new Sorcerers may ride,
Perhaps (for who can guess the Effects of Chance?)
Here *Hunt* may box, or *Mahomet* may dance.
    Hard is his Lot, that here by Fortune plac'd,
Must watch the wild Vicissitudes of Taste,
With every Meteor of Caprice must play,
And chace the new-blown Bubbles of the Day.
Ah! let not Censure term our Fate, our Choice:
The Stage but echoes back the public Voice,
The Drama's Laws, the Drama's Patrons give,
For we that live to please, must please to live.
                    Then

Then prompt no more the Follies you decry,
As Tyrants doom their Tools of Guilt to die:
'Tis yours this Night to bid the Reign commence
Of refcu'd Nature, and reviving Senfe;
To chace the Charms of Sound, the Pomp of Show,
For ufeful Mirth and falutary Woe,
Bid Scenic Virtue form the rifing Age,
And Truth diffufe her Radiance from the Stage.

P R O L O G U E

T O

I R E N E.

YE glitt'ring Train! whom Lace and Velvet
      blefs,
Suſpend the foft Sollicitudes of Drefs;
From grov'ling Bufinefs and fuperfluous Care,
Ye ſons of Avarice! a Moment fpare:
Vot'ries of Fame and Worfhippers of Pow'r!
Difmifs the pleafing Phantoms for an Hour.
Our daring Bard, with Spirit unconfin'd,
Spreads wide the mighty Moral for Mankind.
Learn here how Heav'n fupports the virtuous Mind,
Daring, tho' calm; and vigorous, tho' refign'd.
Learn here what Anguifh racks the guilty Breaft,
In Pow'r dependent, in Succefs depreft.
Learn here that Peace from Innocence muft flow;
All elfe is empty Sound, and idle Show.
    If Truths like thefe with pleafing Language join;
Ennobled, yet unchang'd, if Nature fhine:
If no wild Draught depart from Reafon's Rules,
Nor Gods his Heroes, nor his Lovers Fools:
Intriguing Wits! his artlefs Plot forgive;
And fpare him, Beauties! tho' his Lovers live.
    Be this at leaft his Praife; be this his Pride;
To force Applaufe no modern Arts are try'd.
Shou'd partial Cat-calls all his Hopes confound;
He bids no Trumpet quell the fatal Sound.
Shou'd welcome Sleep relieve the weary Wit,
He rolls no Thunders o'er the drowfy Pit,

No

No Snares to captivate the Judgment spreads;
Nor bribes your Eyes to prejudice your Heads.
Unmov'd tho' Witlings sneer and Rivals rail:
Studious to please, yet not asham'd to fail.
He scorns the meek Address, the suppliant Strain,
With Merit needless, and without it vain.
In Reason, Nature, Truth he dares to trust:
Ye Fops be silent! and ye Wits be just!

PROLOGUE

SPOKEN BY

Mr. GARRICK,

Thursday, April 5, 1750,

At the REPRESENTATION of

C O M U S,

For the Benefit of Mrs. ELIZABETH FOSTER,

MILTON's Grand-daughter, and only furviving
Defcendant.

YE patriot Crouds, who burn for *England's* Fame,
  Ye Nymphs, whofe Bofom's beat at *Milton's*
    Name,
Whofe gen'rous Zeal, unbought by flatt'ring Rhimes,
Shames the mean Penfions of *Auguftan* Times;
Immortal Patrons of fucceeding Days,
Attend this Prelude of perpetual Praife!
Let Wit, condemn'd the feeble War to wage
With clofe Malevolence, or public Rage;
Let Study, worn with Virtue's fruitlefs Lore,
Behold this Theatre, and grieve no more.
This Night, diftinguifh'd by your Smile, fhall tell
That never *Briton* can in vain excel;
The flighted Arts Futurity fhall truft,
And rifing Ages haften to be juft.
  At length our mighty Bard's victorious Lays
Fill the loud Voice of univerfal Praife,
And baffled Spite, with hopelefs Anguifh dumb,
Yields to Renown the Centuries to come.

With

With ardent Haſte each Candidate of Fame
Ambitious catches at his tow'ring Name :
He ſees, and pitying ſees, vain Wealth beſtow
Thoſe pageant Honours which he ſcorn'd below :
While Crowds aloft the laureat Buſt behold,
Or trace his Form on circulating Gold,
Unknown, unheeded, long his Offspring lay,
And Want hung threat'ning o'er her ſlow Decay.
What tho' ſhe ſhine with no *Miltonian* Fire,
No fav'ring Muſe her Morning Dreams inſpire ;
Yet ſofter Claims the melting Heart engage,
Her Youth laborious, and her blameleſs Age :
Hers the mild Merits of domeſtic Life,
The patient Suff'rer, and the faithful Wife.
Thus grac'd with humble Virtue's native Charms,
Her Grandſire leaves her in *Britannia's* Arms,
Secure with Peace, with Competence, to dwell,
While tutelary Nations guard her Cell.
Yours is the Charge, ye Fair, ye Wiſe, ye Brave !
'Tis yours to crown Deſert—beyond the Grave !

PROLOGUE

GOOD-NATUR'D MAN.

PREST by the Load of Life, the weary Mind
Surveys the general Toil of Human-kind;
With cool Submiffion joins the labouring Train,
And focial Sorrow, lofes half its Pain:
Our anxious Bard, without Complaint, may fhare
This buftling Seafon's epidemic Care.
Like Cæfar's Pilot, dignify'd by Fate,
Toft in one common Storm with all the Great;
Diftreft alike, the Statefman and the Wit,
When one a Borough courts, and one the Pit.
The bufy Candidates for Power and Fame,
Have Hopes and Fears, and Wifhes, juft the fame;
Difabled both to combat, or to fly,
Muft hear all Taunts, and hear without Reply,
Uncheck'd on both, loud Rabbles vent their Rage,
As Mongrels bay the Lion in a Cage.
Th' offended Burgefs hoards his angry Tale
For that bleft Year when all that vote may rail;

Their

Their Schemes of Spite the Poet's Foes difmifs,
Till that glad Night when all that hate may hifs.
This Day the powder'd Curls and golden Coat,
Says fwelling *Crifpin*, begg'd a Cobler's Vote.
This Night our Wit, the pert Apprentice cries,
Lies at my Feet, I hifs him, and he dies.
The Great, 'tis true, can charm th' electing Tribe;
The Bard may fupplicate, but cannot bribe.
Yet judg'd by thofe whofe Voices ne'er were fold,
He feels no want of ill-perfuading Gold;
But confident of Praife, if Praife be due,
Trufts without Fear, to Merit, and to you.

LONDON:

L O N D O N:

A P O E M.

In IMITATION of the

THIRD SATIRE OF JUVENAL.

—————*Quis ineptæ*
Tam patiens urbis, tam ferreus, ut teneat se? JUV.

(*a*) THO' Grief and Fondnefs in my Breaft
rebel,
When injur'd THALES bids the Town farewell,
Yet ftill my calmer Thoughts his Choice commend,
I praife the Hermit, but regret the Friend,
Who now refolves from Vice, and LONDON far,
To breathe in diftant Fields a purer Air,
And, fix'd on *Cambria*'s folitary Shore,
Give to St. *David* one true *Briton* more.

JUV. SAT. III.

(*a*) *Quamvis digreſſu veteris confuſus amici;*
Laudo, tamen, vacuis quod fedem figere Cumis
Deſtinet, atque unum civem donare Sibyllæ.

(*b*) **For**

(b) For who wou'd leave, unbrib'd, *Hibernia's* Land,
Or change the Rocks of *Scotland* for the *Strand?*
There none are fwept by fudden Fate away,
But all whom Hunger fpares, with Age decay:
Here Malice, Rapine, Accident, confpire,
And now a Rabble rages, now a Fire;
Their Ambufh here relentlefs Ruffians lay,
And here the fell Attorney prowls for Prey;
Here falling Houfes thunder on your Head,
And here a female Atheift talks you dead.
    (c) While THALES waits the Wherry that contains
Of diffipated Wealth the fmall Remains,
On *Thames's* Banks in filent Thought we ftood,
Where *Greenwich* fmiles upon the filver Flood:
Struck with the Seat that gave † *Eliza* Birth,
We kneel, and kifs the confecrated Earth;
In pleafing Dreams the blifsful Age renew,
And call *Britannia's* Glories back to View;
Behold her Crofs triumphant on the Main,
The Guard of Commerce, and the Dread of *Spain,*
Ere Mafquerades debauch'd, Excife opprefs'd,
Or *Englifh* Honour grew a ftanding Jeft.
    A tranfient Calm the happy Scenes beftow,
And for a Moment lull the Senfe of Woe.
At Length awaking, with contemptuous Frown,
Indignant THALES eyes the neighb'ring Town.

(b) - - - - *Ego vel Prochytam præpono Suburræ,*
Nam quid tam miferum, tam folum vidimus, ut non
Deterius credas horrere incendia, lapfus
Teĉtorum affiduos, et mille pericula fævæ
Urbis, & Augufto recitantes, menfe poetas?
(c) *Sed, dum tota domus rhedâ componitur unâ,*
Subftitit ad veteres arcus. - - - - -

† Queen *Elizabeth* born at *Greenwich.*

(d) Sicne

(d) Since Worth, he cries, in these degen'rate Days
Wants ev'n the cheap Reward of empty Praise;
In those curs'd Walls, devote to Vice and Gain,
Since unrewarded Science toils in vain;
Since Hope but sooths to double my Distress,
And ev'ry Moment leaves my Little less;
While yet my steady Steps no (e) Staff sustains,
And Life still vig'rous revels in my Veins;
Grant me, kind Heaven, to find some happier Place,
Where Honesty and Sense are no Disgrace;
Some pleasing Bank where verdant Osiers play,
Some peaceful Vale with Nature's Painting gay;
Where once the harrass'd *Briton* found Repose,
And safe in Poverty defy'd his Foes;
Some secret Cell, ye Pow'rs, indulgent give.
(f) Let - - - - - live here, for - - - - - has learn'd to
    live.
Here let those reign, whom Pensions can incite
To vote a Patriot black, a Courtier white;
Explain their Country's dear-bought Rights away,
And plead for Pirates in the Face of Day;
With slavish Tenets taint our poison'd Youth,
And lend a Lye the Confidence of Truth.
  (g) Let such raise Palaces, and Manors buy,
Collect a Tax, or farm a Lottery,

(d) *Hic tunc Umbricius: Quando artibus, inquit, honestis*
Nullus in urbe locus, nulla emolumenta laborum,
Res hodie minor est, heri quam fuit, atque eadem cras
Deteret exiguis aliquid: proponimus illuc
Ire, fatigatas ubi Dædalus exuit alas,
Dum nova canities - - - - -
(e) *- - - - - et pedibus me*
Porto meis, nullo dextram subeunte bacillo.
(f) *Cedamus patriâ: vivant Arturius istic*
Et Catulus: maneant qui nigrum in candida vertunt.
(g) *Quis facile est ædem conducere, flumina, portus,*
Siccandam eluviem, portandum ad busta cadaver. - - -
Munera nunc edunt.   With

With warbling Eunuchs fill a licens'd Stage,
And lull to Servitude a thoughtlefs Age.
 Heroes, proceed, what Bounds your Pride fhall
   hold?
What Check reftrain your Thirft of Pow'r and
   Gold?
Behold rebellious Virtue quite o'erthrown,
Behold our Fame, our Wealth, our Lives your own.
 To fuch, a groaning Nation's Spoils are giv'n,
When public Crimes inflame the Wrath of Heav'n:
(*h*) But what, my Friend, what Hope remains for me,
Who ftart at Theft, and blufh at Perjury?
Who fcarce forbear, tho' BRITAIN's Court he fing,
To pluck a titled Poet's borrow'd Wing;
A Statefman's Logick unconvinc'd can hear,
And dare to flumber o'er the *Gazetteer*;
Defpife a Fool in half his Penfion drefs'd,
And ftrive in vain to laugh at *H———y's* Jeft.
 (*i*) Others with fofter Smiles, and fubtler Art,
Can fap the Principles, or taint the Heart;
With more Addrefs a Lover's Note convey,
Or bribe a Virgin's Innocence away.
Well may they rife, while I, whofe ruftick Tongue
Ne'er knew to puzzle Right, or varnifh Wrong,
Spurn'd as a Beggar, dreaded as Spy,
Live unregarded, unlamented die.
 (*k*) For what but focial Guilt the Friend endears?
Who fhares *Orgilio's* Crimes, his Fortune fhares.

(*h*) *Quid Romæ faciam? mentiri nefcio: librum,*
Si malus eft, nequeo laudare & pofcere. - - -
(*c*) *Fere ad nuptas, quæ mittit adulter,*
Quæ mandat, norint alii; me nemo miniftro
Fur erit, atque ideo nulli comes exeo.
(*k*) *Quis nunc diligitur, nifi confcius?*
Carus erit Verri, qui Verrem tempore, quo vult
Accufare poteft. - - - - -

          (*l*) But

(*l*) But thou, ſhould tempting Villainy preſent
All *Marlb'rough* hoarded, or all *Villiers* ſpent,
Turn from the glitt'ring Bribe thy ſcornful Eye,
Nor ſell for Gold, what Gold could never buy,
The peaceful Slumber, ſelf-approving Day,
Unſullied Fame, and Conſcience ever gay.

  (*m*) The cheated Nation's happy Fav'rites, ſee!
Mark whom the Great careſs, who frown on me!
LONDON! the needy Villain's gen'ral Home,
The common Shore of *Paris* and of *Rome*;
With eager Thirſt, by Folly, or by Fate,
Sucks in the Dregs of each corrupted State.
Forgive my Tranſports on a Theme like this;
(*n*) I cannot bear a *French* Metropolis.

  (*o*) Illuſtrious EDWARD! from the Realms of
       Day,
The Land of Heroes and of Saints ſurvey;
Nor hope the *Britiſh* Lineaments to trace,
The ruſtick Grandeur, or the ſurly Grace;
But, loſt in thoughtleſs Eaſe, and empty Show,
Behold the Warrior dwindled to a Beau;
Senſe, Freedom, Piety, refin'd away,
Of *France* the Mimic, and of *Spain* the Prey.

  All that at Home no more can beg or ſteal,
Or like a Gibbet better than a Wheel,
Hiſs'd from the Stage, or hooted from the Court,
Their Air, their Dreſs, their Politicks import;

(*l*) - - - *Tanti tibi non ſit opaci*
Omnis arena Tagi, quodque in mare volvitur aurum,
Ut ſomno careas. - - -
(*m*) *Quæ nunc divitibus gens acceptiſſima noſtris,*
Et quos præcipue fugiam, properabo fateri.
(*n*) - - - - *Non poſſum ferre, Quirites,*
Græcam urbem. - - - -
(*o*) *Ruſticus ille tuus ſumit trechedipna, Quirine,*
Et cromatico fert niceteria collo.

                 (*f*) Obſe-

(*p*) Obſequious, artful, voluble and gay,
On *Britain*'s fond Credulity they prey.
No gainful Trade their Induſtry can 'ſcape;
(*q*) They ſing, they dance, clean Shoes, or cure a Clap;
All Sciences a faſting Monſieur knows,
And bid him go to Hell, to Hell he goes.

  (*r*) Ah! what avails it, that, from Slav'ry far,
I drew the Breath of Life in *Engliſh* Air;
Was early taught a *Briton*'s Right to prize,
And liſp the Tales of HENRY's Victories;
If the gull'd Conqueror receives the Chain,
And Flattery ſubdues when Arms are vain?

  (*s*) Studious to pleaſe, and ready to ſubmit,
The ſupple *Gaul* was born a Paraſite:
Still to his Int'reſt true, where-e'er he goes,
Wit, Brav'ry, Worth, his laviſh Tongue beſtows;
In ev'ry Face a thouſand Graces ſhine,
From ev'ry Tongue flows Harmony divine.
(*t*) Theſe arts in vain our rugged Natives try, ⎫
Strain out with fault'ring Diffidence a Lye, ⎬
And gain a Kick for aukward Flattery. ⎭

  Beſides, with Juſtice this diſcerning Age
Admires their wond'rous Talents for the Stage:

(*p*) *Ingenium velox, audacia perdita, ſermo*
Promptus————

(*q*) *Augur, ſchœnobates, medicus, magus, omnia novit,*
Græculus eſſuriens in cœlum, ſi juſſeris, ibit.

(*r*) *Uſque adeo nihil eſt, quod noſtra infantia cœlum*
Hauſit Aventini?

(*s*) *Quid, quod adulando gens prudentiſſima laudat*
Sermonem indocti, faciem deformis amici?

(*t*) *Hæc eadem licet & nobis laudare: ſed illis*
Creditur.

(*u*) Well may they venture on the Mimick's Art;
Who play from Morn to Night a borrow'd Part;
Practis'd their Master's Notions to embrace,
Repeat his Maxims, and reflect his Face;
With ev'ry wild Absurdity comply,
And view each Object with another's Eye;
To shake with Laughter ere the Jest they hear,
To pour at Will the counterfeited Tear,
And as their Patron hints the Cold or Heat,
To shake in Dog-days, in December sweat.
(*x*) How, when Competitors like these contend,
Can surly Virtue hope to fix a Friend?
Slaves that with serious Impudence beguile,
And lye without a Blush, without a Smile;
Exalt each Trifle, ev'ry Vice adore,
Your Taste in Snuff, your Judgment in a Whore;
Can *Balbo's* Eloquence applaud, and swear
He gropes his Breeches with a Monarch's Air.

For Arts like these preferr'd, admir'd, caress'd,
They first invade your Table, then your Breast;
(*y*) Explore your Secrets with insidious Art,
Watch the weak Hour, and ransack all the Heart;
Then soon your ill-plac'd Confidence repay,
Commence your Lords, and govern or betray.

(*z*) By Numbers here from Shame or Censure free,
All Crimes are safe, but hated Poverty.
This, only this, the rigid Law pursues,
This, only this, provokes the snarling Muse.

(*u*) *Natio commœdia est. Rides? majore cachinno*
Concutitur, &c.
(*x*) *Non sumus ergo pares: melior qui semper & omni*
Nocte dieque potest alienum sumere vultum:
A facie jactare manus, laudare paratus,
Si bene ructavit, si rectum minxit amicus.
(*y*) *Scire volunt secreta domûs, atque inde timeri.*
(*z*) - - - - *Materiem præbet causasque jocorum*
Omnibus hic idem si fœda & scissa lacerna, &c.

5   The

The fober Trader at a tatter'd Cloak
Wakes from his Dream, and labours for a Joke ;
With brifker Air the filken Courtiers gaze,
And turn the varied Taunt a thoufand Ways.
(a) Of all the Griefs that harrafs the Diftrefs'd,
Sure the moft bitter is a fcornful Jeft ;
Fate never wounds more deep the gen'rous Heart,
Than when a Blockhead's Infult points the Dart.

   (b) Has Heaven referv'd, in Pity to the Poor,
No pathlefs Wafte, or undifcover'd Shore ?
No fecret Ifland in the boundlefs Main ?
No peaceful Defart, yet unclaim'd by Spain ?
Quick let us rife, the happy Seats explore,
And bear Oppreffion's Infolence no more.
This mournful Truth is ev'ry where confefs'd,
(c) Slow rifes Worth, by Poverty deprefs'd :
But here more flow, where all are Slaves to Gold,
Where Looks are Merchandife, and Smiles are fold,
Where won by Bribes, by Flatteries implor'd,
The Groom retails the Favours of his Lord.   [Cries

   But hark ! th' affrighted Crowd's tumultuous
Roll through the Streets, and thunder to the Skies :
Rais'd from fome pleafing Dream of Wealth and Pow'r,
Some pompous Palace, or fome blifsful Bow'r,
Aghaft you ftart, and fcarce with aching Sight
Suftain th' approaching Fire's tremenduous Light :

(a) *Nil habet infelix paupertas durius in fe,*
Quam quod ridiculous homines facit.
(b) - - - - - - - *Agmine facto*
Debuerant olim tenues migraffe Quirities.
(c) *Haud facile emergunt, quorum virtutibus obftat*
Res angufta domi. Sed Romæ durior illis
Conatus - - - - -
- - - - - - *OMNIA Romæ*
Cum pretio - - - - -
Cogimur, & cultis augere peculia fervis.

        Swift

Swift from pursuing Horrors take your Way,
And leave your little ALL to Flames a Prey;
(d) Then thro' the World a wretched Vagrant roam,
For where can starving Merit find a Home?
In vain your mournful Narrative disclose,
While all neglect, and most insult your Woes.
(e) Should Heaven's just Bolts *Orgilio's* Wealth con-
And spread his flaming Palace on the Ground, [found,
Swift o'er the Land the dismal Rumour flies,
And publick Mournings pacify the Skies;
The laureat Tribe in servile Verse relate,
How Virtue wars with persecuting Fate;
(f) With well-feign'd Gratitude the pension'd Band
Refund the Plunder of the beggar'd Land.
See! while he builds, the gaudy Vassals come,
And crowd with sudden Wealth the rising Dome;
The Price of Boroughs and of Souls restore,
And raise his Treasures higher than before:
Now bless'd with all the Baubles of the Great,
The polish'd Marble, and the shining Plate,
(g) *Orgilio* sees the golden Pile aspire,
And hopes from angry Heav'n another Fire.

(h) Could'st thou resign the *Park* and play content,
For the fair Banks of *Severn* or of *Trent*:

There

(d) - - - - - *Ultimus autem*
Ærumnæ cumulus, quod nudum, & frustra rogantem
Nemo cibo, nemo hospitio, tectoque juvabit.
(e) *Si magna Asturici cecidit domus, horrida mater,*
Pullati proceres. - - - -
(f) *Jam accurrit, qui marmora donet,*
Conferat impensas: hic, &c.
Hic modum argenti. - - - -
(g) - - - - - *Meliora, ac plura reponit*
Persicus orborum lautissimus. - - - -
(h) *Si potes avelli Circensibus, optima Soræ,*
Aut Frabrateriæ domus, aut Frusinone paratur,

Quant:

There might'ft thou find fome elegant Retreat,
Some hireling Senator's deferted Seat;
And ftretch thy Profpects o'er the fmiling Land,
For lefs than rent the Dungeons of the *Strand* :
There prune thy Walks, fupport thy droopingFlow'rs,
Direct thy Rivulets, and twine thy Bow'rs ;
And, while thy Beds a cheap Repaft afford,
Defpife the Dainties of a venal Lord ;
There ev'ry Bufh with Nature's Mufick rings,
There ev'ry Breeze bears Health upon its Wings ;
On all thy Hours Security fhall fmile,
And blefs thy Evening Walk and Morning Toil.

(*i*) Prepare for Death, if here at Night you roam,
And fign your Will before you fup from Home.

(*k*) Some fiery Fop, with new Commiffion vain,
Who fleeps on Brambles till he kills his Man ;
Some frolick Drunkard, reeling from a Feaft,
Provokes a Broil, and ftabs you for a Jeft.

(*l*) Yet ev'n thefe Heroes, mifchievoufly gay,
Lords of the Street, and Terrors of the Way ;
Flufh'd as they are with Folly, Youth, and Wine,
Their prudent Infults to the Poor confine ;
Afar they mark the Flambeau's bright Approach,
And fhun the fhining Train, and golden Coach.

(*m*) In

Quanti nunc tenebras unum conducis in annum.
Hortulus hic - - - - - -
Vive bidentis amans, & culti villicus horti,
Unde epulum poffis centum dare Pythagoræis.
(*i*) *- - - Poffis ignavus haberi,*
Et fubiti cafus improvidus, ad cœnam fi
Inteftatus eas.
(*k*) *Ebrius, ac petulans, qui nullum forte cecidit,*
Dat pœnas, noctem patitur lugentis amicum
Pelidæ - - - -
(*l*) *Sed, quamvis improbus annis*
Atque mero fervens, cavet hunc, quem coccina lœna

Vitari

(*m*) In vain, thefe Dangers paft, your Doors you
And hope the balmy Bleffings of Repofe :   [clofe,
Cruel with Guilt, and daring with Defpair,
The Midnight Murd'rer burfts the faithlefs Bar ;
Invades the facred Hour of filent Reft,
And plants, unfeen, a Dagger in your Breaft.

(*n*) Scarce can our Fields (fuch Crowds at *Tyburn*
With Hemp the Gallows and the Fleet fupply. [die,
Propofe your Schemes, ye fenatorian Band,
Whofe Ways and Means fupport the finking Land ;
Left Ropes be wanting in the tempting Spring,
To rig another Convoy for the K—g.

(*o*) A fingle Jail, in *Alfred*'s golden Reign,
Could Half the Nation's Criminals contain ;
Fair *Juftice* then, without Conftraint ador'd,
Held high the fteady Scale, but deep'd the Sword ;
No Spies were paid, no fpecial Juries known,
Bleft age ! but ah ! how diff'rent from our own !

(*p*) Much could I add, but fee the Boat at hand,
The Tide retiring, calls me from the Land :
(*q*) Farewel ! — When   Youth,   and   Health,   and
          Fortune fpent,
Thou fly'ft for Refuge to the Wilds of *Kent* ;

                                        And

Vitari jubet, et comitum longiffimus ordo :
Multum præterea fiammarum, atque ænea lampas.
(*m*) *Nec tamen hoc tantum metuas : nam qui fpoliet te*
Non deerit : claufis domibus, &c.
(*n*) *Maximus in vinclis ferri modus : ut timeas ne*
Vomer deficiat, ne marræ et farcula defint.
(*o*) *Felices proavorum atavos, felicia dicas*
Secula, quæ quondam fub regibus atque tribunis
Viderunt uno contentam carcere Romam.
(*p*) *His alias poteram, & plures fubnectere caufas :*
Sed jumenta vocant. - - - -
(*q*) *- - - Ergo vale noftri memor : & quoties te*
Roma tuo refici propetantem reddet Aquinos.

                                        Me

And tir'd like me, with Follies and with Crimes,
In angry Numbers warn'ft fucceeding Times;
Then fhall thy Friend, nor thou refufe his Aid,
Still Foe to Vice, forfake his *Cambrian* Shade;
In Virtue's Caufe once more forfake his Rage,
Thy Satire point, and animate thy Page.

Me quoque ad Eleufinam Cererem, veftramque Dianam
Convelle a Cumis: fatirarum ergo, ni pudet illas
Adjutor gellidos veniam caligatus in agros.

X 4   T H E

THE

VANITY of HUMAN WISHES.

THE

TENTH SATIRE OF JUVENAL.

LET (*a*) Obfervation with extenfive View,
Survey Mankind, from *China* to *Peru*;
Remark each anxious Toil, each eager Strife,
And watch the bufy Scenes of crowded Life;
Then fay how Hope and Fear, Defire and Hate,
O'erfpread with Snares the clouded Maze of Fate,
Where wav'ring Man, betray'd by vent'rous Pride,
To tread the dreary Paths without a Guide,
As threach'rous Phantoms in the Mift delude,
Shuns fancied Ills, or chafes airy Good.
How rarely Reafon guides the ftubborn Choice,
Rules the bold Hand, or prompts the fuppliant Voice,
How Nations fink, by darling Schemes opprefs'd,
When Vengeance liftens to the Fool's Requeft.
Fate wings with ev'ry Wifh th' afflictive Dart,
Each Gift of Nature, and each Grace of Art,
With fatal Heat impetuous Courage glows,
With fatal Sweetnefs Elocution flows,
Impeachment ftops the Speaker's pow'rful Breath,
And reftlefs Fire precipitates on Death.
    (*b*) But fcarce obferv'd the Knowing and the Bold,
Fall in the gen'ral Maffacre of Gold;
Wide-wafting Peft! that rages unconfin'd,
And crowds with Crimes the Records of Mankind;

(*a*) *Ver.* 1—21.   (*b*) *Ver.* 12—22.

For

For Gold his Sword the hireling Ruffian draws,.
For Gold the hireling Judge diftorts the Laws;
Wealth heap'd on Wealth, nor Truth nor Safety buys,
The Dangers gather as the Treafures rife.
   Let Hift'ry tell where rival Kings command,
And dubious Title fhakes the madded Land,
When Statutes glean the Refufe of the Sword,
How much more fafe the Vaffal than the Lord;
Low fculks the Hind beneath the Rage of Pow'r,
And leaves the wealthy Traytor in the Tow'r;
Untouch'd his Cottage, and his Slumbers found,
Tho' Confifcation's Vultures hover round.
   The needy Traveller, ferene and gay,
Walks the wild Heath, and fings his Toil away.
Does Envy feize thee? crufh th' upbraiding Joy,
Increafe his Riches and his Peace deftroy,
New Fears in dire Viciffitude invade,
The ruftling Brake alarms, and quiv'ring Shade,
Nor Light nor Darknefs bring his Pain Relief,
One fhews the Plunder, and one hides the Thief.
   Yet (c) ftill one gen'ral Cry the Skies affails,
And Gain and Grandeur load the tainted Gales;
Few know the toiling Statefman's Fear or Care,
Th' infidious Rival and the gaping Heir.
   Once (d) more, *Democritus*, arife on Earth,
With chearful Wifdom and inftructive Mirth,
See motley Life in modern Trappings drefs'd,
And feed with varied Fools th' eternal Jeft: [price
Thou who couldft laugh where Want enchain'd Ca-
Toil crufh'd Conceit, and Man was of apiece;
Where Wealth unlov'd without a Mourner dy'd;
And fcarce a Sycophant was fed by Pride;
Where ne'er was known the Form of mock Debate,
Or feen a new-made Mayor's unwieldy State;
Where Change of Fav'rites made no Change of Laws,
And Senates heard, before they judg'd a Caufe;

   (c) *Ver.* 23—27.   (d) *Ver.* 28—55.

How

How wouldſt thou ſhake at *Britain*'s modiſh Tribe,
Dart the quick Taunt, and edge the piercing Gibe?
Attentive Truth and Nature to decry,
And pierce each Scene with philoſophic Eye.
To thee were ſolemn Toys or empty Shew,
The Robes of Pleaſure and the Veils of Woe:
All aid the Farce, and all thy Mirth maintain,
Whoſe Joys are cauſeleſs, or whoſe Griefs are vain.

Such was the Scorn that fill'd the Sage's Mind,
Renew'd at ev'ry Glance on human Kind;
How juſt that Scorn ere yet thy Voice declare,
Search every State, and canvaſs ev'ry Prayer.   [Gate,
(*e*) Unnumber'd Suppliants crowd Preferment's
Athirſt for Wealth, and burning to be Great;
Deluſive Fortune hears th' inceſſant Call,
They mount, they ſhine, evaporate, and fall.
On ev'ry Stage the Foes of Peace attend,
Hate dogs their Flight, and Inſult mocks their End.
Love ends with Hope, the ſinking Stateſman's Door
Pours in the morning Worſhipper no more;
For growing Names the weekly Scribbler lies,
To growing Wealth the Dedicator flies,
From ev'ry Room deſcends the painted Face,
That hung the bright Palladium of the Place,
And ſmoak'd in Kitchens, or in Auctions ſold,
To better Features yields the Frame of Gold;
For now no more we trace in ev'ry Line
Heroic worth, Benevolence divine:
The Form diſtorted juſtifies the Fall,
And Deteſtation rids th' indignant Wall.

But will not *Britain* hear the laſt Appeal,
Sign her Foes doom, or guard her Fav'rites Zeal;
Thro' Freedom's Sons no more Remonſtrance rings,
Degrading Nobles and controuling Kings;
Our ſupple Tribes repreſs their Patriot Throats,
And aſk no Queſtions but the Price of Votes;

(*e*) *Ver.* 56—107.

With

With weekly Libels and feptennial Ale,
Their Wifh is full to Riot and to Rail.
 In full-blown Dignity, fee *Wolfey* ftand,
Law in his Voice, and Fortune in his Hand:
To him the Church, the Realm, their Pow'rs confign,
Thro' him the Rays of regal Bounty fhine,
Still to new Heights his reftlefs Wifhes tow'r,
Claim leads to Claim, and Pow'r advances Pow'r;
Till Conqueft unrefifted ceas'd to pleafe,
And Rights fubmitted left him none to feize.
At length his Sov'reign frowns—the Train of State
Mark the keen Glance, and watch the Sign to hate.
Where-e'er he turns he meets a Stranger's Eye,
His Suppliants fcorn him, and his Followers fly;
At once is loft the Pride of awful State,
The golden Canopy, the glitt'ring Plate,
The regal Palace, the luxurious Board,
The liv'ried Army, and the menial Lord.
With Age, with Cares, with Maladies opprefs'd,
He feeks the Refuge of monaftic Reft.
Grief aids Difeafe, remember'd Folly ftings,
And his laft Sighs reproach the Faith of Kings.
 Speak thou, whofe Thoughts at humble Peace re-
     pine,
Shall *Wolfey's* Wealth, with *Wolfey's* End be thine?
Or liv'ft thou now, with fafer Pride content,
The wifeft Juftice on the Banks of *Trent?*
For why did *Wolfey* near the Steeps of Fate,
On weak Foundations raife th' enormous Weight?
Why but to fink beneath Misfortune's Blow,
With louder Ruin to the Gulphs below?
 What (*f*) gave great *Villiers* to th' Affaffin's Knife,
And fix'd Difeafe on *Harley's* clofing Life?
What murder'd *Wentworth,* and what exil'd *Hyde?*
By Kings protected, and to Kings ally'd?
What but their Wifh indulg'd in Courts to fhine,
And Pow'r too great to keep, or to refign?
                                        When

(*f*) *Ver.* 108—213.

When *(g)* firſt the College-rolls receive his Name,
The young Enthuſiaſt quits his Eaſe for Fame;
Through all his Veins the Fever of Renown
Spreads from the ſtrong Contagion of the Gown;
O'er *Bodley*'s Dome his future Labours ſpread,
And * *Bacon*'s Manſion trembles o'er his Head.
Are theſe thy Views? proceed, illuſtrious Youth,
And Virtue guard thee to the Throne of Truth!
Yet ſhould thy Soul indulge the gen'rous Heat,
Till captive Science yields her laſt Retreat;
Should Reaſon guide thee with her brighteſt Ray,
And pour on miſty Doubt reſiſtleſs Day;
Should no falſe Kindneſs lure to looſe Delight,
Nor Praiſe relax, nor Difficulty fright;
Should tempting Novelty thy Cell refrain,
And Sloth effuſe her opiate Fumes in vain;
Should Beauty blunt on Fops her fatal Dart,
Nor claim the Triumph of a letter'd Heart;
Should no Diſeaſe thy torpid Veins invade,
Nor Melancholy's Phantoms haunt thy Shade;
Yet hope not Life from Grief or Danger free,
Nor think the Doom of Man revers'd for thee:
Deign on the paſſing World to turn thine Eyes,
And pauſe awhile from Letters, to be wiſe;
There mark what Ills the Scholar's Life aſſail,
Toil, Envy, Want, the Patron, and the Jail.
See Nations ſlowly wiſe, and meanly juſt,
To buried Merit raiſe the tardy Buſt.
If Dreams yet flatter, once again attend,
Hear *Lydiat*'s Life, and *Galileo*'s End.

Nor deem, when Learning her laſt Prize beſtows,
The glitt'ring Eminence exempt from Woes;
See when the Vulgar 'ſcape, deſpis'd or aw'd,
Rebellion's vengeful Talons ſeize on *Laud*.

(g) *Ver.* 114—132.

* There is a Tradition, that the Study of Friar *Bacon*, built on an Arch over the Bridge, will fall, when a Man greater than *Bacon* ſhall paſs under it.

From

From meaner Minds, tho' fmaller Fines content
The plunder'd Palace, or fequefter'd Rent;
Mark'd out by dangerous Parts he meets the Shock,
And fatal Learning leads him to the Block:
Around his Tomb let Art and Genius weep,
But hear his Death, ye Blockheads, hear and fleep.

The (i) feftal Blazes, the triumphal Show,
The ravifh'd Standard, and the captive Foe,
The Senate's Thanks, the *Gazette*'s pompous Tale,
With Force refiftlefs o'er the Brave prevail.
Such Bribes the rapid *Greek* o'er *Afia* whirl'd,
For fuch the fteady *Romans* fhook the World;
For fuch in diftant Lands the *Britons* fhine,
And ftain with Blood the *Danube* or the *Rhine*;
This Pow'r has Praife, that Virtue fcarce can warm,
Till Fame fupplies the univerfal Charm.
Yet Reafon frowns on War's unequal Game,
Where wafted Nations raife a fingle Name,
And mortgag'd States their Grandfires Wreaths re-
    gret,
From Age to Age in everlafting Debt,
Wreaths which at laft the dear-bought Right convey
To ruft on Medals, or on Stones decay.

On (k) what Foundation ftands the Warrior's
    Pride,
How juft his Hopes let *Swedifh Charles* decide;
A Frame of Adamant, a Soul of Fire,
No Dangers fright him, and no Labours tire;
O'er Love, o'er Fear extends his wide Domain,
Unconquer'd Lord of Pleafure and of Pain;
No Joys to him pacific Scepters yield,
War founds the Trump, he rufhes to the Field;
Behold furrounding Kings their Pow'r combine,
And one capitulate, and one refign;
Peace courts his Hand, but fpreads her Charms in vain;
' Think nothing gain'd, he cries, till Nought remain,

(i) *Ver.* 133—146.   (k) *Ver.* 147—167.
    ' On

' On *Mofcow*'s Walls till *Gothick* Standards fly,
' And all be mine beneath the polar Sky.'
The March begins in military State,
And Nations on his Eye fufpended wait;
Stern Famine guards the folitary Coaſt,
And Winter barricades the Realm of Froſt;
He comes, not Want and Cold his Courfe delay;—
Hide, bluſhing Glory, hide *Pultowa*'s Day:
The vanquiſh'd Hero, leaves his broken Bands,
And ſhews his Miferies in diſtant Lands;
Condemn'd a needy Supplicant to wait,
While Ladies interpofe, and Slaves debate.
But did not Chance at length her Error mend?
Did no fubverted Empire mark his End?
Did rival Monarchs give the fatal Wound?
Or hoſtile Millions prefs him to the Ground?
His Fall was deſtin'd to a barren Strand,
A petty Fortrefs, and a dubious Hand;
He left the Name, at which the World grew pale,
To point a Moral, or adorn a Tale.
　　All (*l*) Times their Scenes of pompous Woes af-
　　　　ford,
From *Perfia*'s Tyrant, to *Bavaria*'s Lord.
In gay Hoſtility, and barb'rous Pride,
With half Mankind embattled at his Side,
Great *Xerxes* comes to feize the certain Prey,
And ſtarves exhauſted Regions in his Way;
Attendant Flatt'ry counts his Myriads o'er,
Till counted Myriads footh his Pride no more;
Freſh Praife is try'd till Madnefs fires his Mind,
The Waves he laſhes, and enchains the Wind;
New Pow'rs are claim'd, new Pow'rs are ſtill beſtow'd,
Till rude Refiſtance lops the fpreading God;
The daring *Greek* derides the martial Show,
And heaps their Vallies with the gaudy Foe;

(*i*) *Ver.* 168—187.

　　　　　　　　　　　　　　Th'

Th' infulted Sea with humbler Thoughts he gains,
A fingle Skiff to fpeed his Flight remains ;
Th' incumber'd Oar fcarce leaves the dreaded Coaft
Through purple Billows and a floating Hoft.
　　The bold *Bavarian*, in a lucklefs Hour,
Tries the dread Summits of *Cefarean* Pow'r,
With unexpected Legions burfts away,
And fees defencelefs Realms receive his Sway;
Short Sway! fair *Auftria* fpreads her mournful
　　　　Charms,
The Queen, the Beauty, fets the World in Arms ;
From Hill to Hill the Beacons roufing blaze,
Spreads wide the Hope of Plunder and of Praife:
The fierce *Croatian*, and the wild *Huffar*,
And all the Sons of Ravage crowd the War ;
The baffled Prince in Honour's flatt'ring Bloom
Of hafty Greatnefs finds the fatal Doom,
His Foes Derifion, and his Subjects blame,
And fteals to Death from Anguifh and from Shame.
　　Enlarge (m) my Life with Multitude of Days,
In Health, and Sicknefs, thus the Suppliant prays ;
Hides from himfelf his State, and fhuns to know,
That Life protracted, is protracted Woe.
Time hovers o'er, impatient to deftroy,
And fhuts up all the Paffages of Joy :
In vain their Gifts the bounteous Seafons pour,
The Fruit autumnal, and the vernal Flow'r,
With liftlefs Eyes the Dotard views the Store,
He views, and wonders that they pleafe no more ;
Now pall the taftelefs Meats, and joylefs Wines,
And Luxury with Sighs her Slave refigns.
Approach, ye Minftrels, try the foothing Strain,
And yield the tuneful Lenitives of Pain :
No Sounds, alas, would touch th' impervious Ear,
Tho' dancing Mountains witnefs *Orpheus* near,

(m) *Ver.* 188—283.

Nor

Nor Lute nor Lyre his feeble Pow'r attend,
Nor sweeter Musick of a virtuous Friend,
But everlasting Dictates crowd his Tongue,
Perversely grave, or positively wrong.
The still returning Tale, and ling'ring Jest,
Perplex the fawning Niece and pamper'd Guest,
While growing Hopes scarce awe the gath'ring Sneer,
And scarce a Legacy can bribe to hear ;
The watchful Guests still hint the last Offence,
The Daughter's Petulance, the Son's Expence,
Improve his heady Rage with treach'rous Skill,
And mould his Passions till they make his Will.

Unnumber'd Maladies his Joints invade,
Lay Siege to Life, and press the dire Blockade ;
But unextinguish'd Av'rice still remains,
And dreaded Losses aggravate his Pains ;
He turns, with anxious Heart and crippled Hands,
His Bonds of Debts, and Mortgages of Lands ;
Or views his Coffers with suspicious Eyes,
Unlocks his Gold, and counts it till he dies.

But grant, the Virtues of a temp'rate Prime,
Bless with an Age exempt from Scorn or Crime ;
An Age that melts in unperceiv'd Decay,
And glides in modest Innocence away ;
Whose peaceful Day Benevolence endears,
Whose Night congratulating Conscience chears ;
The gen'ral Fav'rite as the gen'ral Friend ;
Such Age there is, and who could wish its End ?

Yet ev'n on this her Load Misfortune flings,
To press the weary Minutes flagging Wings :
New Sorrow rises as the Day returns,
A Sister sickens, or a Daughter mourns.
Now kindred Merit fills the sable Bier,
Now lacerated Friendship claims a Tear.
Year chases Year, Decay pursues Decay,
Still drops some Joy from with'ring Life away ;
New Forms arise, and different Views engage,
Superfluous lags the Vet'ran on the Stage,

Till

Till pitying Nature figns the laft Releafe,
And bids afflicted Worth retire to Peace.
  But few there are whom Hours like thefe await,
Who fet unclouded in the Gulphs of Fate.
From *Lydia*'s Monarch fhould the Search defcend,
By *Solon* caution'd to regard his End,
In Life's laft Scene what Prodigies furprife,
Fears of the Brave, and Follies of the Wife?
From *Marlb'rough*'s Eyes the Streams of Dotage flow,
And *Swift* expires a Driv'ler and a Show.
  The (*n*) teeming Mother, anxious for her Race,
Begs for each Birth the Fortune of a Face:
Yet *Vane* could tell what Ills from Beauty fpring;
And *Sedley* curs'd the Form that pleas'd a King.
Ye Nymphs of rofy Lips and radiant Eyes,
Whom Pleafure keeps too bufy to be wife,
Whom Joys with foft Varieties invite,
By Day the Frolick, and the Dance by Night,
Who frown with Vanity, who fmile with Art,
And afk the lateft Fafhion of the Heart,
What Care, what Rules your heedlefs Charms fhall
            fave,
Each Nymph your Rival, and each Youth your Slave?
Againft your Fame with Fondnefs Hate combines,
The Rival batters, and the Lover mines.
With diftant Voice neglected Virtue calls,
Lefs heard and lefs, the faint Remonftrance falls;
Tir'd with Contempt, fhe quits the flip'ry Reign,
And Pride and Prudence take her Seat in vain.
In crowd at once, where none the Pafs defend,
The harmlefs Freedom, and the private Friend.
The Guardians yield, by Force fuperior ply'd;
By Int'reft, Prudence; and by Flattery, Pride.
Now Beauty falls betray'd, defpis'd, diftrefs'd,
And hiffing Infamy proclaims the reft.

(*n*) *Ver.* 289—345.

Where (*o*) then shall Hope and Fear their Objects
    find?
Must dull Suspence corrupt the stagnant Mind?
Must helpless Man, in Ignorance sedate,
Roll darkling down the Torrent of his Fate?
Must no Dislike alarm, no Wishes rise,
No Cries attempt the Mercies of the Skies?
Enquirer, cease; Petitions yet remain,
Which Heav'n may hear, nor deem Religion vain.
Still raise for Good the supplicating Voice,
But leave to Heav'n the Measure and the Choice.
Safe in his Pow'r, whose Eyes discern afar
The secret Ambush of a specious Pray'r.
Implore his Aid, in his Decisions rest,
Secure whate'er he gives, he gives the best.
Yet when the Sense of sacred Presence fires,
And strong Devotion to the Skies aspires,
Pour forth thy Fervours for a healthful Mind,
Obedient Passions and a Will resign'd;
For Love, which scarce collective Man can fill;
For Patience Sov'reign o'er transmuted Ill;
For Faith, that panting for a happier Seat,
Counts Death kind Nature's Signal of Retreat:
These Goods for Man the Laws of Heav'n ordain,
These Goods he grants, who grants the Pow'r to
    gain;
With these celestial Wisdom calms the Mind,
And makes the Happiness she does not find.

(*o*) *Ver.* 346—366

THE

THE

BATTLE OF THE WIGS.

IN THREE PARTS.

Dabiturque LICENTIA *fumpta pudenter.*—HOR.

WRITTEN IN THE YEAR 1768.

To the READER..

THOUGH the Writer of the following little
Piece has chofen to call it *An Additional Canto
to Dr.* Garth's *Poem of the Difpenfary,* he by no
Means pretends to afpire to an Imitation of that
Work, much lefs would he prefume to affect a Ri-
valfhip with the ingenious Author. The Subject
being in fome Meafure fimilar, he was induced to
make Ufe of this Title.

The Difputes, at prefent fubfifting between the
Fellows and *Licentiates* of the *College of Phyficians,*
concerning their refpective Rights, feemed to be no
improper Topic for an innocent Laugh. Nothing
that fhould in the leaft offend any Individual, is intended by it. No Character is defigned to be per-
fonally pointed out. As to the common Sarcafm,
' The Killing of Numbers of Patients,' fays Dr.
Garth, ' is fo trite a Piece of Raillery, that it ought
' not to make any Impreffion.'

It is difficult, and perhaps in fome Degree prefumptuous, to attempt following, in a confined
Walk, the Steps of any Author of Eminence. If

Y 2

fome

some Expressions or Sentiments in this Piece should be found to be the same with, or somewhat similar to any in Dr. *Garth*'s Poem, the Writer begs he may not lay under the Imputation of Plagiarism. One or two Instances, which he has discovered, of a Similarity, he has carefully pointed out.

One Part of the *Machinery* is founded upon Fact. A *Blacksmith* was employed to break open the College Gate, in order to try the Rights of the *Licentiate*. The Circumstances of the *Butchers* and the *Engine* charged with *Blood*, were jocular. Reports at that Time.

The Writer begs leave to enter a *Caveat* against the Critics finding Fault with his Rhymes not exactly chiming in some few Places. He cannot, with Submission, but be of Opinion, that the Sense should not be totally sacrificed to the Sound: Besides, he can shelter himself under the Authority and Example of our best Authors. He might also plead in Favour of those *Alliterations*, in which he has indulged himself, if he was not satisfied, that the Use of them is generally allowed in the *Mock Heroick*, however sparingly they ought to be introduced in more serious Compositions.———

P A R T I.

TURN, Muse, once more to *Warwick*'s dismal Lane,
Where Feuds unheard of, and new Uproars reign;
Where *Fellows* with *Licentiates* hold Debate;——
There, (to preserve their Dignity of State)
Admit no Partners in their Councils grave,
Who Titles only from *Diplomas* have;

N O T E.

V. 1. *Turn, Muse, once more to* Warwick's *dismal Lane.*
The College of Physicians is erected in *Warwick-Lane.*

An

An equal Rank the others boldly claim,
Alike their Fortunes, and alike their Fame :—
Each *Æſculapian* Breaſt fell Diſcord warms,
And for awhile the Gown gives place to Arms.   10
     Say, DEATH, what prompted thee to ſpread Debate
Among thy Sons, the Arbiters of Fate?
Thy great Upholders, whoſe unſparing Pen
Crowds *Pluto*'s Realm, and thins the Race of Men?
     'Twas on the Day, held ſacred to *St. Luke,*   15
Rever'd by Sages ſkill'd in Purge or Puke ;—
When in mute State the grave Aſſembly meet,
To hear profound Oration,—and to Eat ;—
Licentiato held it for a Sin
To Faſt without, while others Feaſt within.   20
Hungry and Dry, he mourn'd his hapleſs Fate,
With *Secio* not allow'd to foul a Plate ;
Forbid to cheer his Heart, and warm his Throttle,
With *Hauſtus repetendus* of the Bottle.

N O T E S.

V. 10. *And for awhile the Gown gives Place to Arms.*

Cedunt Arma Togæ, is a well-known Expreſſion.
In the Univerſities the Doctors of Phyſick are in-
veſted with a *Scarlet Gown* ; and it may be a Queſ-
tion with ſome perhaps, whether that or the *Scarlet
Coat* has been productive of moſt Deſtruction among
Mankind.

V. 18. *To hear profound Oration—*

On *St. Luke*'s Day there is a *Latin* Speech pronounced by a *Fellow* in the College of Phyſicians,
called (from Doctor *Harvey,* the original Inſtitutor
of this Ceremony) *Oratio Harveiana.*

V. 24. *With Hauſtus repetendus of the Bottle.*

The medical Gentry, however they may recommend Abſtinence to others, are many of them no
Enemies

Mad'ning at length with Grief, and fir'd with Rage, 25
Which nothing but Admittance could affuage,
‘ Open your Gates, he cries, and let us enter,
‘ Or elfe to force them open we'll adventure.’
    Socio, elated with his high Degree
Of A. B. A. M. M. B. and M. D.
Bids him without, and at a Diftance wait,
Nor deigns he to unfold the facred Gate.
‘ Shall *Scots*, he cries, or *Leyden* Doctors dare
‘ With fapient *Regulars* to claim a Chair?
‘ How can *Diplomatifts* have equal Knowledge?   35
‘ No, no—they muft not Mefs with *Graduates* of a
    He faid, when ftrait *Licentiato* tries   [*College.*’
By Force to gain what ftubborn Pride denies.
And now the pond'rous Peftle beats to Arms,
And the huge Mortar rings with loud Alarms;   40

N O T E S.

Enemies to the Bottle, if taken in *Moderation*, as
they term it. A certain witty Phyfician was advifing
a Friend of his, who had been ufed to be too free
with his Bottle, to take a chearful *Pint* with his
Meals, and no more: ‘ But, fays he, the whole Se-
‘ cret confifts in knowing how much your *Pint* fhould
‘ hold. I myfelf take my *Pint* conftantly after Din-
‘ ner and Supper; but mine is a *Scots Pint*,’—that is,
two Quarts.

    V. 29. *Socio, elated with his high Degree*
        Of A. B. A. M. M. B. *and* M. D.

    A. B. *Artium Baccalaureus*, Batchelor of Arts;
A. M. *Artium Magifter*, Mafter of Arts; M. B.
Medicinæ Baccalaureus, Batchelor of Phyfick; M. D.
Medicinæ Doctor, Doctor of Phyfick.

    V. 39. *And now the pond'rous Peftle beats to Arms,*
        And the huge Mortar rings with loud Alarms.
While lifted Peftles brandifh'd in the Air
Defcend in Peals, and Civil Wars declare.—GARTH.

                            On

On Barber's Pole a Peruke they diſplay
With triple Tail, a Signal for the Fray.
  O could the modeſt Muſe but dare aſpire
To emulate one Spark of *Homer's* Fire,
The Liſt of large-wig'd Warriors ſhe might chaunt, 45
From *Clumſy Tunbelly* to *John o' Gaunt.*
  Nor yet unmindful to defend the Doors
Are *Socio's* Bands, and Force repel with Force.
  Within the Gates cloſe-bolted, lock'd, and barr'd,
Of neighb'ring *Butchers* ſtands an awful Guard ;   50
Each with an azure Apron ſtrung before,
And ſnow-white Sleeves, as yet unſtain'd with Gore :
The Foe the Whetting-iron hears diſmay'd,
Grating harſh Muſick from the ſharp'ning Blade.
  From *Newgate Market* came the bloody Bands, 55
With Marrow-bones and Cleavers in their Hands,
Fram'd to ſplit Skulls, and deal deſtructive Knocks,
To fell a Doctor, or to fell an Ox ; ——

N O T E S.

V. 43. *O could the modeſt Muſe but dare aſpire*
        To emulate one Spark of Homer's *Fire,*
        The Liſt of large-wig'd Warriors ſhe might
        chaunt.

  In the fourth Book of *Homer's Iliad* is a Liſt of the
Forces employed againſt *Troy.*

V. 46. *From* Clumſy Tunbelly *to* John o' Gaunt.
        Clumſy Tunbelly, Doctor ——.
        John o' Gaunt, Doctor ——.

V. 55. *From* Newgate Market *came the bloody Bands.*
  Newgate Market is contiguous to *Warwick Lane.*
The Butchers are therefore called (in V. 50.) *neigh-*
b'ring Butchers.

Fit Instruments to quash a Foe, then ring
A Peal of Triumph;—*Ding dong, ding dong, ding.* 60
   No Wonder Butchers should Physicians aid;
The same their Practice, nor unlike their Trade:
And what Alliance more exactly suits?
Man-killers leagu'd with those who slaughter Brutes.
   Nor yet on these alone the Dons rely,   65
But they prepare a mask'd Artillery.
A Water-Engine, charg'd with beastly Gore,
Stands ready on the Foe its Filth to pour.
And what than this can call a greater Dread,
Design'd to change the sable Coat to red?   70
To save their Cloaths e'en Surgeons step aside,
When from the Puncture spouts the crimson Tide.
   Thou too, dread Officer, of sov'reign Pow'r,
Thou Tyrant-Monarch of the midnight Hour,—
(If haply, when thou tread'st thy watchful Round, 75
Some kind-inviting vagrant Nymph be found;)
Hight Constable, wait there;——Thy magic Staff,
With royal Standard down emblazon'd half;——

NOTES.

V. 59. *Fit Instruments to quash a Foe, then ring*
   A Peal of Triumph, ding dong, ding dong, ding.
  In the *Ode on St. Cecilia's Day,* adapted to the ancient *British* Musick, is the following A I R.
   Hark, how the banging Marrow-bones
     Make clanging Cleavers ring,
   With a ding dong, ding dong,
   Ding dong, ding dong,
Ding dong, ding dong, ding dong, ding.
   Raise your uplifted Arms on high,
     In long-prolonged Tones,
   Let Cleavers sound
   A merry merry Round,
     By banging Marrow-bones.

Enfign of Might, to make wild Uproar ceafe,
And bid tumultous Riot be at Peace.

PART II.

WIthout, th' enrag'd *Licentiato* waits,
   Striving to force a Paffage through the Gates;
In vain he ftrives;--- then drooping with Defpair,
To *Venus* he addreft his humble Pray'r.
  ' O Goddefs!— If thy Vot'ries own my Skill, 5
' If they approve my Lotion, or my Pill;—
' If *Rock*, or *Flugger*, boaft a fairer Name;
' If *Drury*, and *The Garden*, found my Fame;—
' If many a Mother, that would pafs for Maid,
' In Secret calls for my *obftetric* Aid;——   10
' If, to prevent th' affected Sneer of Prude,
' My Juice of S—— can the Shame preclude;—

                     If

NOTES.

V. 7. *If* Rock, *nor* Flugger *boaft a fairer Name,*
  Richard Rock, a very noted Practitioner. We
have not been able to learn the Import of thofe two
fignificant Letters, M. L. which conftantly accom-
pany his Name.
  Flugger. Dr. *Flugger,* no lefs noted, but not of
fo long Standing.

V. 8. *If* Drury, *and* The Garden, *found my Fame.*
  Drury Lane, of ancient Renown. *Covent Garden*
is emphatically ftiled THE *Garden,* as the principal
Singers in the *Opera* are called THE *Guarducci,* THE
Lovatini, &c.

V. 12. *My Juice of* S—— *can the Shame preclude.*

  Doctor *Mead,* in his Effay on Poifon, fays, ' I
' had once in my Poffeffion, given me by an inge-
                  nious

' If with my *Drops* I rouse th' enervate Rake,
' And Wives unfruitful happy Mothers make ; —
' () help !—Let *Mars*'s Arms a while be staid,   15
' And send your Cuckold to my instant Aid.'

   The Goddess heard, and, hast'ning to her Spouse,
With Protestations and repeated Vows
Of strict Fidelity in Time to come,
('No more she'd wander, but would cleave to Home,')
Prevail'd upon her fond and easy Dear
On Earth in Form of *Blacksmith* to appear.
The tedious Hours of Absence to beguile,
'Tis said, with *Mars* she solac'd all the while.

   To Earth the God descending stood confest   25
By the black Bristles of his Beard and Breast :
A leathern Apron ty'd about his Waist,
And on his Head a woollen Nightcap plac'd ;

N O T E.

' nious Chemist, a clear Liquor, which though pon-
' derous, was so volatile, that it would all fly away
' in the open Air, without being heated ; and so
' corrosive, that a Glass Stopple of the Bottle, which
' contained it, was in a short Time so eroded, that
' it could never be taken out. The Fume of it was
' so thin, that if a Candle was set at some Distance
' from the Bottle, upon a Table, the Heat would
' direct its Course that Way ; so that it might be
' poisonous to any one that sat near to the Light, and
' to no-body else. I know (adds the Doctor) the
' Composition of this *Stygian* Spirit ; *but it is better*
' *that the World should not be instructed in such Arts of*
' *Death.*'

   For the same Reason the Author, as a Lover of
his King and Country, and consequently a Friend
to *Population*, chuses not to print the Word S——
at full Length.

                                    A massy

A maſſy Hammer in his Hand he held,
Which ſcarce two Men of modern Strength could
   weild.   30
 With this advancing, at one pond'rous Stroke,
Forthwith th' inhoſpitable Bars he broke :
Then to next Alehouſe did his Godſhip ſteer,
To quaff the earthly Nectar of Butt Beer.
 Soon as he ſaw the Gates wide open ſtand, 35
In ruſh'd *Licentiato* with his Band ;
Through Conſtables, through Butchers onward preſt
To *Fuming Chamber,* an unwelcome Gueſt ;

          Where,

N O T E S.

V. 29. *A maſſy Hammer in his Hand he held,*
   Which ſcarce two Men of modern Strength could
   weild.

A pond'rous Stone bold *Hector* heav'd to throw,
Pointed above, and rough and groſs below ;
Not two ſtrong Men th'enormous Weight could raiſe,
Such Men as live in theſe degenerate Days.
        Pope's Homer, B. XII.

V. 33. *Then to next Alehouſe did his Godſhip ſteer,*
    To quaff the earthly Nectar of Butt Beer.

 In Juſtice to the honeſt Landlord that keeps the
Houſe, and the worthy Alderman that ſerves it, we
think ourſelves obliged to acquaint all true Lovers of
Entire Butt, that they will be ſure to meet with an
excellent Tankard of it at the *Three Jolly Butchers,*
the Corner of *Warwick-Court.*
 The Author ingeniouſly acknowledges, that ſome
of the beſt Lines (if any may be called ſo) in his
Poem, are owing to the Inſpiration of this excellent
Liquor.

V. 38. To *Fuming Chamber,*
    Vulgarly called, *Smoaking Room.*

            We

Where, from Intrusion (as they thought) secure,
In lolling Posture, and with Look demure,   40
Immers'd in Politicks and sober Chat,
The Dons serenely o'er their Bottle sat ;
In ' customary Suits of solemn Black,'
Save that the Peruke whitens down the Back.
Slow from their Lips proceeds the puff'd Perfume, 45
And Sleep-inviting Vapours cloud the Room.
   Licentiato enters.—With Appall
Each was struck dumb, as Mute at Funeral.—
So sat the *Roman Curules*, dully wise,
When *Gauls* rush'd in, and view'd them with
      Surprize,   50
Taking their awful Forms for Deities.

                              Choak'd

NOTES.

We cannot but take Notice here of an infamous
Addition to those admirable Lines, in Favour of
this noble exotic Plant ; to wit,

   Tobacco Hick, Tobacco Hick,
   'Twill make you well, if you are sick.

An Enemy to *Tobacconists* has reversed the Sentiment, by saying,

   Tobacco Hick, Tobacco Hick,
   If you are well will make you sick.

V. 43. ' *In customary Suits of Solemn Black,'*
         Or customary Suits of solemn Black. *Hamlet*.

V. 49. *So sat the* Roman Curules, *dully wise,*
         When Gauls *rush'd in, and view'd them with*
            Surprize,
         Taking their awful Forms for Deities.

' When the Crowd of superannuated Patriots
' had, by their Advice and Exhortations to the Sol-
' diers, done all that was in their Power towards
                                          ' the

Choak'd with the Fume, *Licentiato* broke
The folemn Silence, and thus, coughing, fpoke :

                            ' Give

N O T E.

' the Defence of the Capital [*Rome*] they returned
' to their Houfes, there to wait, with fteady Refo-
' lution, the coming of the Enemy, and Death.
' Such of them as had *triumphed* for Victories, or
' had been *Curule* Magiftrates, that they might die
' with the greater Dignity, adorned themfelves with
' the *Infignia* of thofe Honours which they had ac-
' quired by their Virtue. Cloathed in their tri-
' umphal Robes, or thofe of their Magiftracies, they
' repaired to the *Forum*, and feating themfelves there
' in their *Curule* Chairs, maintained the fame re-
' fpectable Air of Greatnefs, as when in the Ful-
' nefs of their former Power.

  ' As the *Gauls* had met with little Refiftance from
' the *Romans* in the Field, and were not put to the
' Trouble of an Affault to take the City, they en-
' tered it (at the Gate *Collina*) without any Thing,
' in their Appearance, of hoftile Anger, that raging
' Flame, kindled by Oppofition, Difficulty, and
' Danger. Moving on, they beheld, with Amaze-
' ment, the Streets unpeopled as a Defert ; and
' when they came to the *Forum*, and caft their
' Eyes all around, they could obferve no Shew of
' War but in the Citadel alone. What chiefly
' drew and fixed their Attention, was the Company
' of venerable Victims, who had devoted them-
' felves to Death. *Their magnificent purple Robes,*
' *their long white Beards, their Air of Greatnefs, their*
' *Silence, Stilnefs, and Serenity, all thefe aftonifhed the*
' *Gauls, held them at an awful Diftance, and infpired*
' *them with the fame Refpect which they would have*
' *had for fo many Gods.* It chanced, however, that
' one of the Soldiers (who was, probably, lefs apt

                                       ' to

' Give us, *(hem, hem,)* one Drop to clear our Lungs,
' *(Hem,hem)* one little Drop to cool our Tongues.' 55
' No ; not a fingle Drop, 'ftern *Socio* roar'd,
And up he fnatch'd the Bottle from the Board.
' How dares *Licentiato* force our Gate ?'
He faid, and hurl'd the Bottle at his Pate.
The Glafs, lefs hard, quick from his Front rebounds, 60
Scarce leaving on the Skin fome fuperficial Wounds.

Thrice happy thou, whofe tender Brain's immur'd
In thickeft Cafe, by leaden Skull fecur'd !
Drug-venders elfe had rued th' Adventure crofs,
And callous Undertakers mourn'd thy Lofs.   65

N O T E.

' to be religioufly affected than his Comrades) took
' the Freedom gently to put his Hand towards the
' Beard of *Manlius Papirius,* as if he meant to
' ftroke it ; a Familiarity which fo much offended
' the *majeftick Figure,* that, with a fmart Blow of
' his *Ivory Truncheon,* he broke the Fellow's Head.
' There needed no more to put an End to all Re-
' verence for fuch a cholerick Deity.   The *Gauls*
' inftantly killed *Papirius* ; and, as if he had given
' the Signal for a general Maffacre, all the reft were
' now flain, *fitting, like him, in State, in their Curule*
' *Chairs.'*

HOOKE's *Rom. Hift.* Book II. Chap. XXXVIII.

Let the Reader figure to himfelf the *Doctors,*—
their *magnificent full-trim'd Black,*—their *long white
Perukes,*—their *Air of Greatnefs,*—their *Silence, Still-
nefs,* and *Serenity,*—their *Gold-headed Canes,* (no lefs
refpectable than the *Ivory Truncheon*)—their *fitting
in State, in their Elbow Chairs* ;—Let the Reader,
I fay, figure to himfelf thefe *Majeftick Figures,* and
we are confident, he muft be ftruck with Awe and
Admiration.

Yet

Yet with the Shock *Licentiato* lies
Stun'd—from the Floor unable to arife;
And, as when Cupping-utenfil's applied,
The trickling Streams from narrow Sluices glide,
So down his Face flow flows a purple Flood :— 70
The Mufe affirms not, whether Wine or Blood.

PART III.

A ND now a general Tumult reigns thro' all;
"To Arms, to Arms," on ev'ry Side they
bawl.
Each grave Bafhaw, that bears three deathful Tails,
Rous'd from his Torpor joins in fierce Aflails;
Foregoes his wonted Solemnefs of Mein, 5
While Wig meets Wig, and Cane encounters Cane.

NOTE.

V. 67. *Yet with the Shock* Licentiato *lies*
        Stun'd—*from the Floor unable to arife.*

The Sound is here defignedly made to echoe to the
Senfe.
So *Virgil.*
——*procumbit humi Bos.*
Many Inftances may be brought, not only from the
Greek and *Latin* Poets, of fimilar Attention, but al-
fo from our own. Let one fuffice.——
Shakefpear, in his King Lear, has the following
Line.
    " Many a Fathom down precipitating,"
the *Precipitation* of which *Tate* has chofen to *flop* (in
his Alteration of this Play) by fubftituting

    " Many a Fathom *tumbling down,*"
O what a *tumbling down* is here!
                                    The

The ruffled Hairs on fretful Perukes rise,
Like Quills on Hedge-hog, when he roll'd up lies;
Their Knots on either Side the Tyes unfold,
And pendent Midmoft ftands erectly bold.   10

So when *Medufa's* Head bore Snakes for Hair,
(Curl'd like the *Tétes* our Dames of Fafhion wear,)
Their Folds untwifting, with Amaze and Dread
They ftruck the Foe, and inftant ftar'd him dead.

The Cane, for Sapience rever'd of old,   15
(With Head of Amber, or with Head of Gold,)
Sage Nurfe of Thought, that gently kifs'd the Nofe,
On the crack'd Cranium deals defcending Blows.
The fhort fnug Sword, of Meafure Larks to fpit,
With modeft Hilt juft peeping thro' the Slit   20
From peaceful Scabbard ftarts a warring Blade,
' By a mere Bodkin the *Quietus* made.'

N O T E S.

V. 7. *The ruffled Hairs on fretful Perukes rise,*
Like Quills on Hedge-hog, when he roll'd up lies.

Make thy young Hairs to ftand on End,
Like Quills upon the fretful Porcupine.
                              HAMLET.

V. 12 *Curl'd like the Tétes our Dames of Fafhion wear.*

Thefe prepofterous Ornaments of falfe Hair,
twifted and twirled into a thoufand unnatural Shapes,
may indeed be very properly called *Medufa Tétes*,
though it muft be confeffed they are (in the Language of *Enamoratos*) not quite fo *killing.* For the
Story of *Medufa*, fee the End of the *Latin* Dictionary, under the Letter M.

V. 22. ' *By a mere Bodkin the* Quietus *made.*'

When himfelf might his *Quietus* make
With a bare Bodkin.   HAMLET.
                                        So

So when a Taylor on the Shopboard fits,
Of Galligafkins to repair the Slits,
Tormented by the Foe, he Vengeance vows,   25
And with his Spear, a Needle, pricks a Loufe.
   And now a general Tumult reigns thro' all,
' To Arms, to Arms,' on ev'ry Side they bawl.
So loud the Din, fo terrible the Roar,
It pierc'd the Earth to *Lethe*'s farther Shore ;   30
Shook *Pluto*'s Throne,--who trembled for his Friends,
So fkill'd, fo prompt to ferve their mutual Ends.
Refolv'd to part them, he afcends to Light,
Enters the Room, in folemn Veft bedight.
   A fable Truncheon his Right-hand difplays,   35
And in his Left four flaming Torches blaze ;
Rings on his Fingers for departed Friends ;
Athwart his Breaft a filken Scarf defcends ;
Plumes on his Head, and on his Back he bore,
Like Herald's Coat, a Robe efcutcheon'd o'er.   40
An *Undertaker* aptly he appears :—
Black is the conftant Drefs *Hell*'s Monarch wears.
   Thus have we feen, in *Pantomimick* Tricks,
Grim *Pluto* thro' the Trap-door come from *Styx* ;
Black and all black, all difmal is his Suit,   45
And powder'd feems the Peruke's felf with Soot :
His Legs alone, with emblematic Aim,
In fcarlet-colour'd Hofe affect to Flame.
   ' Hold, hold, (he cries,) what means this def-
       p'rate Fray?
' Will ye yourfelves inftead of others flay?   50
' Has *Beaume* purg'd *Autumn* of each fad Complaint?
' The Air in vain does *Influenza* taint?
                        ' What!'

N O T E.

V. 52. *Has* Beaume *purg'd* Autumn *of each fad*
     Complaint ?
    The Air in vain does Influenza *taint ?*

‘ What! no acute, no chronical Difeafe,
‘ No Fevers want your Aid? No Pleurifies, 55
‘ No Coughs, Confumptions, Atrophies, Catarrhs?
‘ No foul Mifhaps from Love's intemp'rate Wars?
‘ If ye neglect *Your* Bufinefs, there will be,
‘ Alas! I fear, but little Work for *Me.*
   ‘ What's in a Name? That which we call a Wig, 60
‘ By any other Name would look as big.
‘ What's in a Place? Where'er ye had Degrees,
‘ The fame the *Latin* in your *Recipes:*
‘ The Scrawl, illegible to vulgar Eyes,
‘ Denotes you deeply learn'd, and wond'rous wife.
                     65

N O T E S.

Beaume de Vie. A Medicine fo called, which is
advertifed as a fovereign Remedy *againft* autumnal
Complaints.

Influenza. A Diftemper which rages in *Italy,* in
the *Summer* Months. The Term has been adopted in *England.*

V. 58. *If ye neglect* Your *Bufinefs, there will be,*
     Alas! I fear, but little Work for Me.

The two Trades are fo intimately connected, that
an eminent Apothecary, whofe eldeft Son is brought
up to the Father's Profeffion, has, with a prudent
Forecaft, bound his youngeft Son Apprentice to an
Undertaker.

V. 60. *What's in a Name? That which we call a Wig,*
     By any other Name would look as big.

A Parody on the following Lines;

What's in a Name? That which we call a Rofe,
By any other Name would fmell as fweet.
               ROMEO *and* JULIET.
                      ‘ Think

' Think on the Meed, that tickles fweet your Hand,
' The glitt'ring Meed, no Doctor can withftand.
  ' Tho' Doctors differ ;—for the human Tripe
' Tho' fome the Purge prefer, and fome the Pipe ;
' Or in th' Inteftines raife the fharp Commotion, 70
' Some with a Pill, and others with a Potion ;
' Tho', to apply the Flayer of the Skin,
' Some hold a Virtue, others hold a Sin ;
' In *Antimony* fome their Truft repofe,
' And fome in *Mercury*—to fave a Nofe ;   75
' In this one Point ye never difagree,—
' Ye're all unanimous—about the Fee.
  ' Come then, my Friends, (for now methinks I fpy
' A mild Complacency in ev'ry Eye,)
' Think on the Meed, that tickles fweet your Hand, 80
' The glitt'ring Meed, no Doctor can withftand.
                  ' Like

NOTES.

V. 72. *The Flayer of the Skin.*

A poetical Expreffion for *Emplaftr. Epifpaftic.*—
In plain *Englifh*, a Blifter.

V. 76. *In this one Point ye never difagree,*
        Ye're all unanimous—about the Fee.

    About each Symptom how they difagree,—
    But how unanimous in cafe of Fee. GARTH.

V. 80. *Think on the Meed that tickles fweet your Hand,*
    The glitt'ring Meed, no Doctor can withftand.

    To corroborate the Truth of this Maxim, we
fhall take the Liberty of fetting down the two following fhort Stories, by Way of Illuftration.   The

' Like to the Cur in *Æsop*'s Tale difplay'd,
' Ye quit the Subftance, and embrace the Shade.
' *Licentiato Licence* has—to kill:
' Can *Socio* boaft a greater Pow'r, or Skill?   85
' While ye difpute, and quarrel for a Word,
' Behold! your Patients are to Health reftor'd.

NOTES.

Circumftances required the Stile of the Narration to
be more familiar than would fuit with the Dignity of
the Reft of the Poem, to have them interwoven in
the Body of it.

A Doctor once (no Matter whence I ween,
From *Oxford*, *Leyden*, *Cam*, or *Aberdeen*,)
Was call'd to vifit one with utmoft Speed;
But, when he came, behold! the Patient's dead.
' What! dead?'—' Yes, Doctor,—dead,—but here's
            ' your Fee.'—
' Oh, very well:—'tis all the fame to me.'

A Doctor once (O tell it not in *Bath*,
Left Doctor *Somebody* be much in Wrath,)
Soon as he faw the fick Man, fhook his Head,—
No Pulfe—no Breath—the Man in fhort was dead.—
Now as our Doctor kept his filent Stand,
The tempting *Shiner* in the dead Man's Hand
He faw, he touch'd—and feizing, ' 'Tis for me,'
He cried, and took his Farewell,—and the Fee.

V. 87. Behold! your Patients are to Health reftor'd.

It is very remarkable, that the * *Decreafe* of *Bu-
rials* within the Bills of Mortality for the Year 1767,
is not lefs than 1299, owing (it may perhaps be
fuppofed) to the Phyficians having been fo much
taken up with Squabbles among themfelves.

* See the *General Bill of Mortality*, fet forth by the Parifh Clerks,
from *December* 15, 1766, to *December* 16, 1767.

' Ye

' Ye three-tail'd Sages, ceafe your Difputation,
' Be Friends, and focial join in Confultation ;
' Each fhake his loaded Noddle with the other,   90
' And Brother gravely fmell his Cane with Brother.'
  He ended, and forthwith to Sight appears
A Car triumphal in the Form of Hearfe :
Six coal-black Steeds ' drag'd its flow Length along,'
Deaf to *Aight, Aight,* and heedlefs of the Thong.   95
Thefe with dull Pace th' infernal Monarch drew,
(Laid flat upon his Back, and hid from View,)
In awful Pomp, flow, folemn, fad, and ftill,
Thro' *Warwick-Lane,* and on, (down *Ludgate-Hill,*)
To the *Fleet-Market,*—whofe ftupendous Ditch   100
A lazy Current rolls, as black as Pitch ;
From whence a Paffage, difmal, dark, and dank,
Leads underneath to *Acheron*'s gloomy Bank.
Twelve fable Imps the Vehicle furround,
And with lethiferous Nightfhade ftrew the Ground :
                      105

N O T E S.

V. 90. *Each fhake his loaded Noddle with the other,*
      And Brother gravely fmell his Cane with Brother.

  An Imitation of the following Lines ;

One Fool lolls his Tongue out at another,
And fhakes his empty Noddle at his Brother.

V. 94. *Six coal-black Steeds* ' drag'd its flow Length
        along,
      A needlefs *Alexandrine* ends the Song,
      And like a wounded Snake, ' drag'd its flow
      ' Length along.'

V. 95. *Deaf to* Aight, Aight, *and heedlefs to the Thong.*

  Aight, Aight—an Expreffion in the *Huynhym* Language, made Ufe of by Coachmen, *&c.* in fpeaking to the Horfes, fignifying, *Go on.*

         Z 3   A ftrong

A ſtrong Perfume, as in his Car he rode,   106
Of *Aſſa Fœtida* proclaim'd the God.
   Their Feuds forgot, the Doctors, with Amaze
And rev'rent Awe, on the Proceſſion gaze.

N O T E.

V. 106. *A ſtrong Perfume, as in his Car he rode,*
       Of Aſſa Fœtida *proclaim'd the God.*

Aſſa Fœtida, vulgarly called *Devil's Dung*; Abundance of which is found about the *Peak* in *Derbyſhire.* [See *Cotton's* Natural Hiſtory of that Place.]

S H A K E-

SHAKESPEARE:

A N

EPISTLE to D. GARRICK, Esq.

Nil Admirari.———— HOR.

Quod ſi tam Graijs, Novitas *inviſa fuiſſet,*
Quam nobis, *quid nunc eſſet vetus?* Idem.

THANKS to much Induſtry and Pains,
　Much Twiſting of the Wit and Brains,
Tranſlation has unlock'd the Store,
And ſpread abroad the *Grecian* Lore,
While *Sophocles* his Scenes are grown,
E'en as familiar as our own.
　No more ſhall Taſte preſume to ſpeak,
From its Encloſures in the *Greek*;
But, all its Fences broken down,
Lie at the Mercy of the Town.
　Critic, I hear thy Torrent rage,
＇ 'Tis Blaſphemy againſt that Stage,
＇ Which *Æſchylus* his Warmth deſign'd,
＇ *Euripides* his Taſte refin'd,
＇ And *Sophocles* his laſt Direction,
＇ Stamp'd with the Signet of Perfection.'
　Perfection's but a Word ideal,
And bears about it nothing real,
And Excellence was never hit
In the firſt Eſſays of Man's Wit.
Shall *ancient* Worth, or *ancient* Fame
Preclude the Moderns from their Claim?

Muſt

Muſt they be Blockheads, Dolts, and Fools,
Who write not up to *Grecian* Rules?
Who tread in Buſkins or in Socks,
Muſt they be damn'd as Hetorodox,
Nor Merit of good Works prevail,
Except within the claſſic Pale?
'Tis Stuff that bears the Name of Knowledge,
Not current half a Mile from College;
Where half their Lectures yield no more
(Before I ſpeak of Times of Yore)
Than juſt a niggard Light, to mark
How much we all are in the Dark.
As Ruſhlights in a ſpacious Room,
Juſt burn enough to form a Gloom.

　　When *Shakeſpeare* leads the Mind a Dance,
From *France* to *England*, hence to *France*,
Talk not to me of Time and Place;
I own I'm happy in the Chace.
Whether the Drama's here or there,
'Tis Nature, *Shakeſpeare* every where.
The Poet's Fancy can create,
Contract, enlarge, annihilate,
Bring paſt and preſent cloſe together,
In Spite of Diſtance, Seas, or Weather.
And ſhut up in a ſingle Action,
What coſt whole Years in its Tranſaction.
So, Ladies at a Play, or Rout,
Can ſlirt the Univerſe about,
Whoſe geographical Account
Is drawn and pictur'd on the Mount.
Yet, when they pleaſe, contract the Plan,
And ſhut the World up in a Fan.

　　True Genius, like *Armida's* Wand,
Can raiſe the Spring from barren Land.
While all the Art of Imitation,
Is pilf'ring from the firſt Creation;
Tranſplanting Flowers with uſeleſs Toil,
Which wither in a foreign Soil.

As

As Confcience often fets us right,
By its interior active Light,
Without th' Affiftance of the Laws
So combat in the moral Caufe ;
To Genius, of itfelf difcerning,
Without the myftic Rules of Learning,
Can from its prefent Intuition,
Strike at the Truth of Compofition.
   Yet thofe who breathe the claffic Vein,
Enlifted in the mimic Train,
Who ride their Steed with double Bit,
Not run away with by their Wit,
Delighted with the Pomp of Rules,
The Specious Pedantry of Schools ;
(Which Rules, like Crutches, ne'er became
Of any Ufe but to the Lame)
Purfue the Method fet before 'em,
Talk much of Order and Decorum,
Of Probability of Fiction,
Of Manners, Ornament, and Diction,
And with a Jargon of hard Names,
(A Privilege which Dulnefs claims)
And merely us'd by way of Fence,
To keep out plain and common Senfe,
Extol the Wit of antient Days,
The fimple Fabric of their Plays ;
Then from the Fable, all fo chafte,
Trick'd up in antient-modern Tafte,
So mighty gentle all the While,
In fuch a fweet defcriptive Stile,
While Chorus marks the fervile Mode
With fine Reflexion, in an Ode,
Prefent you with a perfect Piece,
Form'd on the Model of old *Greece*.
   Come, prithee Critic, fet before us,
The Ufe and Office of a Chorus.
What! filent! Why then, I'll produce
Its Services from antient Ufe.

I

'Tis

'Tis to be ever on the Stage,
Attendants upon Grief or Rage,
To be an arrant Go-between,
Chief-Mourner at each difmal Scene;
Shewing its Sorrow, or Delight,
By fhifting Dances, left and right.
Not much unlike our modern Notions,
Adagio or *Allegro* Motions;
To watch upon the deep Diftrefs,
And Plaints of Royal Wretchednefs;
And when, with Tears, and Execration,
They've pour'd out all their Lamentation,
And wept whole Cataracts from their Eyes,
To call on Rivers for Supplies,
And with their *Hais* and *Hees* and *Hoes*
To make a Symphony of Woes.
  Doubtlefs the Antients want the Art
To ftrike at once upon the Heart.
Or why their Prologues of a Mile
In fimple — call it — humble Stile,
In unimpaffion'd Phrafe to fay
' 'Fore the beginning of this Play,
' I, haplefs *Polydore*, was found
' By Fifhermen, or others, drown'd!
' Or, I, a Gentleman, did wed,
' The Lady I wou'd never bed,
' Great *Agamemnon*'s royal Daughter,
' Who's coming hither to draw Water.'
  Or need the Chorus to reveal
Reflexions, which the Audience feel;
And jog them, left Attention fink,
To tell them how and what to think?
  Oh, where's the Bard, who at one View,
Cou'd look the whole Creation through,
Who travers'd all the human Heart,
Without Recourfe to *Grecian* Art?
He fcorn'd the Modes of Imitation,
Of Altering, Pilfering, and Tranflation,

Nor

Nor painted Horror, Grief, or Rage,
From Models of a former Age;
The bright Original he took,
And tore the Leaf from Nature's Book.
'Tis *Shakespeare*, thus who stands alone—
Why need I tell what *You* have shown?
How true, how perfect, and how well,
The Feelings of our Hearts must tell.

ODE

ODE TO GENIUS.

.

I.

THOU Child of Nature, Genius ſtrong,
  Thou Maſter of the Poet's Song,
Before whoſe Light, Art's dim and feeble Ray
Gleams like the Taper in the Blaze of Day:
Thou lov'ſt to ſteal along the ſecret Shade,
  Where Fancy, bright aërial Maid!
  Awaits thee with her thouſand Charms,
  And revels in thy wanton Arms.
  She to thy Bed, in Days of Yore,
  The ſweetly-warbling *Shakeſpeare* bore;
Whom every Muſe endow'd with every Skill,
  And dipt him in that ſacred Rill,
Whoſe ſilver Streams flow muſical along,
Where *Phœbus*' hallow'd Mount reſounds with raptur'd
  Song.

II.

 Forſake not Thou the vocal Choir,
Their Breaſts reviſit with thy genial Fire,
Elſe vain the ſtudied Sounds of mimic Art,
Tickle the Ear, but come not nigh the Heart.
Vain every Phraſe in curious Order ſet,
On each Side leaning on the [ſtop-gap] Epithet.
Vain the quick Rime ſtill tinckling in the Cloſe,
While pure Deſcription ſhines in meaſur'd Proſe.
 Thou bear'ſt a-loof, and look'ſt with high Diſdain,
  Upon the dull mechanic Train;
Whoſe nerveleſs Strains flag on in languid Tone,
Lifeleſs and lumpiſh as the Bag-pipe's drowzy Drone.

III. No

III.

No longer now thy Altars blaze,
No Poet offers up his Lays;
Infpir'd with Energy divine,
To worfhip at thy facred Shrine.
Since TASTE * with abfolute Domain,
Extending wide her leaden Reign,
Kills with her melancholy Shade,
The blooming Scyons of fair Fancy's Tree;
Which erft full wantonly have ftray'd,
In many a Wreath of richeft Poefie.
For when the Oak denies her Stay,
The creeping Ivy winds her humble Way;
No more fhe twifts her Branches round,
But drags her feeble Stem along the barren Ground.

IV.

Where then fhall exil'd Genius go?
Since only thofe the Laurel claim,
And boaft them of the Poet's Name,
Whofe fober Rimes in even Tenour flow;
Who prey on Words, and all their Flowrets cull,
Coldly correct, and regularly dull.
Why fleep the Sons of Genius now?
Why *Wartons* refts the Lyre unftrung?
‡ And thou, bleft Bard! around whofe facred
Great *Pindar*'s delegated Wreath is hung;   [Brow,
Arife, and fnatch the Majefty of Song,
From Dullnefs' fervile Tribe, and Arts unhallow'd
Throng.

* By TASTE, is here meant the modern Affectation of it.
‡ The fpirited and truly poetical Dr. *Akenfide*.

TRANSLATION;

A

POEM.

'SUCH is our Pride, our Folly, or our Fate,[1]
'That few, but such who cannot write, tranf-
   late.'
So *Denham* fung, who well the Labour knew ;
And an Age paft has left the Maxim true.
Wit as of old, a proud imperious Lord,   5
Difdains the Plenty of another's Board ;
And haughty Genius feeks, like *Philip*'s Son,
Paths never trod before, and Worlds unknown.
Unmov'd by thefe, whilft Hands impure difpenfe
The facred Streams of ancient Eloquence,   10
Pedants affume the Tafk for Scholars fit,
And Blockheads rife Interpreters of Wit.
 In the fair Field th' vet'ran Armies ftand,
A firm, unconquer'd, formidable Band,
When lo ! 'Tranflation comes and levels all ;   15
By vulgar Hands the braveft Heroes fall.
On Eagle's Wings fee lofty *Pindar* foar ;
Cowley attacks, and *Pindar* is no more.

LINE 18. *Cowley attacks,* &c. Nothing can be
more contemptible than the Tranflations and Imitations of *Pindar* done by *Cowley*, which yet have had
their Admirers.

O'er

O'er *Tibur*'s Swan the Mufes wept in vain,
And mourn'd their Bard by cruel *Dunfter* flain.   20
By *Ogilby* and *Trap* great *Maro* fell,
And *Homer* dy'd by *Chapman* and *Ozell*.

In bleft *Arabia*'s Plains unfading blow
Flow'rs ever fragant, Fruits immortal grow.
To Northern Climes th' unwilling Guefts convey, 25
The Fruit fhall wither, and the Flow'r decay ;
Ev'n fo when here the Sweets of *Athens* come,
Or the fair Produce of imperial *Rome*,
They pine and ficken in th' unfriendly Shade,
Their Rofes droop, and all their Laurels fade.   30

The modern Critic, whofe unletter'd Pride,
Big with itfelf, contemns the World befide,
If haply told that *Terence* once could charm,
Each feeling Heart that *Sophocles* cou'd warm,
Scours ev'ry Stall for *Eachard*'s dirty Page,   35
Or pores in *Adam* for th' *Athenian* Stage ;
With Joy he reads the fervile Mimics o'er,
Pleas'd to difcover what he guefs'd before ;

LINE 20. See *Horace*'s Epiftles, Satires, and Art
of Poetry, *done into Englifh* by S. *Dunfter*, D. D.
Prebendary of *Sarum*.

LINE 21, 22. See their Tranflations of *Homer*
and *Virgil*.

LINE 31. *The modern Critic,* &c. Les belles
traductions (fays *Boileau*) font des preuves fans re-
plique en faveur des anciens, qu'on leur donne les
Racines pout interpretes, & ils fcauront plaire au-
jourdhui comme autrefois. Certain it is, that the
Contempt, in which the Ancients are held by the
illiterate Wits of the prefent Age, is in a great
Meafure owing to the Number of bad Tranflations.

LINE 36. See *Adams*'s Profe Tranflation of *Sophocles*.

Concludes

Concludes that *Attic* Wit's *extremely low*;
And gives up *Greece* to *Wotton* and *Perrault*.   40
  Our fhallow Language, fhallow'r Judges fay,
Can ne'er the Force of ancient Senfe convey.
  As well might *Vanbrugh* ev'ry Stone revile,
That fwells enormous *Blenheim*'s awkward Pile;
The guiltlefs Pen as well might *Mauro* blame,   45
For writing ill, and fullying *Arthur*'s Fame;
Succefslefs Lovers blaft the Maid they woo'd,
As thefe a Tongue they never underftood;
That Tongue which gave immortal *Shakefpeare* Fame,
Which boafts a *Prior*'s, and a *Thomfon*'s Name;   50
Graceful and chafte which flows in *Addifon*,
With native Charms, and Vigour all its own;
In *Bolinbroke* and *Swift*, whofe Beauties fhine,
In *Rowe*'s foft Numbers, *Jonfon*'s nervous Line,
Dryden's free Vein, and *Milton*'s Work divine.
  But, fuch, alas! difdain to borrow Fame,   55
Or live like Dulnefs in another's Name;
And hence the Tafk for nobleft Souls defign'd,
Giv'n to the Weak, the Taftelefs, and the Blind;
To fome low Wretch, who, proftitute for Pay,
Lets out to *Curll* the Labours of the Day,   60
Carelefs who hurries o'er th' unblotted Line,
Impatient ftill to finifh, and to dine;

  LINE 39. *Extremely low.* A favourite Coffee-
houfe Phrafe.
  LINE 40. *Wotton and Perrault.* See *Wotton*'s
Difcourfe on ancient and modern Learning, and
Perrault's Defence of his *Siecle de Louis* XIV.
  LINE 46. *Arthur's Fame.* See *Blackmore*'s *King
Arthur*, an Heroic Poem.
  LINE 60. *To Curll*, &c. Moft of the bad Tranf-
lations, which we have of eminent Authors, were
done by Garreteers under the Infpection of this
Gentleman, who paid them by the Sheet for their
hafty Performances.

                                        Or

Or some pale Pedant, whose encumber'd Brain
O'er the dull Page hath toil'd for Years in vain,
Who writes at last ambitiously to shew   65
How much a Fool may read, how little know;
Can these on Fancy's Wing with *Plato* soar?
Can these a *Tully's* active Mind explore?
Great Nature's secret Springs can these reveal,
Or paint those Passions which they ne'er cou'd feel? 70
Yet will they dare the pond'rous Lance to wield,
Yet will they strive to lift the seven-fold Shield;
The Rock of *Ajax* ev'ry Child would throw,
And ev'ry Strippling bend *Ulysses'* Bow.

    There are, who timid Line by Line pursue, 75
Anxious to keep th' Original in View;
Who mark each Footstep where their Master trod,
And after all their Pains have miss'd the Road.

    There are, an Author's Sense who boldly quit,
As if asham'd to own the Debt of Wit: 80
Who leave their Fellow-trav'ller on the Shore,
Launch in the Deep, and part to meet no more.

    Some from Reflection catch the weaken'd Ray,
And scarce a Gleam of doubtful Sense convey,
Present a Picture's Picture to your View,   85
Where not a Line is just, or Feature true.

LINE 75, 79. *There are*, &c. The Reader will
easily recollect Instances to illustrate each of these Remarks, more especially the last; half our Translations
being done from Translations by such as were never
able to consult the Original. One of these Gentlemen
having Occasion in his Version to mention *Dionysius*
of *Halicarnassus*, not having the good Fortune to be
acquainted with any such Writer, makes Use of the
French Liberty of Curtailing, and without Scruple
calls him *Dennis* of *Halicarnassus*. Mistakes as gross
as this often occur, though perhaps not many altogether so ridiculous.

Thus *Greece* and *Rome*, in modern Drefs array'd,
Is but Antiquity in Mafquerade.
Difguis'd in *Oldfworth*'s Verfe or *Watfon*'s Profe,
What Claffic Friend his alter'd *Floccus* knows?　95
Whilft great *Longinus* gives to *Welfted* Fame,
And *Tacitus* to *Gordon* lends his Name,
Unmeaning Strains debafe the *Mantuan* Mufe,
And *Terence* fpeaks the Language of the Stews.

In Learning thus muft *Britain*'s Sons decay,　95
And fee her Rival bear the Prize away,
In Arts as well as Arms to *Gallia* yield,
And own her happier Skill in either Field?
See where her boafted *d'Ablancourt* appears,
Her *Mongualts*, *Brumoys*, *Olivets*, *Daciers*;　100

'Careful

LINE 91. See *Welfted*'s Tranflation of *Longinus*,
done almoft Word for Word from *Boileau*,

LINE 62. *To Gordon*.—This Gentleman tranflated *Tacitus* in a very ftiff and affected Manner,
tranfpofing Words, and placing the Verb at the
End of the Sentence, according to the *Latin* Idiom.
He was called in his Life-Time *Tacitus-Gordon*.

LINE 97. *To Gallia yield*. It was faid by a great
Wit in the laft War, that he fhould never doubt
of our Succefs, if we could once bring ourfelves to
hate the *French* as heartily as we do the Arts and
Sciences. It is indifputable, that they are more
warmly encouraged, and confequently more cultivated
and improved in *France* than amongft us. Their
Tranflations (efpecially in Profe) are acknowledged
to be more faithful and correct, and in general more
lively and fpirited than ours.

LINE 99. The *French* had fo high an Opinion of
d'Ablancourt's Merit, as to think him deferving of
the following Epitaph:

L'illuftre d'Ablancourt repofe en ce tombeau,
Son genie à fon fiécle fervi de flambeau,

Dans

Careful to make each Ancient's Merit known,
Who, juft to others Fame, have rais'd their own;
No Wonder thefe fhou'd claim fuperior Praife;
A Nation thanks them, and a Monarch pays.
Far other Fate attends our hireling Bard,   105
A Sneer his Praife, a Pittance his Reward;
The Butt of Wit, and Jeft of every Mufe,
Foes laugh to Scorn, and even Friends abufe;
The great Tranflator bids each Dunce tranflate,
And ranks us all with *Tibbald* and with *Tate*.   110
   But know, whate'er proud Art hath call'd her own,
The breathing Canvas, and the fculptur'd Stone,
The Poet's Verfe, 'tis Imitation all;
Great Nature onlyis Original.
Her various Charms in various Forms exprefs'd, 115
They beft have pleas'd us, who have copy'd beft;
And thofe ftill fhine more eminently bright,
Who fhew the Goddefs in the faireft Light.
   So when great *Shakefpeare* to his *Garrick* join'd,
With mutual Aid confpire to roufe the Mind,   120
'Tis not a Scene of idle Mimickry,
'Tis *Lear's*, *Hamlet's*, *Richard's* felf we fee;

    Dans fes fameux ecrits toute la France admire
    Des Grecs & des Romains les precieux trefors;
     A fon trepas on ne peut dire
    Qui perd le plus, des vivans ou des morts.

LINE 109. *The great Tranflator*, &c. *Pope*, in his Epiftle to *Arbuthnot*, after his Enumeration of Dunces, concludes with thefe two Lines:

    All thefe my modeft Satire bade *tranflate*,
    And own'd that nine fuch Poets made a *Tate*.

I make no Doubt but the very defpicable Light in which Tranflation is here reprefented, may have deterr'd many from engaging in it, who would, per-haps, have made no contemptible Figure in that Branch of Literature.

                                   We

We feel the Actor's Strength, the Poet's Fire;
With Joy we praise, with Rapture we admire,
To see such Pow'rs within the Reach of Art,   125
And Fiction thus subdue the human Heart.

   When *Sarto*'s Pencil trac'd the faithful Line,
So just each Stroke, so equal the Design,
That pleas'd he saw astonish'd *Julio* stand,
Nor knew his own, nor *Raphael*'s magic Hand; 130
Blushing to find himself enamour'd grown
Of rival Charms and Beauties not his own.

   Theirs be the Task to comment and translate,
Like these who judge, like these who imitate.

   Unless an Authour like a Mistress warms,   135
How shall we hide his Faults, or taste his Charms,
How all his modest, latent Beauties find,
How trace each lovelier Feature of the Mind,
Soften each Blemish, and each Grace improve,
And treat him with the Dignity of Love?   140

   'Tis not enough that, fraught with Learning's Store,
By the dim Lamp the tasteless Critic pore;
'Tis not enough that Wit's misguiding Ray
Uncertain glance, and yield a doubtful Day,

LINE 129. *Andrea del Sarto* being desired by *Frederic*, Duke of *Mantua*, to copy a Picture of *Leo* X. did it with so much Justness, that *Julio Romano*, who drew the Drapery of that Piece under *Raphael*, took his Copy for the Original, and said to *Vasari*, 'Don't I see the Strokes that I struck with 'my own Hand; but *Vasari* shewing him *Del Sarto*'s Mark, he was convinced of his Mistake.

   The Story is told at large in the 27th Chapter of the first Book of *De Pile's Art of Painting*.

   LINE 135. *Unless*, &c. *Roscommon* says,

   'Chuse then an Author as you chuse a Friend.'

Perhaps the Image is better drawn from the more lively Passion.

Not

Not ev'n when both by partial Nature giv'n,   145
United bless the Favourite of Heav'n ;
Unless, by secret Sympathy combin'd,
The faithful Glass reflects its kindred Mind ;
Unless from Soul to Soul th' imparted Fire
Congenial catch, and kindle warm Desire;   150
Ev'n such as lives in *Rowe's* enraptur'd Strain,
And gives *Pharsalia* to our Eyes again;
Where glowing in each animated Line,
We see the fiery Soul of *Lucan* shine ;
Or such as gilds the fair historic Page,
For *Smith* reserv'd, to grace our latter Age ;
Such as o'er *Dryden* all its Influence shed,
And bade his Muse recall the mighty Dead,
Such as in *Pope*'s extensive Genius shone,
And made immortal *Homer* all our own.   160
  View all that proud Antiquity displays,
Count o'er her boasted Heirs of endless Praise,
Who thought so nobly, or who wrote so well,
Britain can shew th' illustrious Parallel.
Methinks I hear each venerable Shade
For base Neglect his genuine Sons upbraid.
Why would not *Congreve Afer'* Charms revive,
Or tender *Hammon* bid *Tibullus* live?

LINE 147. *Unless by secret*, &c.] A Bias of Inclination towards a particular Author, and a Similarity
of Genius in the Translator, seem more immediately necessary than Wit or Learning.

LINE 154. See *Rowe's* Translation of *Lucan's
Pharsalia*, at the End of which is a short Supple-
ment written in the true Spirit of the Original.

LINE 156. See *Smith*'s Translation of *Thucydides*,
lately published.

LINE 168. *Hammond*, Author of *Love Elegies*.

Plautus

Plautus had pleas'd in *Vanbrugh's* loofer Page,
And *Otway* fhould have trod the *Grœcian* Stage; 179
Lucian wou'd fhine unveil'd by *Swift* alone,
And *Tully* calls in vain for *Middleton* ;
A *Livy's* Senfe demands a St. *John's* Style,
And *Plato* afks a *Melmoth* or a *Boyle*.

Ev'n now there are, ere Learning take her Flight,
And Gothick Darknefs fpread a fecond Night ;
Tho' Science droop, and ling'ring Arts decay,
There are, who gild the Evening of our Day.
Once more behold, majeftic in her Tears,
By *Gray* adorn'd, fair *Elegy* appears,
Whilft by her Side the foft *Elfrida* ftands,
And all our Love and all our Grief demands ;
With *Roman* Spirit *Johnfon's* manly Page
Rifes fevere to fcourge a venal Age;
Brown draws the Pen in facred Truth's Defence, 185
And *Armftrong* paints his own Benevolence.
From ancient Models thefe exalted few
Their faireft Forms and bright Ideas drew;

LINE 180. See Elegy in a Country Church-yard.

LINE 181. *Elfrida*, by Mr. *Mafon*.

LINE 183. *Samuel Johnfon*, Author of the *Ram-bler*, and alfo of two fine Imitations of *Juvenal*.

LINE 185. See Effay on the Characteriftics of Lord *Shaftefbury*.

LINE 186. See an Epiftle on Benevolence, by Dr. *Armftrong* ; fo well known for his celebrated Poem on Health, one of the beft Performances in the *Englifh* Language.

We

We know the Fountain whence the Waters came,
Nor wonder at the Clearnefs of the Stream.   190
    Yet ftill, fair *Greece*, we fee thy Garlands torn,
We fee there ftill thy widow'd Altars mourn;
On us thy Heroes ftill fuperior frown,
Or look with awful Indignation down;
The Tears of *Rome* for injur'd Learning flow,   195
And *Athens* grieves that *Britain* is her Foe.
    Will you not rife then, Oh! you Sons of Fame
To vindicate the *Greek* and *Roman* Name?
On Friends opprefs'd your gen'rous Aid beftow,
And pay the Debt of Gratitude you owe?   200
Or can you ftill their Wrongs unpitying fee,
Nor focial join with *Warton* and with Me?
    Whilft round his Brows the *Mantuan* Ivy twine,
Cautious to tread in *Attic* Paths be mine;
To Fame unknown, but emulous to pleafe,   205
Trembling I feek th' immortal *Sophocles*.
    Genius of *Greece* do thou my Breaft infpire
With fome warm Portion of thy Poet's Fire,
From Hands profane defend his much-lov'd Name;
From cruel *Tibbald* wreft his mangled Fame;   210
Give him once more to bid the Heart o'er-flow
In graceful Tears, and fympathizing Woe;
A Father's Death while foft *Electra* mourn,
Or fhed her Sorrows o'er a Brother's Urn;

LINE 202.   Mr. *Warton* has lately publifhed a
new Tranflation of the Eclogues and Georgics of
Virgil, and joined it to Mr. *Pit*'s excellent Tranflation of the *Æneid*.

LINE 210.   *Tibbald* (or *Theobald*) tranflated two
or three Plays of *Sophocles*, and threatened the Publick with more.

Or

Or fair *Antigone* her Griefs relate ; 215
Or poor *Tecmeſſa* weep her hapleſs State ;
Or *OEdipus* revolve the dark Decrees of Fate.
Could I like him the various Paſſions move,
Granville wou'd ſmile, and *Cheſterfield* approve ;
Each letter'd Son of Science wou'd commend, 220
Each gentle Muſe wou'd mark me for her Friend ;
Iſis well pleaſed wou'd join a Siſter's Praiſe,
And *Cam* applauding conſecrate the Lays,

END of the SECOND VOLUME.

www.ingramcontent.com/pod-product-compliance
Lightning Source LLC
Chambersburg PA
CBHW051117120726
47905CB00005B/1316